D1568374

PAST PRESENT FUTURE

How to read and interpret

Dreams, Handwriting, Palms, Cards, Tea Leaves, Dice, Doodles, Numbers

The Bobbs-Merrill Company, Inc.
Indianapolis/New York

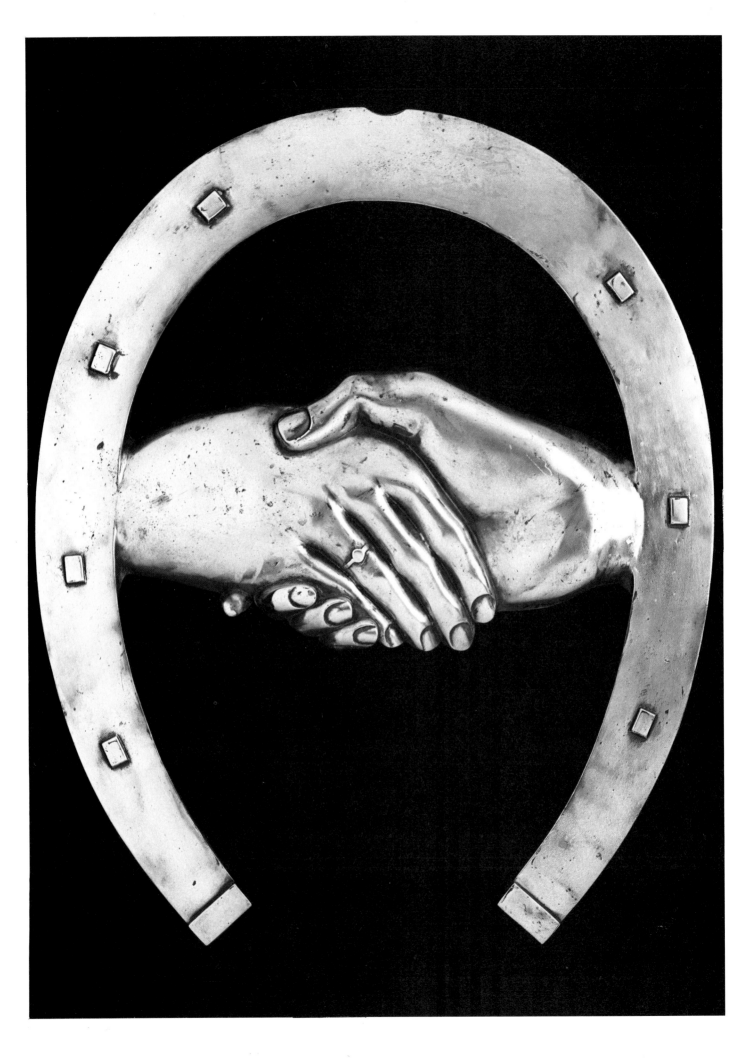

Part 1
How to tell your Fortune

Peter Brent

Credits: Fortune
Frontispiece Don McAllester.
Chris Barker pp. 15, 25, 49, 50, 51
52-53, 55, 64. Steve Bicknell p. 34.
The Bodleian Library, Oxford pp. 9.
32, 33. The British Museum, London
pp. 32, 64. Alan Duns pp. 22-23.
Mary Evans Picture Library pp. 7, 29,
62. Malcolm Scoular pp. 26, 37, 45,
60, 53. Snark International p. 8.
Michael James Ward p. 14.
Illustrations by Maggie Raynor.
Artwork makeup by Roy Flooks.

Credits: Handwriting
David Bailey/Sunday Times p 6. Chris
Barker p. 16. Bettman Archive p. 31.
Bodleian Library, Oxford p. 55.
Camera Press p. 7. John Garrett pp.
60-61, 62. Keystone pp. 7, 14. Chris
Lewis p. 5. Ben Manchipp MSIA p. 34.
The Mansell Collection pp. 8, 13.
National Portrait Gallery, London
pp. 8, 9. David Newson p. 4. Pictorial
Press p. 6. Popperfoto p. 14. Malcolm
Scoular p. 43. Transworld Publishers
p. 56. Warner Bros. p. 59. Dick
Zimmerman p. 21.
Marion Richardson copy card on p. 9
from *Writing and Writing Patterns*,
reproduced by permission of the
University of London Press Ltd. Other
school models reproduced from
Blumenthal's *Schulschriften der
Verschidenen Laender* by permission of
Hans Huber Verlag, Berne. Samples of
Sir Winston S. Churchill's handwriting
on p. 9 reproduced by kind permission
of C & T Publications Ltd. Other
historical samples supplied by John
Wilson and Mary Evans Picture Library.

Credits: Dreams
The Bodleian Library, Oxford p. 49.
Larry Burrows/Aspect p. 55. Roger
Charity p. 17. Salvador Dali/
A.D.A.G.P., Paris p. 60. John Fernley
pp. 25, 52. Fox-Rank p. 61. John
Garrett pp. 8, 16, 18, 26, 31. The
Mansell Collection pp. 52, 53. M.G.M./
C.I.C. p. 61. Oslo Kommunes
Kunstsamlinger p. 59. Popperfoto pp.
25, 52. F. Jurgen Rögner pp. 7, 12-13.
Sanders p. 33. Kim Sayer p. 63. John
Seymour p. 4. Trevor Sutton p. 6. The
Tate Gallery, London pp. 10, 21, 40.
Victoria and Albert Museum/Crown
Copyright p. 45. John Watney p. 43.
Chris Yates pp. 5, 15, 22, 29, 36, 39, 51,
57, 62, 64. ZEFA/Pictor Ltd p. 35.

Published in the United States by the Bobbs-Merrill
Company, Inc, Indianapolis/New York

Published in Great Britain by Marshall Cavendish
Publications Limited

ISBN 0 672 52130 X
Library of Congress catalog card number 74 29205

Printed in Great Britain

First printing 1975

Introduction

Everything you want to know about yourself, your past and your future is contained within these pages. Your fortune and how to tell it; your handwriting and what it means; your dreams and the innermost secrets they can reveal; all of these are explained fully and simply to help you discover yourself more completely than ever before.

Part One covers many different methods of fortune telling. Cards, hands, tea-leaves, dice and dominoes—even the bumps on your head—any of these can be used. Whether you take it seriously or just think of it as an amusing pastime, you will be able to try all the various methods to entertain your friends with your newfound talent. There are details of the background and techniques needed for the different ways of telling fortunes and revealing character.

Here you can find out about frivolous superstitions, like the meaning of moles or itches on various parts of the body, and more serious methods too, like palmistry and I Ching. The sample palm analyses included were made by experts who know nothing at all about their clients and yet were astonishingly accurate.

Much of fortune telling depends on interpretation of the 'signs' in the cards or at the bottom of the cup, so to help you develop your skills to the full there are many examples to show you how to weave seemingly unconnected meanings and symbols into fascinating readings.

Contents

Q

What is fortune telling?

Fortune telling falls into two parts: the divining of the future and the reading of character and how it has been shaped by events in the past. Palmistry alone combines both of these facets — the other methods in this book are concerned solely with one or the other. This book can be used in several different ways — for serious attempts to read character or the future; for fun and entertainment among friends, or simply for the curiosity value of a collection of past beliefs. There are sections which fall into each of these categories. Numerology uses the logic of mathematics to bring order out of apparent chaos. Palm reading and phrenology — the reading of lumps on the head — can be amusing to try out on friends and the collection of past beliefs — the meanings of moles, for example — and the section on tea-leaf reading, make fascinating reading.

Methods

Since time immemorial man has tried to give Fate an opportunity to make its intentions known by using the operations of Chance. And it is from these that all methods of foretelling the future developed. Some are no longer seriously used; some, however, many people take very seriously. I Ching, one of the oldest methods, has many devoted adherents, and the Tarot pack continues to draw believers. Perhaps it is the more obscure and complicated methods which inspire faith. The pack of cards used in everyday life to play poker, patience or snap has no longer the same aura. We find it difficult to believe it can reveal our future. But the Tarot — its signs and figures clearly fixed in the remote past — we feel can tell us something. It is as though Fate, being mysterious, needs a mysterious vessel to work through.

In the following pages there are fortune telling methods both old and new. All of them are interesting and fun to use even if you do not place much faith in some of them.

Character

If you can tell fortunes or reveal character you will find that people gather around like bees after honey, clamouring to be told about themselves and their character. And this is one sure way to get conversation going at a party! A further dimension

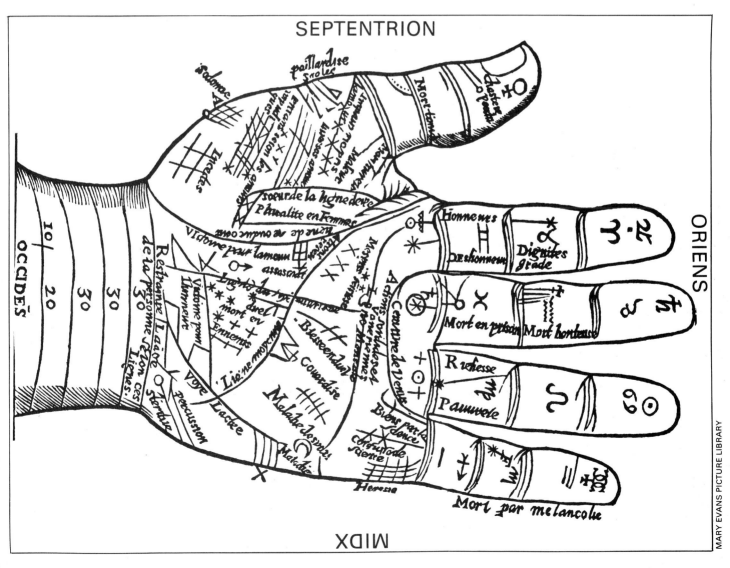

is added to your self-knowledge when your character is told. If the fortune teller is on target there is the surprise of having your views of yourself reinforced or modified or your self-deceptions shattered.

The fascination lies in the fact that things you thought were only known to you are suddenly revealed as apparent to others too. And this is revealed objectively. It is not simply other people's views of your character which happen to coincide with your own. The fortune teller has divined them from an outside source, whether cards, a palm print or the lumps on your head. And even the sceptic can be somewhat unnerved by accuracy obtained like this without rational provision of data.

Yet this is not so strange; finger prints are accepted as unique (they are used regularly in the detection of criminals), so why should not the same apply to palm prints? It could be that what is unique to you might in some way reveal something of your inner self.

The future

The future is fascinating to everyone. You frequently consider the past and remember how often you have been overtaken by surprise, how many opportunities you missed because they presented themselves too suddenly, how may offers of help you spurned because you misunderstood them. 'If only I'd known', you murmur.

As a result even the most sceptical people keep some corner of the mind free for an unacknowledged hope that perhaps, in some way, such knowledge just might be obtainable. There the mind allows itself to accept omens, superstitions, portents and the telling of fortunes. And even if you don't actually believe implicitly in these it is possible that alternative courses of action may be indicated which had not previously occurred to you. You might even consider acting upon them.

On the other hand, if you believe in an underlying pattern in events, that the seeds of the future lie in the present, then you believe in Fate.

Some methods of telling character can be claimed to be scientific because they relate directly to the subject rather than the operations of chance working through cards, say, or tea leaves.

Phrenology, on the other hand, started with scientific pretensions and has now largely fallen into disrepute. But it remains amusing, and a good party

game guaranteed to claim the attention of the person whose lumps you are reading.

Telling your own fortune

You can attempt to peer into your own future by using cards or the I Ching. In general, however, fortune telling demands a 'diviner' and a 'client'. This is because you cannot stand far enough away from yourself to interpret your own future without bending the facts slightly to suit your wishes.

Learning by heart?

It is, of course, better if you can memorize the meanings of the cards — both ordinary and Tarot — tea-leaf formations and so forth. If you do then there will be no hesitations in your readings, no searching through this book for the relevant passage!

On the other hand, you can simply familiarize yourself with the meanings and then refer to the text as necessary. This can be an even more impressive method. Friends and acquaintances might mistrust your reading if they think you are using your imagination rather freely. But they will probably tend to believe and accept your predictions if they see you referring to a text and then interpreting it. Interpretation is, perhaps, the most important factor in fortune telling so the need to refer back to the book does not detract too much from your impact or your claim to be a fortune teller.

Be responsible

Beware when reading other people's futures. Many people, however much they protest disbelief, will half believe or be disturbed by any prognostications of doom and disaster that you may give. Use your tact and discretion in deciding how much to reveal, and when. If reading futures or characters in public — at a party, say — be careful. Your client may be secretly pleased to hear he will change his life, go abroad or marry three times — but his wife may not be.

Intuition and imagination

When you reveal the character or tell the fortunes of others your intuition, sympathy and awareness all come into play. Fortune telling when done face to face depends largely on the interaction of minds. Mutual sympathy is important. If you the fortune teller

are responsive to and aware of the client's reactions, the reading has a better chance of success. Let your subconscious and imagination have full rein. Many of us are more intuitive than we think and if you temporarily discard logical thought processes you may be surprised at your own powers of discernment.

At the simplest level fortune telling can be an amusing party trick and a very good way of getting to know people. It can also offer clues to greater self-knowledge and a chance to glimpse future possibilities.

The language of signs

Long before writing was invented, man used a rich vocabulary of signs to express hopes and fears about his own life and the world that surrounded him.

The five pointed star is one of the most ancient signs — certainly older than writing. It was believed to be a protection against witches.

Three arrows bound together — a sign of unity.

A sign used to cast out evil spirits.

Omens, oracles and signs

There is hardly anything which moves which has not at one time served as an omen, hardly any human activity which was not surrounded with its own superstitions. The direction a bed faced has been thought significant — for riches, the head should be to the East, for a long life, to the South. Money was supposed to come to you if you sneezed to the right, good news if you dropped and smashed an egg or had a shoelace which kept coming undone.

Fortune might attend you if you picked up a pin, met the same person twice on the same journey or broke uncoloured glass (but if that glass was a mirror or a bottle then bad luck would follow). The sight of bellows and the burning of bones was once considered unlucky. If you wanted to avoid evil fortune you had, apparently, to not cut your hair before the new moon, avoid meeting grave-diggers, be careful never to cross two forks or two knives, and not mend clothes while you were wearing them. You should also never — unless you wanted to tempt fate — put your left shoe on before your right, break a pair of scissors, sit on a table without keeping one foot on the ground and, of course, never open an umbrella indoors.

It is as though everyone felt they were on the verge of disaster all the time, kept from ill-fortune only by a series of inconsequential yet desperately important actions. At any moment one might unknowingly trigger off disaster. The spilling of salt, the breaking of a plate, even a sneeze — especially, it seems, on a Monday or Friday — could summon bad luck which had been lying in wait. If one believed all this then every action, every occurrence became an oracular pronouncement. All that was necessary was to know the appropriate meaning and one was then forewarned and prepared for what the future held in store.

Omens

People believed that Fate was constantly active and, therefore, that every-

thing which occurred had a fateful message to convey. Every passing cloud, bird or breeze, every accident of nature, became part of the code by which one's future fate could be revealed so men scanned the earth and sky for omens.

Even now sometimes you probably catch yourself out not walking under a ladder, feeling slightly worried about breaking a mirror or waiting for the second magpie to appear. It is not necessarily that you believe in such omens, just that having heard them from childhood there is a vague feeling that perhaps you might, after all, be tempting fate. And people who do disregard them — walking deliberately under every ladder they see — often do so with a certain air of defiance!

However, whether or not you choose to believe in them, certain events and phenomena have, over the centuries, been given particular meanings. Some of the better-known ones are given below.

Animals

Carrying their unconscious forecasts of a good or a disastrous future, these too were thought to be the innocent messengers of Fate.

Bat Bad luck, especially if it cries while flying.

Cat There is doubt about the significance of this mysterious beast. Black, it may be good or bad; experience would have to tell. But to kill one is thought to be disastrous, and if one unaccountably leaves your house, it could mean catastrophe.

Dog Much less involved with fortune telling, but an omen of death if it howls at the moon, although it offers no precise warning of where death intends to strike.

Goat Good luck.

Hare Unfortunate, especially if one crosses your path.

These charming animal drawings are taken from a medieval manuscript. Even today country dwellers still think of animals as harbingers of fate.

Hedgehog Good fortune, especially if met going in the opposite direction.

Horse Piebald, a good omen. (If seen tail first, however, a friend may meet misfortune.) A white horse seen by lovers will bring them good luck.

Mouse White or brown, it means happiness, especially in love; grey, danger threatens.

Pig A bad omen, especially if met immediately after marriage.

Rat Good, if white; bad, if black.

Sheep In a flock, good fortune, especially if approaching.

Squirrel Happiness will be found soon after seeing one.

Birds

Because the flight of birds is so unpredictable, yet so apparently purposeful, their appearance has often been taken as a portent of good or evil fortune.

Crow A bad omen, especially if seen to the left.

Cuckoo Not seen, but heard, it foretells prosperity, especially if it is heard to the right.

Dove A happy omen, particularly for those about to marry.

Gull Settling on a ship, a happy sign for those about to sail in her. But to be touched by a gull in flight is said to foretell the death of someone close.

Hawk Be watchful — powerful enemies threaten. (This is supposed to be especially true if the bird is seen to the left.)

Kingfisher A scandal threatens.

Magpie One, especially on the left, is an omen of death. Two, however, are very lucky and signify that good fortune will follow within three days.

Owl Always bad luck. If it hoots three times, be especially careful.

Robin Good luck.

Sparrow Bad luck, except for lovers.

Swallow Very good fortune, especially early in Spring. If they build under your roof, good will follow. If you kill one, expect disaster.

Wagtail Fortunate, especially if approaching from the left.

Wren Good luck. (But at your peril either harm or frighten it.)

Insects

Their movements are difficult to forecast and their purposes obscure. Perhaps for this reason insects have always been taken to be messengers of Fate.

Ants A nest near your home is a good augury, but to be bitten by one means quarrels and strife.

Bee Good luck if it is trapped for a while in the house.

Cockroach If seen in an unusual place, it foretells a death.

Cricket Always and everywhere thought of as lucky. But if they suddenly abandon a house where they have been settled, disaster follows.

Grasshopper A journey, and good news.

Ladybird A good omen, especially if it has seven spots on its back.

Spider A doom-laden creature: seen in the morning, it means grief; at noon anxiety; in the evening, financial loss. A spider spinning a web means people are plotting. To kill one brings misfortune. However, if found on the body it is a harbinger of prosperity.

Wasp To be stung by a wasp indicates danger, probably through jealousy.

Patterns and shapes

As the patterns made by tea-leaves offer an irresistible temptation to look into the future so, too, did other apparently random formations. These were read in the same way as a tea-cup (see later for the meaning of the symbols). As with reading tea-leaves, it took some imagination and a great deal of concentration to understand the message offered by the symbols!

Egg whites
Take an egg, separate the white from the yolk, and pour the white into a bowl almost brimful of water. After 24 hours, clots will have formed which you should then be able to read.

Sealing wax
Heat a little sealing wax in a serving spoon or ladle. When it is melted, pour the wax into a bowl of clean water. The shapes that the wax forms will give you symbols which contain the answer you need.

Seeds
To discover the order in which certain events will occur, plant a seed for each event — but never enquire about more than five things. Put each seed in a separate pot. As far as possible give each pot the same amount of sunshine and water. The order in which the seedlings appear will give you the information you want. This process is likely to be somewhat lengthy so it is best not to enquire about events in the immediate future.

Simple questions

Several different methods were developed to answer questions which require only a simple affirmative or negative.

Burning paper
Write out a wish or a question on a slip of paper, place it face down on a plate and light it with a match. If all the paper is burnt, you will get what you want. But if only a part of it burns, though your wish may eventually be granted, this will not be for some time.

Cat's paw
If you have a cat, it too can give you a yes-or-no reply. Think of your question, then call your pet. If the right forepaw appears first around the door, the answer to your question is Yes.

Paper pieces
Write a different question on each of a number of pieces of paper (usually thirteen) and then place all the slips at the bottom of a bowl. Pour water into the bowl and wait for the first slip of paper to rise to the surface. The answer to the question on it will be Yes.

Paper squares
Cut two squares of paper, both the same size, and colour one black. Drop them both at the same time from an upstairs window. If the white one lands first, the answer is Yes.

Stones
Fill a wide bowl with water and murmur a question aloud as you drop a small stone into it. Count the ripples in the water — if the number is odd, the answer will be Yes.

Wedding ring
Tie a length of black thread around a gold wedding ring. Hold the other end of the thread in your left hand and then lower the ring into a glass of water. If it touches the right side of the glass then the answer to your question is Yes. If it touches the left, No. If it touches the side either nearest you or furthest away, you may take it that the oracle refuses to answer and should not be consulted for another 24 hours.

Itches

If one believes that all things have a meaning, then even a sudden irritation which demands to be scratched might be able to enlighten you in some way about your future. The message can be precisely deciphered by the place on the body where it has settled. Next time you have an itch, consider the significance it might have.

Top of head Promotion.

Right cheek Someone is slandering you.

Left cheek Someone is complimenting you.

Right eye You will meet an old friend.

Left eye Disappointment awaits.

Inside nose Problems, grief.

Outside nose The saying is 'Kissed, cursed or meet with a fool', this to take place within the hour.

Lips Someone insults you behind your back.

Back of neck A relative will fall ill.

Right shoulder Legacy.

Left shoulder Sorrow.

Right elbow Goods news.

Left elbow Bad news.

Right palm Money comes your way.

Left palm Bills come your way.

Back Disappointment.

Stomach Invitation.

Loins Reconciliation.

Thighs A move.

Right knee Happy voyage.

Left knee Voyage beset with difficulty.

Shins An unpleasant surprise.

Ankles Marriage and/or a rise.

Sole (right foot) A journey with profit.

Sole (left foot) A journey which brings a loss.

Moles

Because one is born with these curious marks upon the body they were often thought significant. The essential information which they give depends

The position of significant moles on different parts of the body.

upon where the moles are placed. The bigger the mole, the more emphatically the attributes and fortunes it foretells will come into being. There are general points to watch for, too, because the shape of the mole has its importance. The rounder it is the more good fortune is implied. If the mole is raised, that means very good fortune indeed; an oval or pointed mole means bad luck, made even worse if its colour is dark, and worse again if it is hairy.

Forehead Right: intelligence, leading to fame and prosperity. Left: extravagance, fecklessness.

Eye Near the outer corner of either eye, placidity of temperament, frugality and thriftiness.

Eyebrow Right: happy and probably early marriage. Left: difficult marriage.

Ear Recklessness.

Cheek Right: happiness, especially in marriage. Left: difficulties, struggles.

Chin Success, prosperity, good fortune.

Mouth Happy, sensual disposition.

Jaw Bad health.

Nose Great fortune, travel, a developed sexuality.

Throat Rich marriage; ambitions attained.

Neck Many ups and downs, unexpected legacies, early set-backs but ultimate success.

Hand Natural ability, leading to success.

Arm Right: success. Left: financial anxiety.

Shoulder Hard and difficult times.

Breast Right: ups and downs of fortune. Left: in a man — fortune and happiness, in a woman — ardent temperament, sometimes leading to foolish attachments. Centre: adequate income, but no great wealth.

Abdomen A nature selfish and self-indulgent, lazy and perhaps greedy.

Back Frankness and generosity, but also arrogance and self-display. If very low: sensuality and self-indulgence.

Ribs Right: cowardice, indolence, insensitivity, boorishness. Left: the same, but less so and modified by humour.

Hips Strong, healthy children and numerous grandchildren.

Thigh Right: warmth of temperament, wealth, happiness in marriage. Left: loneliness, loss, poverty, although the temperament is equally warm.

Knee Right: ease in marriage and with finances. Left: rashness.

Ankle Refinement, leading in a man to dandyism. In a woman a sign of energy and hard work.

Foot Right: love of travelling. Left: swift intelligence.

Leg Right or left: laziness.

The trial of destiny

Use this chart to tell your
own fortune as well as other people's.
The instructions are in the text.

Choose which subject you want to ask a question about — you can, if you like ask a question on each subject. Then take a pin, close your eyes and prick the pin into the section of your choice. The number the pin lands on gives the answer to your question. The inner point sections give a general indication of something about to happen to you — and here again you can choose a section. Close your eyes and proceed in the same way. If the pin fails to hit a number, fate is unwilling to answer your query.

Love
1. Many lovers.
2. One sincere lover, one false one.
3. A flirtation.
4. A senseless jest.
5. A lover who has not the courage to speak his mind.
6. You love and are not beloved again, — so banish the flame.

Courtship
1. The lover is sincere.
2. No wedlock is intended.
3. They are wavering in love.
4. A long courtship, to end in nothing.
5. It will end in marriage.
6. A sudden break.

Marriage
1. Happy, and of long duration.
2. Short, but prosperous and peaceful.
3. Not so soon as you expect, but happy in itself.
4. Not so happy in the end as the beginning promises.
5. A separation or divorce before death.
6. A paradise on earth awaits you in this respect.

Children
1. They will surround your table like olive-branches.
2. Several in number, — some as roses to you, and some will prove thorns.
3. One at most.
4. Not many.
5. One amongst your children will raise you to affluence, — they will all prove acceptable.
6. Illegitimate children will trouble you, yet perhaps not your own.

Kin
1. They will enrich you.
2. They will improverish you.
3. They will exalt you.
4. They will degrade you.
5. Some of your kindred will leave you a valuable remembrance.
6. A death in the family.

Trade
1. You will never be indebted to it in your own person.
2. You will suddenly embark on it.
3. You will form a friendship with a trader.
4. You will lose by trade.
5. You will enter into partnership.
6. You will get rich by commerce.

Fortune
1. Changes every seven years will occur to you.
2. A steady life.
3. Sudden riches.
4. Fatal extravagance.
5. False promises will undo your peace.
6. A sudden fall and a great rise will mark your life.

Speculation
1. Success in the lottery.
2. Never speculate.
3. Chance luck.
4. Fortunate at cards.
5. You will be lucky at ventures in trade.
6. Luck in a wager to come.

The points
A a letter.
B a reproof.
C a loss.
D a gain.
E new appeal.
F a gift.
G a journey.
X a disappointment.
Y a feast.

1. A comfortable hour.
2. A change.
3. Bad news.
4. Good tidings.
5. A voyage.
6. A present of money.
7. A valentine.
8. A gift to wear.
9. A present for which you will pay dear.
10. You have lately practised some unworthy deception.
12. A period of anxiety.
13. Moment inauspicious. Try again.
15. You will soon lose something good by passion.
17. A long walk on a sudden occasion — try again. A cross betokens great joy — try once more.

Know that these points only refer to minor affairs, and such as will be speedily verified.

The reading of tea cups

The sediment in the cup one drinks from has in the past often been thought to provide clues to the drinker's fate, because it involves both the random and the personal.

Many people once thought that only those with 'psychic powers' could read cups. But no one has ever been able to define precisely what these powers are. You just may, whether consciously or not, possess them so do not let such a doctrine put you off. With knowledge and practice you may arrive at levels of perception which surprise you. This is by no means a precise science, however, and if you attempt it you will need to exercise your imagination and let your mind wander freely. Learning the meanings will not be enough.

Method

There are one or two basic points to remember. First, use a cup which can be easily read: one that is plain, and not straight-sided. Second, avoid a dusty tea. China tea is supposed to be the best, but any large-leaved mixture will do. (You can, of course, follow exactly the same procedure to read coffee grounds.) To provide the necessary personal link it is also thought to be vital that the subject actually drinks the cup of tea or coffee. In order to obtain the pictures you need, let your client drink almost the whole cup and then swill the remaining teaspoonful around a few times. (Some people insist on a ritual element in this

swirling of the dregs, and say it must be done only with the left hand and either three or seven times.)

Next turn the cup upside down on its saucer. When the final drop of tea has drained away, turn the cup the right way up again and begin your reading. Do not hurry. Give your imagination a chance to work. Turn the cup, tilt it, consider it from every angle. The clearer a symbol appears, the greater its importance. Do not, however, expect the images ever to be totally clear. Sometimes the leaves offer no more than a suggestion and it is up to you to interpret such hints. If you really cannot discern any pattern or symbol, tell your client the truth. Although you may allow yourself to add that the confusion of the leaves probably mirrors the state of mind.

Reading the symbols

The meaning of the various symbols is the most important thing. The list that follows gives some of the most commonly used, but your own imagination and, in time, experience, may lead you to add more of your own. The position and size of the symbols are also significant.

The client

The cup-handle represents the client. If a symbol is near the handle it indicates an occurrence close to the person's home. The direction taken by symbols which suggest movement is also important. Some will point to the handle, suggesting approach; and some away, suggesting departure. There is also one theory that, when holding the cup with the handle towards you, symbols to the left of the handle concern events in the past and those on the right events in the future.

Time

The sides of the cup, from rim to bottom, are taken as a time scale. Thus the position of the symbols is important: *near the rim* — they indicate events which will occur in the near future, *near the bottom* — events distant in time, *in the bottom* — ill-fortune at any time.

Proportion

The size of the symbol is also important, for example, the proportions of the symbol will give some indication of the size of the house your client might move to or the legacy he might receive.

Overall reading

First, consider which kind of symbols predominate and make a general assessment of good or bad fortune. This will give a logical structure to your reading. It will tell you whether any bad news the cup foretells will be no more than a minor blemish on a period of happiness, or whether the good will only lighten a bad period.

Remember that the message lies in the combination of all the symbols. Only when you have put them together will what they have to tell become clear.

If an ant and an eye, pointing to perseverance and watchfulness, are combined with a large and very clear gun near the cup's handle, this suggests that it is in the domestic arena that these qualities will be best deployed. If, however, the third symbol is a broken necklace, then the problems through which one has to persevere and over which one must watch arise from a love relationship. And an open book would translate the same effort into the legal field.

Every combination of signs has a different significance, making reading from cups a fairly exacting business, but also a rewarding one.

Left: This seems to be the cup of an unmarried person, for the horse's head on the right suggests that there is a lover in the offing — possibly a rich lover. Yet the head faces away, and that is not a good sign. There may be danger of a swift parting. Opposite the handle there stands a swaddled baby, indicative of a multiplicity of small worries, and the arrow-head which suggests that bad news is impending.

To the left, the signs indicate that a bad time has been passed through: a flying bat, pointing to the plots of false friends: the square, implying unwelcome restriction, and the jester's head which tells us that this situation was taken very seriously indeed.

Right: A period of domestic happiness has come to an end. In the past, to the left of the handle one finds the fish, a symbol of happiness, and a table,

suggesting meetings, dinner parties and all manner of pleasant gatherings. But to the right of the handle, danger threatens: a hand grasps a gun, the muzzle toward the cup handle — domestic bliss is threatened, and very determinedly, by an outsider. (A gun can also indicate a call to arms.) Terror follows, for a devil-tailed monster leaps up from the disaster-cluttered bottom of the cup.

Meanings of the symbols

Acorns
An excellent symbol. The good fortune it foretells varies according to its position in the cup:
near the top — financial success
towards the middle — good health
near the bottom — improvement either in health or finances

Aircraft
A sudden journey, unexpected and not without risk
alternatively there will be a rise to new heights
if the aircraft seems broken — danger threatens, either physically or in one's career

Alligator
Treachery lies in wait

Anchor
Success awaits. Again the position in the cup is important:
at the top of the cup — success in business, augmented by the support of a faithful love
towards the middle — a voyage ending in prosperity (increased if dots surround the symbol)
at the bottom — good fortune socially. If the symbol is obscured — anticipate difficulties

Ant
With perseverance, success will arrive

Arc
Ill health threatens either career or

other plans, projects may be abandoned, accidents threaten

Arrow
Bad news is on the way

Axe
Difficulties face you, especially if only the axe-head appears

Baby
Many small worries threaten
alternatively, there may be an addition to the family

Bag
A trap awaits, likely to be successful if the bag is closed

Ball
Variable fortunes await you in life

Basket
A very good sign. Again pay attention to its position:
near the handle — a baby will soon be announced
near the top of the cup — your possessions will be added to
if flowers lie in the basket — a very good sign, suggesting happiness, social success, parties and festivities
if the basket is surrounded by dots — finances will be unexpectedly augmented, perhaps by a legacy

Bat
Beware of plots and of false friends

Bear
Irrational decisions will bring difficulties and even danger in their train
if the bear is turned away from the handle a long journey is indicated

Bed
if neat — a tidy mind
if disordered — an undisciplined mind which leads to problems

Bee
Success, both social and financial; good news
near the handle — a gathering of friends
a swarm of bees — possible success with an audience

Bell
News is expected, good or bad according to the significance of the surrounding symbols
near the top of the cup — promotion
near the bottom of the cup — sad news
two bells — great joy

Bird
This is particularly lucky if there are two or more birds
flying birds — good news
standing birds — a successful voyage

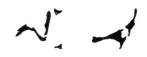

Boat
Refuge in time of trouble

Book
If the book is open expect litigation, if closed difficult researches

Boot
Protection from pain
pointing away from the handle sudden removal, perhaps dismissal
broken — failure and disgrace threaten

Bottle
Take care of health

Bridge
Opportunity to be seized for short-cut to success

Broom
Small worries disappear

Butterfly
Frivolous but innocent pleasure
if surrounded by dots this indicates the frittering away of wealth

Cabbage
Jealousy entails complications

Candle
Helpfulness, zeal for education

Castle
Strong character, rising to position of authority

Cat
Someone lies in treacherous ambush, probably a false friend

Chair
Improvement and, if the chair is surrounded by dots, financial improvement

Circle
A successful outcome

Clock
Avoid delay and hesitation
alternatively — recovery from illness
in the bottom of the cup — a death

Clouds
Doubts, unsolved problems
if the clouds are very heavy, misfortune is indicated

Column
Success. Also a danger of resultant arrogance

Comet
A visitor from overseas

Cross
Suffering, sacrifice, tribulation. Two crosses indicate severe illness or other major affliction

Crown
Great success
If the crown is neat expect a legacy

Dagger
Impetuosity
alternatively — the dangerous plotting of enemies

Dog
Rely on friends
Pay attention to the position and attitude of the dog:
running — good news and happy meetings
subdued — you may be slandering a friend
at the bottom of the cup — a friend is in trouble

Dot
A single dot emphasizes the meaning of the symbol it is nearest to. Dots in groups indicate money

Drum
Scandal and gossip threaten. Quarrels are in the air.

Egg
Prosperity, success, fertility. The more eggs the better

Elephant
Wisdom, strength and slow, but solid, success

Eye
Take care and be watchful, especially in business

Feather
Instability and lack of concentration

Fence
Limitation imposed on plans and activities

Fern
Unfaithfulness is possible in a lover

Fir tree
Success, especially in the arts. The higher the tree the better

Fire
Avoid over-hasty reactions, especially anger

Fish
One of the very best omens, this indicates good luck in everything

Flag
Danger threatens, particularly if the flag is black

Flower
A wish will be granted

Fly
Worry, especially domestic. The more flies there are the more varied the swarm of misfortunes

Forked line
Decisions must be taken. (Whether these will be successful or not depends upon the attendant symbols)

Frog
Avoid self-importance as it may cause trouble

Fruit
This is a lucky symbol, especially if the fruit is in season

Garland
Success and great honour

Glass
Integrity

Goat
Enemies threaten

Gun
near the handle — an attack will threaten domestic happiness
at the bottom of the cup — slander undermines the client
for military personnel — cancelled leave

Hammer
Ability to overcome obstacles and perhaps a tendency to ruthlessness

Hare
Over-timidity

Harp
Domestic harmony
for single people a harp indicates a love affair with a successful outcome

Hat
New possibilities, and probable success
if the hat is bent and holed — failure is more likely
if the hat is in the bottom of the cup — a rival

Hawk
Sudden danger threatens

Hill
Obstacle to progress. (Especially if clouds obscure it)

Horse
galloping — good news, especially from a lover
the head only — a lover

House
Secure conditions, especially in business, so a good time for new ventures
if the sign is near the handle and obscured — domestic strife or illness may threaten the family

Human figures
Consider these carefully and take your cue from their appearance, activities and the surrounding symbols

Insect
Minor worries, soon overcome

Jester
Avoid frivolity, it might be a disadvantage. A time for seriousness

Jug
Influence, enabling the client to give help to another
near the handle — excellent health

Kettle
near the handle domestic contentment
near or at the bottom of the cup — domestic strife

Key
Intelligent appraisal can see and seize new opportunities
double, or near the bottom of the cup — danger of robbery

Knife
Separation, broken contracts, ended friendships
near the handle — divorce
crossed knives — bitter argument

Ladder
Promotion, probably through hard work

Leaf
News
if the leaves are in clusters — happiness and good fortune

Letter
News
if obscured —bad news
if near dots — news concerning financial affairs

Light-house
Trouble threatens but will be averted before it strikes

Lines
Progress, especially if clear and straight

Lion
Influential friends and consequent success

Lock
Obstacle to your advancement

Man
near the handle — a visitor
with arms outstretched — bearing gifts

Mask
Take care, people are trying to deceive you

Mermaid
Take care, people are trying to tempt you

Monkey
Flatterers represent danger; they intend mischief

Monster
In any shape or form this indicates terror

Moon
full — a love affair
in first quarter — new projects
in last quarter — a decline in fortune
obscured — depression
surrounded by dots — marriage for money

Mountains
High ambition which will be successful if the peaks are very clear

Mushroom
Growth, expansion
near the handle — a new home in the country

Nail
Malice threatens and injustice may be inflicted

Necklace

complete — many supporters and admirers
broken — marriage or love affair may break up

Net

Beware of traps

Nurse

Illness threatens
if near the handle — dependants may fall sick

Owl

This evil omen indicates that new ventures will fail
at the bottom of the cup — disease and financial failure
near the handle — unfaithfulness destroys domestic harmony

Palm

Success, honour and respect

Parachute

Escape from danger

Parcel

This is represented by an oblong leaf and indicates a surprise. (The surrounding symbols will offer a clue as to the nature of the surprise)

Parrot

Scandal and gossip threaten

Peacock

with tail spread — possession of an estate
surrounded by dots — a life of luxurious ease
near ring — a rich marriage

Pear

Comfort and financial ease

Pentagon

Mental and intellectual balance

Pig

Mixed fortune. (Material success may bring spiritual or psychological disaster)

Pistol

Danger, perhaps moral danger, threatens

Pot

Service to society

Profile

Temporary friendship, or acquaintanceship

Pump

A generous nature

Purse

Profit, usually material
at the bottom of the cup — this indicates an unexpected loss

Question mark

Hesitancy

Rabbit

Timidity

Rake

Attempts should be made to tidy things up and regulate life-style and work methods

Rat

Treachery and loss, deceitful friends and resourceful enemies

Reptile

Treachery and malice threaten, especially from false friends

Ring

Self-sufficiency, completion, eternity
near the top of the cup — a marriage is indicated
near the middle — marriage is offered
at the bottom — a long engagement (but if a cross is nearby it is doomed to be broken)
two rings — plans come to fruition, projects work out

Saw

Outsiders will theaten domestic tranquillity

Scales

A lawsuit is likely
balanced scales — justice will be done
unbalanced scales — injustice will be suffered

Scissors

Separation, quarrelling
near the handle — domestic bickering

Ship
Good fortune and/or good tidings are on their way

Skeleton
Ill health, poverty

Snake
Hatred and enmity, vicious plots

Spade
Hard work, but success at the end of it

Spider
This indicates a determined, persistent character (but with some guile and cunning)

Square
Restriction, even imprisonment: either external, of the body; or internal, of the mind

Sun
Great happiness, success and power

Star
six-pointed — good fortune
eight-pointed — a bad omen, accidents and reverses may be suffered
five stars — success, but no joy
seven stars — grief

Swallow
Swiftness of decision
This also indicates unexpected journeys, leading to a happy outcome

Swan
Smooth and contented life

Table
Dinner, party, feast, social gathering
dots nearby — a conference on financial matters

Toad
Beware of flattery and flatterers

Tortoise
Over-sensitivity to criticism

Trees
Plans will be fruitful, ambitions fulfilled

Triangle
pointing upwards — success
pointing downwards — plans go awry

Trunk
A journey and fateful decisions

Umbrella
Shelter will be needed
if the umbrella is open it will be found,
if closed, denied

Violin
Individualism, perhaps egoism

Volcano
Passions may erupt and cause harm

Vulture
Loss, perhaps through theft; danger, possibly from an enemy in authority

Whale
Pre-eminence and success, especially in business

Windmill
Success will be achieved through industry and hard work, not brilliance

Wings
News is expected. (The attendant symbols will suggest whether this will be good or bad)

Woman
Happiness and pleasure
more than one woman, scandal and gossip

Yoke
Domination threatens, so avoid being too submissive

Zebra
Adventures overseas. (An unsettled life is indicated)

Dice

These deceptively simple little cubes with numbers marked upon them have been held to be responsible for making and breaking men's fortunes. The random nature of Fate is believed to be nowhere more clearly expressed than in the throwing of dice. Every throw is apparently completely unpredictable. The Egyptians knew these ancient toys, so did the Greeks. And throughout Asia precious woods and metals were used to make them in order to add to their latent power.

Method of reading

Dice have been used for divination for thousands of years, and methods of reading them have passed through many variations. There are, however, two absolute rules. For divination there must be three numbered dice, and they must be thrown in complete silence. It is also generally believed that they run more freely when the weather is calm and the atmosphere cool.

The most common method is to draw a simple chalk circle on a table and then throw the dice on behalf of the person whose fortune you are telling. Dice that roll beyond the circle have nothing to say. Those that fall on the floor indicate that disturbed and vexing times are ahead, which will probably be darkened by quarrels. If all the dice roll out of the circle, they should be picked up and thrown again. However, should the second throw also yield no result, it might be as well to assume that Fate has nothing to communicate that day, and wait until a more propitious moment.

There are two general points to remember. If a number turns up more than once during a reading, it presages the arrival of significant news. And on the very rare occasions when one dice lands on top of another it is always a warning that extreme caution should be exercised in all commercial and romantic ventures.

Meaning of numbers

Once the three dice have been rolled, add together the numbers shown on them. If one has rolled outside the circle and the total is less than three, the dice have nothing to say. The list which follows gives the most familiar meanings of the total numbers.

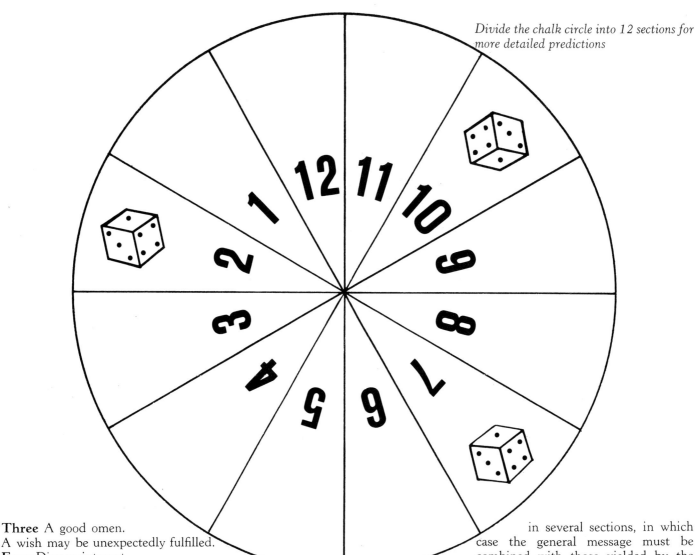

Divide the chalk circle into 12 sections for more detailed predictions

Three A good omen.
A wish may be unexpectedly fulfilled.

Four Disappointment

Five A stranger will bring joy

Six Material loss from which some spiritual advantage may be gained

Seven Unfounded gossip will cause unhappiness

Eight A contemplated action has not been thought through, and may produce an injustice

Nine Success, particularly in amorous affairs. If there has been a quarrel, expect reunion, forgiveness, reconciliation

Ten Domestic contentment, and perhaps some professional or business advancement

Eleven Someone — not necessarily a member of the family or close friend — is ill

Twelve A letter will come, and an answer be demanded. Ask advice before coming to a decision

Thirteen Grief, probably protracted, perhaps even lifelong

Fourteen A stranger will become a close and dear friend

Fifteen Temptation to enter into a shady or unjust deal

Sixteen A journey. Take it, for it will pass pleasantly and end in profit

Seventeen A man from overseas, prob-ably a foreigner, will suggest a course of action to you. His suggestion will be sound

Eighteen A very good omen — promotion, profit and joy

Specific predictions

In order to make predictions more precise, you may divide the chalk circle into twelve parts. These twelve sections represent the following:

First section Next year's happenings
Second section Money matters
Third section Travel
Fourth section Domestic matters
Fifth section Present schemes
Sixth section Health
Seventh section Marriage
Eighth section Deaths — and legacies
Ninth section Present state of mind
Tenth section Work or profession
Eleventh section Friends
Twelfth section Enemies

Continue to take notice of the general message, read as above, offered by the three dice added together, and apply this to the particular sections in which the dice fall. They will probably fall in several sections, in which case the general message must be combined with those yielded by the separate sections. If two or three dice fall into one section this, of course strengthens the message they offer. The numbers on the individual dice are read as follows:

One Search whatever the dice say about this matter for indications of success

Two Success depends on friendly relations continuing

Three Success is bound to follow

Four Things will go badly, as far as this section's affairs are concerned

Five The indications are good

Six The problem under general discussion will in its outcome have a good effect on the matter covered by this particular section

There are no hard-and-fast rules about giving an overall prediction under this more specific method. The general message offered by the three dice must somehow be combined with the particular ones from the individual sections. Use your subtlety and intuition to bring this sometimes fragmented and almost incoherent information into an ordered and relevant meaning. It will be enjoyable to discover how much skill you have.

Dominoes

The pieces used in the game of dominoes can, like dice, reveal possible expressions of the operations of Fate. Here the diviner shuffles the pieces, face downwards, and draws one on behalf of the client. The piece is turned upwards and read according to the table below. It is then returned, face down, to the rest of the pieces, which again are shuffled. A second piece is then drawn and read. This operation may be repeated for a third time, but no more. If one draws more than three pieces at a consultation, or allows more than one consultation per person a day, the dominoes become tired and are liable to mislead you!

Meanings

Double Six Success in every way
Six/Five Charitable works
Six/Four Litigation which is unlikely to be successful
Six/Three Short voyage with a beneficial outcome
Six/Two A gift, likely to be useful and to be presented soon
Six/One An end to the root of all your troubles

Six/Blank Be careful — especially with those you think are your friends
Double Five A move to a new house or apartment, where happiness awaits
Five/Four Profits. But do not use these for speculative ventures
Five/Three A helpful visitor
Five/Two A child is born, probably within the subject's family
Five/One Love affair — passionate but ending unhappily
Five/Blank Give comfort to a friend in trouble
Double Four A party given by a stranger
Four/Three Expected disappointments need not be feared
Four/Two A swindler — perhaps a philanderer — has entered the client's life
Four/One Debts must be paid — even at risk of temporary poverty
Four/Blank Attempt reconcilliation with estranged friend
Double Three A rival in love. Distress and misery result.
Three/Two Avoid tempting fortune for a few days
Three/One Surprising news, of great usefulness
Three/Blank Jealousy makes trouble and disrupts friendship
Double Two Happy marriage
Two/One Loss of money or property, this to occur in the very near future

Two/Blank Meeting, a new relationship and consequent happiness
Double One Avoid hesitation; a bold decision awaits and should be taken
One/Blank A stranger, probably from overseas, who will be of use
Double Blank A bad omen — indication of loss, disappointment, unhappiness

Sometimes you will draw the same piece twice. This confirms the prediction and at the same time suggests it will happen very soon. Usually however, as so often with predictions, the dominoes offer fragments of information which you yourself must build into a coherent message.

Take as much care and time as you need in order to organize the diverse clues into a clear picture. Concentrate hard. Imagination and those latent psychic powers may very well help you to a surprising degree of accuracy.

Reading

The client is a middle-aged housewife, and Five/Four, Four/One and Six/Two are drawn in that order (see picture below), showing that she will receive a windfall. However, she will have to use it to meet old bills. To take away the sting of that, a present will arrive — which may or may not be all the better for being a useful one.

Phrenology: reading the bumps on the head

Throughout the eighteenth and nineteenth centuries, European scientists were dominated by an urge to classify. They named and separated into groups every creature and object in Nature that they could discover — and human beings were no exception.

It was felt there must be a hidden key by means of which every man or woman could be graded into a specific category. And if this key could only be found society would automatically become rational, tidy and controlled. Those with administrative abilities would enter the civil service, the courageous would become military men, the imaginative would be creative artists, and so on. All that was needed was an instant method of analyzing character.

One of the methods which was tested was phrenology — the interpretation of the bumps on people's skulls. This is now somewhat discredited as a science although it still has its adherents. You need not, however, accept it in its entirety — or even at all — in order to have fun with it: it makes an intriguing icebreaker at a party!

Origins

The man who founded it, a German doctor named Gall, was extremely serious about it. He concluded that the brain was the controlling organ of the body, the seat of the mind, and that different parts of it had special functions. Because the brain lay under the skull and the skull was irregularly shaped, with shallow lumps and hollows which varied from one person to another, Gall argued that the size of these bumps revealed the development, or lack of it, of that part of the brain which lay immediately beneath. If one knew what faculties corresponded to those areas of the brain, one would be able to evaluate character merely by a careful examination of a person's skull.

Having decided how parts of the brain and particular characteristics corresponded, Gall, and an assistant named Spurzheim, persisted in the work of spreading their doctrine and, although they died largely unrecognized and unaccepted, their ideas continued slowly to gain in popularity throughout the nineteenth century. In Britain this happened mainly through the work of a Scotsman named George Combe.

Method

Because your client has to sit very still, the more quickly you can read the bumps, the better. It is helpful to practise first on yourself, and then on any patient friend who can be persuaded to keep still for long enough. First, study the head and features of your subject as a whole. Then, gently, but with the fingertips quite firm against the scalp, feel the contours of the skull, moving across the head in a systematic way.

Remember that there are no absolutes in phrenology. What matters is not how large or small a particular bump may be in itself, but how it compares with the others. It is the prominence of one characteristic against the rest which you are trying to determine.

Meaning of bumps

Combe's *System of Phrenology* listed 37 significant areas of the brain. In each, he stated, was based a particular trait of character which could be discerned by the corresponding bump on the skull. Since the brain has two lobes, each characteristic is represented by two bumps, one on each side of the head. Thus both hands can be used simultaneously in the attempt to discern them.

The four groups
Combe divided the bumps into four groups. The first revealed the basic propensities or qualities of the client. The second corresponded to his sentiments or feelings. The third corresponded to perception. And the fourth group referred to what were called the reflective areas, indicating reason and the mental processes by which we order our knowledge.

The following is a breakdown of the meanings given to the bumps in each area. Check the precise positions of these against the diagram.

Qualities
1. Sexuality If too small, this bump indicates a lack of energy, perhaps even of balance. If too large, it suggests so great an interest in the opposite sex as to prove a handicap — unless it is sublimated, turning the person to religious or charitable works.

2. Self-preservation If very small this indicates possible suicidal tendencies. A relatively small bump suggests recklessness, certainly some disregard for personal safety. A correspondingly large one points to a disinclination to take risks, sometimes amounting to cowardice.

3. Parenthood The larger the bump, the more deeply implanted will be a maternal or paternal instinct.

4. Domesticity Those with a gipsy mentality will probably not show a developed bump in this area. It relates to the delights of staying at home, and people who have it will tend to be faithful to their spouse and their firesides.

5. Friendship This bump displays the qualities of loyalty and trustworthiness we look for in friends.

6. Competitiveness Beware of those who have an over-development of this bump, for they will prove quarrelsome and petulant. If the development is only fairly large, however, such people will have a tendency to push for what they want or believe to be right. A lack of it would be a poor indication of success in careers.

7. Impatience If too large, it suggests destructive traits, a measure of harshness. In moderate size it points to a refusal to tolerate unnecessary impediments and obstacles.

8. Secretiveness Too small a bump here points to insensitive and brutal honesty. Too large a one, to a tendency to conceal and lie. In proportion, however, it suggests tact.

9. Acquisitiveness In a competitive, commercial society this is, perhaps, not a bad quality to have. But if the bump is too large, it hints at hoarding, miserliness and even, in extreme cases, to a tendency to take what is not one's own.

10. Appetite Well-developed, this suggests a discriminating palate. Over-developed, a tendency to gluttony. But under-developed, a lack of vitality and of taste.

11. Achievement This relates to the ability to make or create, whether manually or in the arts or sciences. Too small a bump is a poor indication for success in life. Too large a one suggests the subject will attempt more than he can manage.

Feelings

12. Self-esteem This bump should be easily discernible, but in balance, avoiding indications of vainglory on the one hand, or inferiority feelings on the other.

13. Approbativeness This indicates the wish to do well either in private pursuits or in a career. Too large a bump may indicate vanity and an inflated self-importance, while a small one shows a disregard for society's opinion.

14. Prudence Too large a bump points to over-caution, while a deficiency indicates foolish recklessness.

15. Benevolence Too small a bump indicates a mean and selfish nature, but too large a one points to a mindless, universal charity.

16. Respect This indicates respect for those who deserve it, and perhaps veneration in the religious sense. One that is too large points to an unpleasantly subservient nature, and perhaps religous mania; too small, to a possibly undisciplined revolutionary zeal.

17. Determination This is self-explanatory. But be aware of the possibility of over-development sufficient to indicate obstinacy and unreasonableness.

18. Conscientiousness Again, this is self-explanatory but over-development of this bump could lead to inferiority feelings and a constant sense of guilt.

19. Optimism Too large a bump suggests a credulous person.

20. Belief Too large a bump indicates the fanatic, the acceptor of all superstitions; too small, the sceptic.

21. Beauty A bump denoting ability to appreciate the beautiful, whether in nature or in art. If too large, it can suggest dissatisfaction with the everyday.

22. Humour Self-explanatory. Those who have this bump well-developed are liable to turn their wit caustically on those whom they disapprove. Better that, perhaps, than the solemnity displayed by those in whom this bump is under-developed.

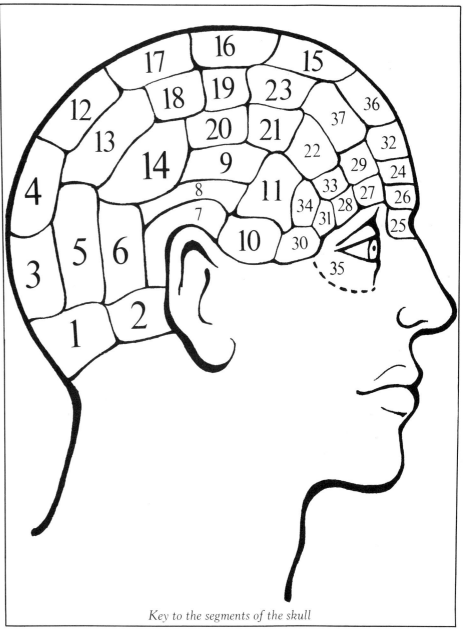

Key to the segments of the skull

23. Emulation This is allied to the ability to learn, so it is especially useful in the young. But if too large it denotes a certain lack of self-assertion.

Perception

24. Observation This denotes the general ability to differentiate between one thing and another, to take in one's environment. If too large, it suggests the spy and the gossip.

25. Shape If well-developed, this bump suggests high mathematical ability, awareness of shape and form and a good memory for them.

26. Size This bump denotes the ability to perceive and evaluate the relative importance of things, not only physically, but in events as well. Architects and draughtsmen will do well if they have such a bump.

27. Weight An understanding of mechanical forces is suggested by this, pointing to balance, both physical and

mental and perhaps some athletic skill.

28. Colour Self-explanatory. This will be developed in painters and country lovers.

29. Place memory Again, self explanatory. Well-developed this bump suggests the eager traveller.

30. Numbers Calculating skill, arithmetical dexterity.

31. Orderliness An understanding of sequence and regularity is denoted here. But in excess, this bump hints at overtidiness and fussiness over details.

32. Memory for events This bump points to a really good memory, particularly for events in the client's personal history, or in history generally. Thus it is a bump denoting a successful student.

33. Time sense A bump indicating an acute sense of time, and thus probably of rhythm. Connected with possible musical ability.

34. Melody Denoting a strong sense of harmony, this bump would confirm

any musical ability indicated by the previous one.

35. Verbal expression A dexterity with words is indicated here. It may be literary, oratorical or linguistic, depending on other characteristics.

Reason

36. Comparison This bump stands for a most important analytical faculty: the one which allows us to compare and contrast objects, events, items of information, ideas and plans.

37. Causality This bump, if developed, suggests logical skill. The ability to argue backwards to first principles, forwards to a rational conclusion. These traits suggest the philosopher, theologian or author.

Analysis

You must always remember that these bumps are not very high, nor very clearly defined. To discover them takes a fair amount of practice. The skull is like a landscape, one feature flowing into another, and to identify each one by touch alone is not easy. If the minor variations in personality are more difficult to discover, you should nevertheless attempt to do so, for the main traits of character are greatly modified by those less important elements which cluster about them. Here again, the information given by the shape and varying thickness of the skull reaches you through the fingers item by item. It is up to you to combine those items into an overall analysis.

For example, a large bump of Self-esteem, a large bump of Benevolence, a small bump of Acquisitiveness, allied to a large lump of Friendship and a small bump of Domesticity, particularly if there is a well-developed bump of

Phrenology was part of the nineteenth-century popular theatre — here 'the Great Baggs' is seen lecturing during a scene from 'Apple Blossoms' at the Vaudeville Theatre.

Appetite, adds up to a character picture which may well be that of a man who spends his evenings buying drinks for everyone, getting his satisfaction from being liked for his material generosity to his friends. But other bumps may modify this picture. Bumps of Conscientiousness, of Humour, of Causality, could materially alter the analysis, and reveal a rather more complex and intelligently thoughtful character.

It is your understanding and intuitive sense which must put everything together to create a final picture, both consistent and accurate, from the contours of your client's head.

Numerology: what numbers reveal

Numbers stand for order. With mathematics a complex problem can be reduced to numerical terms and arrive at a logical conclusion. Because of this, because numbers can bring order out of apparent chaos, people have always attempted to manipulate numbers and use their power to unravel the complexities of human personality and life. Numbers therefore appear in many different ways and in several methods of fortune-telling. The varied Kabbalistic theologians, both of antiquity and the Middle Ages, used numbers, in association with a curious alphabet which was part Hebrew and part Greek, for divination. The Babylonians, skilled astronomers and mathematicians as well as astrologers, magicians and soothsayers, believed that numbers had secrets to reveal. And astrologers in general have always relied on numbers to an extent. Clearly they had to as calculations based on the hour and date of a person's birth played such a large part in their analyses. The methods of analysis which follow are simple and amusing to use. Even if you are a poor mathematician you can use numerology, the 'science' of numbers, to gain some insights into the characters of those around you — and into your own character, too.

Primary numbers

The numbers are each linked to a planet, and it is the planet which suggests the major characteristics associated with the number.

One
The Sun Ambition, action, even aggression; but also creativity, individuality and the positive elements in character.

Two
The Moon Imagination, receptivity,

Each number — usually so ordinary — can have a mysterious power of its own, an individual atmosphere.

artistic qualities; also balance and harmony.

Three
Jupiter Authority, conscientiousness, a strong sense of duty. Because this number also stands for the trinity it shows attachment to the family.

Four
Uranus Opposition, rebellion, reform. These traits are often coupled with idealism and a lack of worldly success.

Five
Mercury Excitable, highly strung, always searching for new adventures.

Six
Venus Attractive, even magnetic, with a love of beauty; easy to make friends with, trusting and to be trusted.

Seven
Neptune Love of travel. This is also the magic number so it stands for psychic powers.

Eight
Saturn Intensity and loneliness, extremism. This often indicates great success but at some cost to private happiness.

Nine
Mars Determination, will, aggression, a hastiness of temper, both courage and impulsiveness. This is the most important of the single numbers and is thought of as having great power.

Secondary numbers

Compound numbers also have their significance, and there are several ways of determining the appropriate number and deciding what it means. In one system, the significant numbers run from 10 to 52, and are arrived at by simply adding together the values of all the letters in either the given or family name of the enquirer.
Another system, below, remembering that the Hebrew alphabet has twenty-

two characters and that Numerology has Kabbalistic associations, considers only the numbers from 10 to 22 as meaningful. In this system it is the second given name, the one which is not normally used, which is coded into numbers. The numbers have the meanings given below.
Ten Attainment, self-confidence, completion.
Eleven Success. But there are hidden dangers, threats of treachery.

Twelve Uncertainty, anxiety, repression, even victimization.
Thirteen Neither lucky nor unlucky. This number is, however, symbolic of power which wrongly used can bring destruction, not least upon the user.
Fourteen Danger overcome, especially natural hazards.
Fifteen Obstinacy, strength of personality, verbal facility.
Sixteen Accident, danger — hence a warning, especially to the over-confident, who need to take more care.
Seventeen Harmony, spirituality.
Eighteen A warning of quarrels and a destructive materialism. Its very association with materialism can, however, mean that it adds strength to what the primary numbers suggest, supporting the good, providing a counterweight to the bad.
Nineteen Good fortune, inspiration, success, new and brilliant ideas.
Twenty Of doubtful influence, suggesting on the one hand zest for new plans; on the other, steadiness in

carrying them out—a steadiness perhaps not strong enough to restrain the impetuous.

Twenty-one Ambition achieved, freedom, independence; but in those whose Primary number is 3, it suggests overconfidence, impatience.

Twenty-two A strong number, increasing the significance of what the Primary number has indicated. It suggests dreams and false judgements, so it may lead to disaster.

Date of birth

In numerology, as in astrology, the subject's date of birth is important. This is to be expected as it is a personal set of numbers relating to the day on which he or she was born.

This date is simply converted to a Primary number. Just write the whole birth date out in figures, add them together once, then add together the result, until you are left with only a single figure. So, if the client was born on April 14th, 1945, the date in figures is 4.14.1945, which you write as the sum, $4+1+4+1+9+4+5$. The answer, 28 gives you the sum $2+8$, which in turn gives you the answer 10. And that, added together, gives the single number you need for the reading — the number 1.

Names

To give a deeper character analysis apply the divinatory power of numbers to the client's name and surname.

Numerical equivalents
This simple key gives a numerical equivalent for each letter.

A	B	C	D	E	F	G	H	I
J	K	L	M	N	O	P	Q	R
S	T	U	V	W	X	Y	Z	
1	2	3	4	5	6	7	8	9

Using this method the name 'Janet', for example, becomes 11552. Proceeding in the usual way this becomes the sum, $1+1+5+5+2=14$. These two figures added together give you the Primary number 5.

Numbers have always had ritual significance, especially in the religions that are based on the Bible. Left top: the Seven Angels bearing plague; bottom left: the Four Horsemen of the Apocalypse; bottom right: the Second Coming of Christ.

Follow exactly the same method to reduce a surname to a Primary number. However, when dealing with the second given name, omit the final stage because for this Secondary number you need a double figure.

When the second given name is too short or has too many A's to give a double figure, use 10 as an equivalent for 1, 11 for 2, 12 for 3, etc. Do the same when the name adds up to more than 22; that is, reduce it to a Primary, then find the double-figure equivalent. So, for example, if the name adds up to the figure 32, that would reduce to the single number 5, which gives you the Secondary number 14.

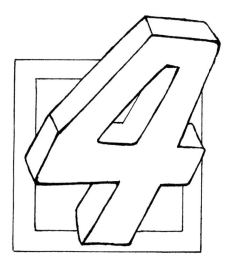

Cheiro's system

Cheiro, the famous French clairvoyant and palmist who lived and worked in the late nineteenth century, gives in his *Book of Numbers* a key which he claims may have originated with the Chaldeans. (Alphabets have changed so much since then that this is difficult to prove or disprove.) Here is his version.

A—1	G—3	N—5	T—4
B—2	H—5	O—7	U—6
C—3	I/J-1	P—8	V—6
D—4	K—2	Q—1	W—6
E—5	L—3	R—2	X—5
F—8	M—4	S—3	Y—1
	Z—7		

A full analysis

Once you have mastered the use of the keys and the meanings of the numbers you can give someone a full reading. To do this you reduce the client's birth-date, name and surname to Primary numbers. These, reduced again to a Primary number, give you the Character number — the key to the client's character. The client's second,

less-used, given name is reduced to a Secondary number and this tells you which character traits are strengthened or weakened.

Suppose, for example, that you have to analyze the character and prospects of a lady named Mary Pamela Waters, who tells you she was born on September 15, 1951. Following the procedure above her birthdate is reduced to the sum $9+1+5+1+9+5+1=31=4$.

Next ask her whether she is normally called Mary or Pamela. This will tell you which name gives you the Primary and which the Secondary influences. If it is 'Mary' which she most often uses, write that name and the name 'Waters' vertically, one below the other, then write beside the letters their equivalents in figures.

Using the first of the two keys above (not Cheiro's system), this would give you the following:

M=4
A=1
R=9
Y=7
Total: 21=2+1=
Primary number 3
W=5
A=1
T=2
E=5
R=9
S=1
Total: 23=2+3=
Primary number 5

Thus: total name number is $3+5=8$
birth date number is 4
—
Total=12
Thus: $1+2=$ Character number 3

You now know that the main characteristics of Mary Waters are those associated with the number Three: conscientiousness, a strong sense of duty, an authoritarian streak. To find out to what extent these traits are modified turn to her less-used middle name. Using the same key this gives you:

P=7
A=1
M=4
E=5
L=3
A=1 Total: 21=Secondary number.

You discover that Mary's already strong personality is given even more force by her secondary characteristics: her individuality, her need for independence. In all, this analysis suggests that she will be a very successful woman, although her personal relationships might suffer.

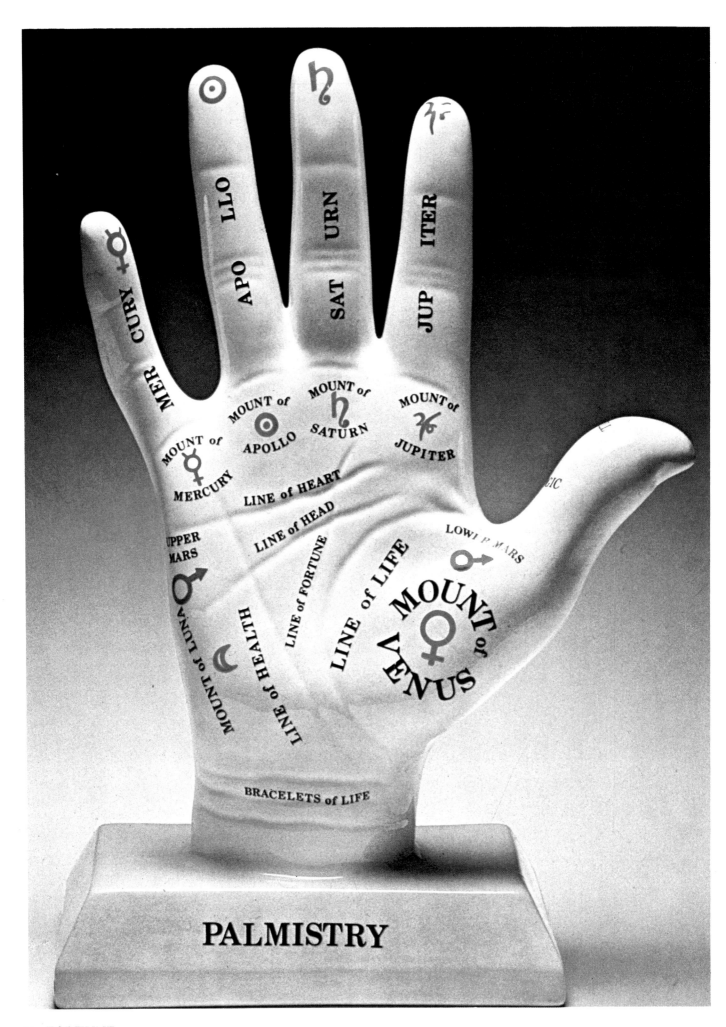

PALMISTRY

Palmistry:reading the hands

There are two aspects to palmistry. The first, called Chirognomy, attempts from the shape of the hand to analyze a person's psychological and emotional make-up. The second, Chiromancy, seeks to use the lines of the hand to foretell a person's future. Palmistry is very old. It was known in China over five thousand years ago, and some people think that it began there. Others believe that it was first practised either in Egypt or India.

Reading of hands is still widespread in modern India, and throughout the Middle East too. The Ancient Greeks knew of it — Aristotle certainly mentioned it, calling the hand 'the organ of organs'. It was known in Western Europe at an early stage, too. The first datable use of the word 'palmistry' was in a book written in English in the fifteenth century, but since books were rare at that time and seldom survived, it was probably used long before.

It is hard to be certain whether the lines of the palm actually foretell the future. That they, and the shape and structure of the hand, should give an indication of character is, however, much more plausible. From the literature on the subject, one can believe that some sort of connection has been more or less proved. Thus an analytical reading is likely to be more accurate, more useful and, in some ways, even more amusing than speculative prognostications of an uncertain future. Not only that: it cannot be repeated too often that such prognostications carry their own dangers. People tend to be credulous in these matters, nor need you believe that they are not when they protest their scepticism. Prophecies may, therefore, prove worrying for them and, in some cases, may alter their attitudes and plans.

Thus the palmist, however temporary and amateur, has responsibilities and should be aware of them and be very careful in the way they are discharged. A cautious silence is wiser than reckless forecasts of disturbing events.

Hand prints

A superficial reading of a hand can be done fairly quickly, but anything more detailed requires time. For this reason, and because it provides you with examples to study and learn from, it is a good plan to take prints of palms you want to examine. If you do this, anyone whose hand you decide to study does not have to sit still for the length of time that it takes to obtain a complete reading. This also has its uses when you want to read the hand of a child. The lines in the palms of children begin to be of significance during the first year — an age when they are not renowned for their willingness to keep still!

For a hand print you will need ink of the kind used in lino-cuts, a five-inch roller, a sheet of glass and a rubber pad not less than twelve inches square. Cover the roller in the ink, then roll it out on the glass to give it an even coating. Then ink the hand you want to examine. Try to cover it as evenly as possible. Have a sheet of good-quality heavy white paper ready on the rubber pad and press the hand to it, making sure that it does not slide sideways and so blur the impression. For the same reason, hold the paper firmly when the hand is raised from the paper. To start with, you may have to make several impressions before you have one good enough to use, but in a little while you will gain in confidence and skill.

There is another quick method, if you have access to certain types of flat copying machine. You can obtain a very good print in a few seconds, simply by laying your hand on the glass plate and operating the machine in the usual way. Care should be taken not to press the palm on the glass as this can obscure the lines. The samples given later in this chapter show how good the results can be.

For a time, most of the palms you examine will look strange and uninformative, but in time, like an explorer, you will learn how to fill in the blank parts of the map. For practice, you may be tempted to use your own palms, but in many ways this is unsatisfactory. We know ourselves — or we think we do. As a result, if we examine our own palms what we see must pass through that mesh of preconceptions, both flattering, and unflattering, that all of us have about ourselves. The habit of clear thought comes better from concentrating on the palms of other people. This is one reason why the ink and roller are so important.

Types of hand

Once you have the print — clear and yours to examine at leisure — what do you actually look for? First, apply the principles of chirognomy and consider the shape of the hand; the shape, length and placing of the fingers; and the position and prominence of the various mounds. This will enable you to assess the character of the subject. Take your time over this.

There are various ways of dividing the types of hand, but basically hands are either square or long.

Square hand

The square hand is one in which square fingers stem strongly from a square palm. This formation indicates practicality, a sense of order, a certain caution. People with square hands are generally practical, with their feet firmly on the ground. Their reliability will make them true friends and faithful lovers. Their liking for hard work, honesty and strength of purpose help them to do well in tasks that require physical effort. Their practicality and application are always indicated by the squareness of the palm, regardless of the length or shape of the fingers.

Long hand

The long hand, also called the conic or the artistic hand, usually has a slightly tapering palm, wider nearer the wrist, narrower at the base of the fingers. The fingers, too, taper gradually to rounded, cone-like tips. As a rule, such hands have small thumbs, and these indicate an impulsive temperament that can be inconstant. People with long hands tend to be very open to external influences and can become infatuated, with ideas and places as much as with people. Their moods can fluctuate between enthusiasm and dejection. Generous and sympathetic, they take up causes, sometimes of a revolutionary nature. They can be furious, but rarely for long, and they are not given to prolonged sulking. Because of the intensity of their feelings, they tend to pursue careers in the arts.

However, a hand that is too long and delicate can suggest that the depth of feelings may be greater than the staying power. For the artist, a better hand-shape might be tapering fingers rooted in a square and practical palm, or a long palm with square-ended fingers. Both these shapes promise a mixture of sensitivity and hard work which can lead to success.

Mixed characteristics

The subject of mixed hands is important in practical terms because not all hands conform to the theoretical purity of types.

Short fingers and long palm This combination suggests energy, speed of reaction, activity — especially if the palm is covered with many fine lines. But it also suggests impatience with the slower and less energetic. A person with this impatience may be somewhat at the mercy of his own versatility and there can be no doubt about his stability and reliability. People with hands of this type tend to choose individualistic, even unconventional occupations, certainly those which offer a variety of challenges and demand flair as much as application.

Long fingers and square palm The combination of long fingers and square palm is found in people who prefer reason to emotion, order to chaos. Such people put a possibly exaggerated emphasis on theory, on how things ought to be, without making enough allowance for how things actually are, influenced by human frailty, feelings and idiosyncracies. The work they choose, however, will usually be interesting and they will often show originality in it. They are, above all, the people to call on in problem situations. They may be teachers, journalists, even philosophers. Certainly they are often found in work that involves communication in one form or another.

Spatulate fingers Some hands, either long or short, have fingers shaped like spatulas, wider in the top segment than lower down. Sometimes their palms are of the same shape. This hand is usually a sign of great originality, combined with self-confidence and, often, creative energy, a mixture of qualities that is not suited to the solitude of a scholarly or artistic life. It is more likely to make people tend towards an outdoor life — an engineer, an explorer, or a successful soldier, for example, might have a palm and fingers of this shape. Some hands are truly mixed. Their fingers — short, long and spatulate — seem to have been brought together from various types of hand. When the mixture is marked, it points to a person of great versatility, someone who might also find it difficult to keep to one goal.

Other general features

Size of hand

There is also the size of the hand to be considered. Large hands suggest a reflective temperament, the ability to take stock before arriving at decisions. Small hands often belong to people who have a swift, intuitive awareness of the characters of those they meet, and of any decisions that must be taken, but who dislike finicky detail or laborious caution. They think big and act fast, and their haste can sometimes create problems for them.

Knotty joints

Knotty joints on the fingers suggest neatness, exactness, a power to observe and concentrate. They are said to be especially common on the hands of scientists.

Texture and elasticity

Make a note, too, of the texture of the skin of the hand you are studying. Fine skin can be a sign of sensitivity. When the skin of the hand is elastic and resistant it can be taken as an indication of energy and willpower. However, if the skin is very hard, this may suggest obstinacy and a lack of perception.

Flexibility

You may also take manual flexibility as an indication of mental flexibility, taking into account the age and occupation of the person whose hand you are studying.

The thumb

When you have come to a decision about the overall character of the hand, it is time to consider some of the details. First of these is the thumb, indicative of energy, symbol of the vital forces within us. A large thumb, therefore, suggests an energetic personality, making a forceful impact on the world.

The top, or nail, segment of the thumb, if it is particularly large, suggests a developed and powerful will and a great deal of staying-power. When this segment is rather narrow — and particularly if it is slightly pointed — the indication is of energies being uncontrolled and wasted.

The second segment, related to logic and reason, is sometimes markedly thinner than the top one, and this can indicate impulsiveness and a lack of control, a tendency to act hastily on impulse. Conversely, a thick, well-developed second segment suggests good control — even too high a degree of it, great reasoning powers and consequent caution.

Consider, too, the relative lengths of the two thumb segments in order to see what balance there may be between energy and reason. When the thumb is set low in the hand, the energy it expresses is likely to be held back.

The fingers

Index finger

Since it is closest to the thumb, the index finger — or 'finger of Jupiter' — is often considered in conjunction with it. Also called 'the finger of ambition', it indicates the kind of desires for which the energy indicated by the thumb will be available and their strength.

A long index finger This suggests the desire to dominate and ambitiousness. If the energy of the thumb supports the ambition, the latter can result in a successful life, although not necessarily in a happy or well-adjusted one. If the energy indicated by the thumb is weak, however, then desire is likely to outreach grasp and this will result in feelings of failure and inadequacy.

Short index finger This, too, suggests feelings of inadequacy. When the finger belongs to a hand indicating a high degree of sensitivity, you can assume that you are studying someone retiring, meek and possibly put upon by others.

Straight index finger If the finger is straight this is a sign of well developed powers of observation, which will not be present if the finger is bent.

Curved index finger An index finger which bends towards the middle finger is a sign of a tendency to hoard and hold on to money. It shows a general lack of openness towards the outside world.

Middle finger

The middle finger, considered to be under the influence of Saturn, is a good indication of overall psychological balance. A long middle finger can be a sign of an over-intellectual approach to life. Conversely, a short middle finger indicates impulsiveness, a tendency to act on inner promptings rather than on a cool consideration of reality. The heavier and more dominating the finger, the more clearly it indicates seriousness and thoughtfulness. If the middle section is markedly larger than the other two, this indicates a love of the

Right: an intriguing and romantic party game — reading the palm of your favourite man.

country and of gardening.

Ring finger
This, the 'finger of Apollo', relates to the emotions and the better its shape and over-all balance, the steadier the psychological balance of the subject is likely to be. If the finger seems out of proportion with the rest of the hand, this may be a sign of an emotional life out of phase with the rest of the subject's existence. A very short finger, for example, can indicate difficulties in adjusting to other people, individual-istic solutions to emotional problems, a nature given to arousing and even provoking conflict with others. A longer finger than expected points to a high degree of introversion and pre-occupation with oneself and one's inner needs.

Little finger
The little finger, dedicated to Mercury, should be looked at in conjunction with the ring finger, the finger of Apollo, for it gives an indication of how well people are able to get on with others. Most important is its placing. If it is isolated from the other fingers, it indicates an inability to relate to other people and to form attachments. A long top segment to the little finger

suggests fluency with words. If the finger as a whole appears a little twisted it can indicate untruthfulness.

Nails
The fingernails also have their sig-nificance. When they are short and broad with square tips, they indicate a high level of irritability and some degree of obstinacy. Short nails which are slightly rounded, however, suggest energy and a developed, even intru-sive, curiosity. The long, oval nails of the dandy or the languid beauty in-dicate, as one might expect, no great energy, but a certain tolerance and an easygoing nature. They also show a high level of idealism and people interested in mysticism may well have nails of this kind. The larger the moons, the healthier the heart is likely to be. When the rest of the nail is very red in colour, the subject is likely to have a quick fierce temper. Better red nails than very pale, white ones perhaps, for the latter are thought to denote selfishness.

Palm contours : the mounts
Now look at the palm of the hand and the pads of flesh which give it its

variations in contour. These are called the mounts.

The Mount of Venus
This lies between wrist and thumb and indicates energy. When it is fleshy and high, energy is strong and needs to be expressed physically rather than through thought or feeling. People with this form of mount, therefore, are often at their best working with their hands and muscles, particularly if they have a square-palmed, square-fingered hand. Alternatively they will tend to be very active sexually, although whether with one partner or with many only the rest of the hand can indicate. A well-developed Mount of Venus also suggests a high level of artistic ability, particularly when it is crossed by lines running towards the thumb from the Life Line.

The Mount of the Moon
Opposite the Mount of Venus, directly below the end of the Head Line, this also indicates energy, the energy of the imagination, which can feed creativity, although it does not guarantee it. In fact, when this mount extends well down the wrist, it suggests a sensitivity so extreme that it may inhibit all artistic work. But on a square hand,

a well developed Mount of the Moon indicates imagination controlled by practicality, consequently it can indicate success in such careers as architecture or journalism. However, study of the rest of the hand may show that the imagination is uncontrolled and expressed in day-dreaming rather than definite action. The qualities of the Moon belong to the subconscious part of the mind and are passive ones.

The finger mounts

The mounts at the bases of the fingers are also significant in a full analysis of the hand.

The Mount of Jupiter
Situated below the index finger, this indicates ambition and a healthy self-confidence. When it is over-developed, however, it is a sign of arrogance and an excessive desire for prestige. If it is practically flat, it shows an almost total lack of drive and even of self-respect.

The Mount of Saturn
Rising below the middle finger, this is often difficult to see. When it is apparent, though, it indicates a serious temperament. If it is rather large, it can be a sign of a mistrustful, pessimistic outlook.

The Mount of Apollo
Lying below the ring finger, this mount suggests an even and cheerful temperament, as well as some artistic ability. If the mount is very high, then these characteristics may blur into one another and become excessive, taking the form of self-indulgence, affectation and greed, especially for attention. A flat mount, however, indicates a rather dull personality, insensitive to beauty and unmoved by anything that is subtle or that needs perception.

The Mount of Mercury
In its normal form this emphasizes the characteristics which are also indicated by the little finger above it — fluency, swiftness in the use of words, wit. When it is too high, it hints at a tendency to lie and to use trickery; when it is too flat, it points to a dull personality — without humour or quickness of thought, too ready to believe and easily tricked.

Mounts of Mars
Finally, there are the Mounts of Mars. The Upper Mount of Mars, between the Mount of Mercury and the Mount of the Moon, gives an indication of moral courage, although when it is over-developed, it can be a sign of bad temper and a tendency to inflict mental cruelty. Someone whose Upper Mount of Mars is flat is unlikely to stand up for any cause — not even his own.

The Lower Mount of Mars, lying between the Mount of Jupiter and the Mount of Venus, suggests self-control and calmness in difficult situations, the sort of cool courage which test pilots or rock-climbers often need. Too big a Lower Mount of Mars may belong to a bully, whereas too flat a mount may be a sign of cowardice.

Mount markings

Often the mounts of the palm and fingers have various shapes on them — crosses, squares, triangles and so on, formed by the fine lines which cover the hand. Of these, the square in particular is thought to be fortunate and to offer protection, while the criss-cross of a grille is thought on the whole to be unfortunate. A triangle is usually taken as a sign that a person has fortune on his side, but when the mount is marked with the cross and the star, the significance of this may depend on where exactly on the mount the marking is located.

Below: the positions of the main lines and mounts. Right: the meanings of the Mount markings.

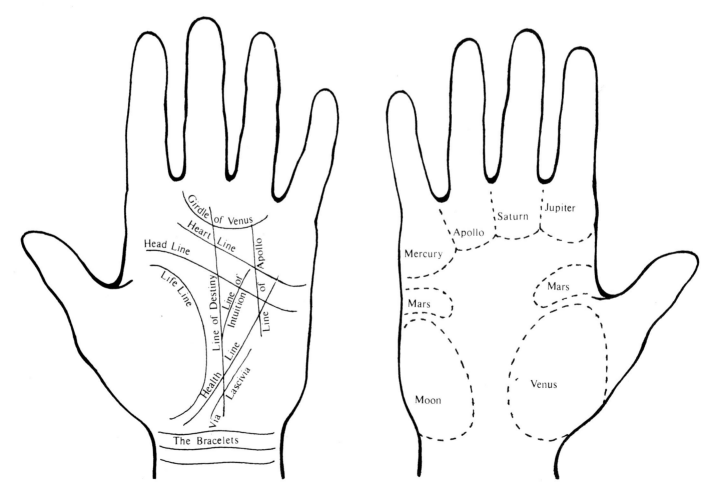

Some of the meanings of these marks are given in the chart below.

The main lines

Having studied the outline and contours of the hand, you will know something about your client, and you can now go on to read the lines of the hand. The three main lines are those of Life, the Head and the Heart. The information they supply will to some extent be modified and added to by the many other lines which cover the palm.

Right versus left hand

In a right-handed person the lines of the left hand indicate the qualities he or she was born with, and those of the right hand the qualities developed and modified by the efforts and accidents of life. In a left-handed person this is, of course, reversed.

Line of life

The Life Line runs from below the Mount of Jupiter and above the Lower Mount of Mars, starting from or bisecting the Head Line, and ending at the heel of the hand, pointing approximately to the middle of the wrist. As its name implies, it gives an indication of physical energy, vitality and strength, but it does not foretell the length of life or the time and nature of death. Nothing read in a palm is certain, partly because the lines themselves alter in varying degrees as time passes.

Life span Because a deep, sharply cut Life Line suggests health, energy and drive, this does indicate the likelihood of a considerable life span. A shorter line is not, in itself, the sign of a short life. It may merely mean a shortage of energy and a need to conserve strength. A line which moves in fits and starts, without being quite broken and with the sections interwoven, indicates variations in levels of energy. A person with such a Life Line will alternate between bursts of energy and periods of fatigue. If the line is really broken, there is a strong possibility that a severe illness or accident has happened at some point.

Ambition Where the Life Line begins has significance, too. If it begins higher than usual, actually on the Mount of Jupiter, it may be a sign of great ambition. Thinner lines cutting the Head Line and reaching up into the Mount of Jupiter also suggest ambition, although ambition probably backed by a sense of proportion.

Calculation If the Life Line begins by forking from the Head Line, the indication is that the energy will be controlled by calculation. The further along the Head Line that this fork occurs, the more control will be exerted. In extreme cases it reaches the point of cunning and results in a complete dependence on calculation, at the life expense of normal feeling and spontaneity. When the line begins below the Head Line, this can be taken as a sign of an impulsiveness that can seem almost uncontrolled at times.

Self-control A chain of lines between Head and Life Lines, before the Life Line breaks away to curve down on its own, suggests a tendency to inward questioning and too much self-control, mixed with periods of excitable, outgoing behaviour.

Line of the head

The Head Line starts halfway between the thumb and index finger, usually right at the edge of the palm, and either runs straight across the palm, stopping anywhere from halfway across to the other edge of the hand, or else curves downward to the Mount of the Moon.

Intelligence There could be some

	Square	Triangle	Star	Grille	Cross
VENUS	Love life without worry	Calculating in love affairs	*Mid-Mount:* sex-appeal; *near wrist:* difficult love life; *near thumb:* long devotion		*One, clearly marked:* a single lifetime love; *many:* a varied love life
MOON	Travel risk-free	Success, fame	Travel risk	Depression and tension	Travel risk
JUPITER	Success	Organizational skill	Unexpected success	Domineering character	Advantageous marriage
SATURN	No money worries	Problem solver	Tragedy threatens	Introspective, undirected	
SUN (APOLLO)	Good name safe	Fame, calmly taken	Influential connections	Vanity, attention-seeker	Disappointment, loss
MERCURY	No tensions	Can influence others, friendly	Success, especially for the studious	Cunning, even dishonest	Beware the dishonesty of others
UPPER MARS	No physical harm			Danger	Danger
LOWER MARS	Danger will not harm	Success in physical combat		Danger	Danger

link between the length and depth of the line and intelligence. It does seem to reflect the type of mind and the way in which this works. A long Head Line may be an indication of a broad and lively understanding. A short Head Line can be a sign of limited intellectual ability, but within the limits there may be intense activity and consequent achievement.

Concentration The depth of the line is what counts here. The deeper and more sharply cut it is, the greater the powers of concentration which it reveals. When the line is chained, this suggests bursts of concentrated mental activity. When it is doubled, with two lines running parallel, it can be a sign of a mind that is disorganized, perhaps to the point of being unbalanced.

Sensitivity A long, straight Head Line suggests a good memory and mental determination. When it slopes down to the Mount of the Moon, it reveals a sensitive temperament, probably in-volved in the arts and certainly creative, but if it continues into the lower part of the Mount, it can be a sign of over-sensitivity, of an inward-looking nature that may suffer from depression.

Caution If the Head Line, as it begins, touches the Life Line, this is an indication of moderation and caution. The longer the two lines remain together, the more pronounced the caution is likely to be, so that decisions will be arrived at slowly and with difficulty.

Irritability If the Head Line crosses the Life Line, having begun on the Lower Mount of Mars, it reveals a tendency to irritability, although a Head Line straight across the hand is a sign that this tendency is at least partly controlled.

Independence Independence and brilliance of mind will show themselves in a slight gap between Head Line and Life Line, but if the Head Line then curves away to the Mount of the Moon, these qualities may be limited by a changeable, over-sensitive temperament. When the space between the two lines is especially wide, there is reason to take this as a sign of recklessness, of a tendency to take independence and courage to the point of foolhardiness.

Self-expression A fork at the end of the Head Line suggests skill in self-expression, particularly through the use of words, and the more the line slopes towards the Mount of the Moon, the more marked that skill becomes. A line curving in this way, with a clear fork at the end, indicates literary ability. A three-pronged fork suggests diverse abilities — intelligence, creativity and also good commercial sense. Too large a fork, however, points to too much versatility.

Right versus left hand Check, too, the variation between the line shown on the left hand and that on the right hand. If there is a marked difference,

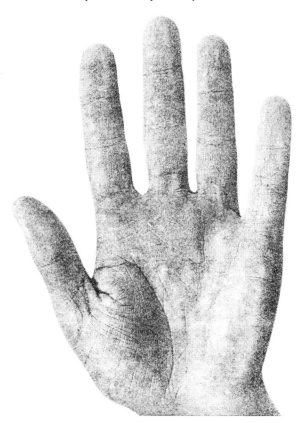 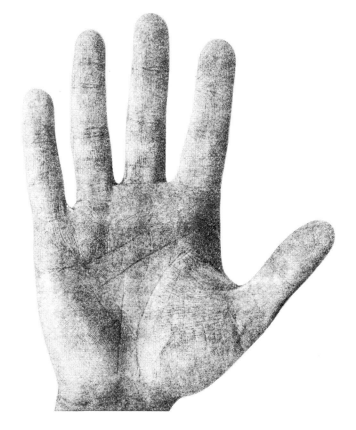

Thom Henvey   Age: 25   Occupation: Writer

Thom has an abundance of energy and strength. The fingers and thumb being fine show a fastidious nature in contrast with his obviously well-developed physique. Only things of quality will interest him for he has a critical eye, but he will be less involved with the material side of life as he gets older and his curiosity about the inner side of things.

His is rather a restless, vacillating nature which does not allow him to sit still for long. He has a lot of ideas, plans and projects which his well developed right hand, giving him energy — shown by the thick base of the hand and heavy finger of Venus — enables him to carry out.

Just about now, an extra Fate line is shown in his hands indicating new responsibilities which he is about to take on himself, but the sound structure of the hands shows that he will cope successfully. It is possible that he is thinking of this new venture right now.

His Head Line is straight, clean cut, long and detached from the Life Line. This indicates success for it shows self-control, speed of thought, attention to detail and a very practical precise execution of work. He is capable of sustained mental effort and can burn the midnight oil with impunity.

His Line of Destiny indicates that at 29 success should be his. After that date Thom can afford to build on the foundation which he has already achieved.

this will show how much basic characteristics have been modified, and even distorted for the sake of making a way in the world.

Line of the heart
The Heart Line rises below the Mount of Mercury and runs across the hand, ending somewhere under or near the Mount of Jupiter. As its name implies, it gives some indication of the depth of feeling of which a person is capable. Its strength, length and depth relate to the profundity and steadiness of the emotions, and its position is important, too. The lower it is on the palm and the more curved the line itself, the more sexuality and sex-appeal will be apparent and the more zest and enjoyment will be shown in love-making. The curve of the line is important, however. If the Heart Line does not rise at the end but finishes a long way below the Mount of Jupiter, this is a sign of reserve and inhibition — an inability to be spontaneous and out-going. If the

line ends by pointing upwards between the fingers of Jupiter and Saturn (the index and middle fingers), take this as showing a great enjoyment of physical pleasure.

Male versus female hands In a male hand, some feminity is indicated by a marked curve downward below the Mount of Jupiter. In a female hand, a similar curve suggests strong masculine elements.

Emotional balance If the line forks on and around the Mount of Jupiter, this has importance, too. A small fork on the Mount of Jupiter points to a steady emotional balance, and to the likelihood of a lasting, harmonious marriage. A wider fork, however, jabbing at the Mount of Saturn as well as the Mount of Jupiter, indicates changeability and self-absorption — a lack of interest in other people. Breaks in the Heart Line may show that there has been an illness of the heart at one time, or an emotional crisis, which probably

ended inconclusively or unhappily.

Romantic predictions
Of course, it is in this connection that people most want to hear prophecies, so here are a few signs to look out for. Little lines branching from the Heart Line indicate romances and affairs — those running upwards being the happy ones, those dropping down from the line the ones which may prove miserable. A chained Heart Line shows at least one affair after marriage.

A break under the finger of Saturn means that a lover has left or will leave. A break under the finger of Apollo shows that it is the person whose hand you are studying who ends the affair.

Overlapping lines point to a quarrel and a break-up, but only a temporary one. A line running from the Heart Line and cutting through the Fate Line points to a marriage which will end unhappily. An island on the line under

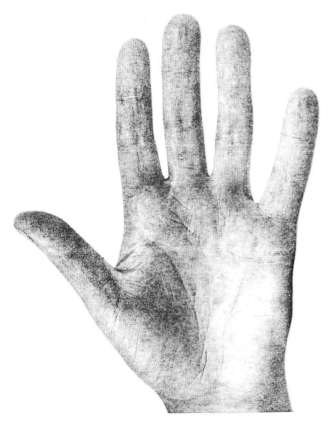

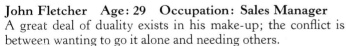

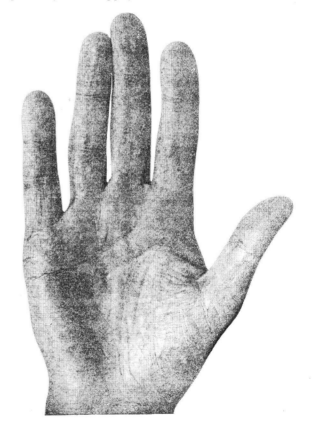

John Fletcher   Age: 29   Occupation: Sales Manager

A great deal of duality exists in his make-up; the conflict is between wanting to go it alone and needing others.

His thumb indicates a very abstract way of looking at life. He likes to ponder things out a good deal. As a youngster, at home, he looked forward to the time when he would be independent. Now he is independent but the finger of Apollo clinging to that of Saturn shows a need for security and a great attachment to the family.

His constitution is not too good and he probably tires easily, but can overcome this by will-power rather than energy potential. This is also borne out by the innate love of fine detail shown in his hand — long Head Line on the left

hand — which is his natural ability; and the desire to delegate such detail — short Head Line on the right hand.

He is very much an individualist and a rebel in his way of expression. His short Head and Heart Lines show he is undemonstrative. He expects to be understood by his actions rather than by his words. This being so, he tends to be misunderstood, but having a good measure of sensitivity (he has fine lines on his hands), he feels this acutely. Consequently his marriage could suffer. Success for John is a matter of harmonizing the dual sides of his nature — shown in the very different appearance of his two hands — and the sharp divergence between his private and public life.

the finger of Saturn suggests an unsatisfactory love affair, one that will bring little happiness. And an island anywhere on the Heart Line points to trouble in love affairs, emotional problems, sexual turmoil, but also to an underlying emotional stability.

Sexual relations The lines which mark sexual relationships run down the edge of the hand, at the side of the Mount of Mercury and between the middle finger. The fainter lines there indicate love affairs, the stronger ones marriages. When they run close to the Heart Line, they show that the affair or the marriage will happen early in life, probably before the age of thirty.

Emotional control Also important is the relation between the Head Line and the Heart Line, for sometimes the temperamental factors that govern these two lines may be in conflict. If the lines lie close together, the emotions are under the control of the mind. If the Heart Line lies very high on the palm, however, this suggests that emotion tends to overrule intelligence and that the subject has a possessive, even a jealous disposition. If a line connects the Head and Heart Lines, it indicates a violent and possibly destructive infatuation. Equally, a line which stretches from the Line of Destiny, the Fate Line, towards the Heart Line without quite reaching it suggests a love affair which will never end in marriage.

Marriage lines The lines indicating marriage also have their own important variations. A break in a marriage line has an obvious meaning, but if the ends overlap, the couple will come together again. If a marriage line curves towards the Heart Line, it is probably that the person whose hand you are looking at will live longer than whoever they marry. If there are tiny downward lines at right angles to a marriage line, your client's marriage-partner may have a long illness. An island on the marriage lines points to infidelity.

Children

Children are indicated by any firm lines which run down to the marriage line from the base of the finger of Mercury — the little finger — and the stronger any of those lines are the greater the likelihood that the child will be a boy.

Girdle of Venus

Sometimes a loosely chained, semi-circular line appears, looping from between the index and middle fingers to between the third and little fingers.

This is known as the Girdle of Venus, for it indicates a deeply passionate nature. The passion need not necessarily show itself sexually, for those with high ideals and an intense involvement in public causes may well have the Girdle on their palms. But it is usually taken as a sign of sexuality. As a result, in the nineteenth century when there was uneasiness about the sexual elements in human make-up, people thought the Girdle of Venus an indication of criminal tendencies and profound instability. Today it can be taken to be no more than a sign of sexual vigour, especially if it is supported by the evidence of a high Mount of Venus. A Girdle broken in the middle shows possible inconstancy, though this would have to be confirmed by other signs in the hand.

Line of Destiny

This line is strongly indicative of the kind of life which a person will live. In terms of character, a well-defined line suggests inner harmony, but a segmented and almost aimless line will be a sign of feelings of inadequacy and an inability to adapt to reality. The place to find the Line of Destiny is near the middle of the hand, running vertically from the wrist towards the middle finger. After adulthood, it changes little, particularly in anyone whose way of life is settled. As a result, the line is much used by palmists making forecasts about their clients' future.

Where it starts Discover where the Line of Destiny starts. If its starting point is almost off the palm, at the first of the lines which run round the wrist, it may belong to someone who has had heavy duties early in life. If it rises from the Life Line, this can be a sign of a cramping early environment, although, if the line continues strongly, this indicates success of life once independence has been achieved. A strong Line of Destiny rising from the Head Line can mean success rather late in life. When it starts from the Mount of Venus, this can show support from a loving family. When the Mount of the Moon is the starting-point, it can mean that help will come from outside the family — and that life will be made exciting but rootless by variety.

Where it ends See how the Line of Destiny ends. If it curves from the Mount of Saturn towards the Mount of Jupiter, you may be looking at the hand of someone who will achieve authority and power over others. If it curves towards the Mount of Apollo, it suggests fame and fortune to come. Any subsidiary line running upward

from the Line of Destiny may be taken as a good sign. Lines that run downward, however, show a likelihood of loss and failure. A Line of Destiny ending at the Head Line suggests eventual failure in life, largely through personal shortcomings and lack of forethought, while one ending at the Heart Line suggests unhappiness in love.

Crosses and linked, chain-like formations If these occur in the Line of Destiny they point to periods of difficulty: a cross at the beginning, for example, suggests a hard childhood, whereas a cross at the end can be a sign that old age will bring difficulties. Breaks in the line are a sign of personal upheavals, but when the fragments overlap, you can assume that the changes which they signify are chosen and not accidental ones.

Line of Apollo

Otherwise known as the Line of the Sun, this runs up from the wrist to the Mount of Apollo. It indicates by its strength good fortune and success. It does not give any clue as to which particular endeavours will bring luck but only indicates that whatever is attempted, good or bad, will have a successful outcome. It overrides by its mere presence many of the negative indications which may exist elsewhere in the palm. If you are reading the hand of someone tempted to become a gambler, a good Line of Apollo might make a sound basis for an otherwise chancy career.

The line should be clear and straight and unflawed. If it is broken or chained, its indications are reversed, for no venture is likely to last long enough to reach success. Naturally, there are few lines which are not flawed in some way, just as there are few lines which are totally successful. If it starts either on the Life Line or the Fate Line, the Line of the Sun indicates high honour and great wealth. When it begins on the Mount of the Moon, however, it tells that this success will be based on approval, amounting to worship, from the opposite sex. Pop stars and film stars are likely to have such a line. If the line rises from the Line of the Head, success will be later in life and will probably be based on intelligence, so the client could be a writer.

Markings on the line A star anywhere along the line of the Sun adds to the amount of luck which the line itself indicates. A series of bars near the beginning of the line shows that early life was hard. When they come later, they indicate the efforts of rivals to discredit your client. A cross, here as elsewhere, is a bad omen and shows that, for a while at least, luck can run out even for the most fortunate people. If the line breaks, look to see how strongly it continues after the break. This indicates no more than a temporary setback if the line is still clearly marked. But there is one sign which overshadows the good fortune shown by the line of Apollo — a deeply hollow palm. A very concave palm always indicates a continuing run of bad luck.

Line of intuition
The line indicating intuitiveness starts just below the little finger. It ends, having traced a shallow, semi-circular course, near the edge of the palm on the Mount of the Moon. If clear, it may be taken to show well-developed psychic powers, and a strong interest in the mystical and the supernatural. See if the lines on the two palms differ. Someone who has the line deeply engraved on the right hand has worked at these intuitive gifts and developed them consciously. If the lines appear only, or in a much more developed form, on the left hand, intuition is rarely consciously resorted to, but operates subconsciously, prompting decisions which may later be rationalized.

Bracelets
These are the three lines running across the wrist that, if they are clear and distinct, indicate good health and a fortunate and peaceful future. If faint, they signify the opposite of this and if the one nearest the hand is chained, this suggests that a life full of struggle will be crowned by success. Marks in that top bracelet have their significance, too. A star there tells you that a legacy may be expected. An angle, like a tick beside a correct sum, means something similar — money and honour — but not until after middle age, while a cross indicates a happy old age after a lifetime's struggle.

The lines which begin in the top bracelet are also important. The one leading to the Mount of Apollo indicates a journey to the tropics, while that to the Mount of Mercury predicts unexpected wealth. Look for lines reaching up to the Mount of the Moon, for every one of them indicates that a journey will be taken.

Minor lines

There are a number of other lines, which are by no means invariably present in the palm. This does not matter, since their meaning will not affect a general interpretation.

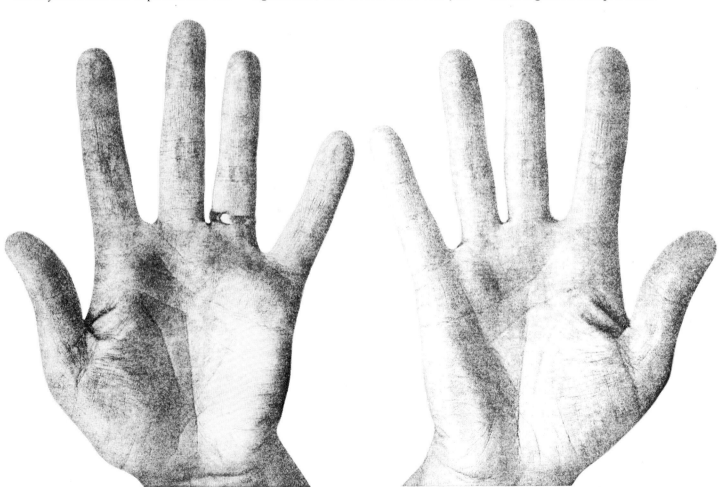

Nicky Hayden   Age: 28   Occupation: Housewife
An impulsive, down to earth, and uncomplicated make-up is shown in the short, straight-set fingers and square palm.
Although she is very independent, she is also warm and instinctive. She could have married early, say at eighteen or nineteen years of age. And her strong Heart Line, taken together with the lines for children, seem to indicate a happy, meaningful relationship with probably three children — two boys and a girl.
She has a strong analytical ability — shown in her long finger of Mercury — and should be good at working with figures as this would use her selective capacities to the full. She can discriminate and sort out what is relevant to the work on hand.
She can expect a change for the better at 28 as her Line of Destiny turns then to the left, and this will make her career more satisfying. And as she gets older she appears to develop the intuitive powers shown in her hand by the strong Line of Intuition.

Fortune in the cards

All playing cards are mysterious. Their curly-bearded kings stare up at us enigmatically, cryptic smiles on their faces. The familiar spades, diamonds, hearts and clubs are potent symbols with many hidden meanings. But what was their beginning? One tradition has it that they were invented by a concubine of the Chinese Emperor S'eun-Ho in 1120 AD. Another indicates that cards may have been used for divination in China two centuries earlier, having possibly come to China from India, crossing the Himalayas to enrich Chinese culture as Buddhism and Yoga had also done. In ancient India, cards were certainly used for augury, the packs being divided into ten suits — one for each incarnation of the Hindu god, Vishnu.

From the start, however, cards seem to have been used as oracles to help resolve people's personal problems. This function almost certainly preceded their association with play and gambling. Most of the skills of early civilizations had a religious aspect, and divination, as the word implies, involves the intervention of the gods.

Some of the European names for cards have derived from Middle Eastern words connected with prediction. The Hebrew word *naibi*, meaning sorcery, and the Arabic *nabi*, meaning to foretell, have given their name to an old Italian card game *naïb*, from which comes the Spanish word for cards, *naipes*. Indeed the Middle East provides another contender to the claim of having invented cards — the ancient Egyptian magician, Hermes Trismegistus. Whether he actually existed, or whether the stories surrounding him are mythical, is not certain, but there remains the possibility that it was under the Pharaohs of the Nile that cards were first employed in the endeavour to throw a little light on human destiny. This theory seemed to make sense when it was believed that the Gypsies originated in Ancient Egypt, for it was certainly the gypsies who spread the use of cards across Europe. But it is now known that the Gypsies first came from India, and so perhaps they brought cards with them from there, over two thousand years ago. Whatever may be the truth of their earliest origins, by the late Middle Ages cards were widespread throughout Europe. And there was a ready audience eagerly seeking their hidden messages—and has been ever since.

The pack

It was probably for the sake of convenience that the seventy-eight cards of the full pack were in the course of time reduced to the familiar fifty-two which we use today. For the art of foretelling the future by cards, known as cartomancy, it is usual to reduce the number to thirty-two. From the full pack, therefore, take the thirty-two cards which have a value of seven or higher, the ace counting as high.

What the individual cards mean

Each card has a meaning, and if you are going to be convincing it will be as well to familiarize yourself thoroughly with these.

It is necessary to remember, however, that certain combinations of cards have a meaning of their own, some of which are given later on. And any card may have its meaning altered by those which lie alongside it.

Since for centuries cartomancy has been mainly an oral tradition, there is bound to be a certain lack of precision, and there is some confusion about the exact meaning of a few of the cards. The most generally agreed meanings of what each of them stands for are given below.

Hearts

Ace Love, warmth, romantic and/or domestic happiness. Good news.
King A generous, handsome man, fair-complexioned.
Queen King's female counterpart, golden-haired and loving.
Jack Friend or lover — but perhaps not always to be trusted.
Ten Success. Good fortune — perhaps unexpected. Happiness.
Nine Fulfilment of hopes. A happy outcome.
Eight Invitation. Perhaps a journey or a visit. Often domestic contentment.
Seven Contentment, especially in marriage.

Spades

Ace Legal matters. A proposition in love or business.
King Lawyer — perhaps a little shady.
Queen Widow or divorcee, subtle and cunning.
Jack A dark, devious, even treacherous, young man.
Ten Worry, begun by a letter. Perhaps a journey — or even imprisonment.
Nine Failure and misfortune.
Eight Sorrow, usually caused by the receipt of bad news.
Seven Quarrels, turbulence — and the receipt of boring advice.

Diamonds

Ace Important letter — and/or ring.
King A man of power and strength.
Queen A gossip. Good-looking, but spiteful.
Jack A messenger, or a man in uniform.
Ten A change, probably a journey.
Nine News, probably concerning money and associated with some new enterprise.
Eight A short, happy journey. (In summer, perhaps a picnic.)
Seven An unexpected gift, or alternatively, hurtful criticism.

Clubs

Ace Success, particularly financial.
King A dark man, friendly and helpful.
Queen Warm, dark woman, affectionate and helpful. Perhaps a widow.
Jack A dark young man, sincere in love.
Ten Sudden money, as in an unexpected legacy.
Nine Financially good marriage.
Eight A dark girl or woman, who brings joy and good fortune.
Seven A small child, perhaps associated with money.

Meaning of suits

Sometimes, when you are laying out the cards, one suit figures more prominently than the others. When this happens, that suit's predominant influence to some extent alters the significance of the other cards. This means that they must be read in the light of that influence. Consequently, it is necessary to know what general feeling is conveyed by each suit.

Hearts

Love, affection, friendship, family and marriage. The emotions, particularly

the warmer, more positive ones. Court cards correspond to people with blond or auburn hair.

Spades
Misfortune and warnings of misfortune. Enemies, scandal and betrayal, suffering and loss. Court cards correspond to people with dark hair.

Diamonds
World affairs, but rarely touching the

extremes of either circumstance or emotion. Court cards correspond to people with blond or auburn hair.

Clubs
Information mainly about friendship, loyalty and money. Thus also worry, anxiety and betrayal. Court cards correspond to brown-haired people.

Client card
The corespondence of court cards to

particular complexions and hair-colourings makes a basis for the selection of one card to represent the person whose fortune you are telling. This card is known as the 'client card'. A fair-haired young woman will be represented by the Queen of Hearts, a fair-haired young man by the King.

An elderly woman with fair, red or grey hair will be represented by the Queen of Diamonds, and a man of similar type by the King.

Dark-haired young men and women are represented respectively by the King and Queen of Clubs.

Dark-haired elderly men and women are represented by the King and Queen of Spades.

The meaning of the other cards can then be related to the way they lie in juxtaposition to the client card.

Here are some examples of the way this works. If your subject is a man and his client card lies next to the Queen of his own suit, this suggests that he will marry soon. If the Queen of Hearts lies next to it, his love will be true, deep and long-lasting. If the Queen of Spades, it suggests a furtive and perhaps guilty affair. If the Queen of Clubs, that he will form a relationship, perhaps a deep friendship, with a wealthy woman.

The Jack of Diamonds next to his client card points to a secret love affair; the Jack of Clubs to money troubles; the Jack of Hearts to some unfaithfulness, and the Jack of Spades to the threat of dishonesty by work colleagues, particularly subordinates. If your subject is a woman, marriage is indicated when her client card lies beside a King of the same colour. A King of the opposite colour suggests a secret love affair. The Jack of Hearts points to a flirtation. The Jack of Diamonds indicates a short-lived infatuation, and the Jack of Spades means an unhappy involvement with a predatory male. If Jacks keep appearing in her cards, the indications are that she may be somewhat indiscriminate in distributing her favours. Whether you mention this will depend on your sense of honesty.

Interconnected meanings

Certain other juxtapositions of cards have an especial significance. The Ten of Diamonds near the client card points to a journey. Near to the Ten of another suit, it suggests a legacy. Near to the Ace of Diamonds, it means a letter, probably from abroad. The Ace of Diamonds itself, when next to the Nine of Spades, indicates a threatened illness. And when next to the Seven of Diamonds, an impending quarrel of some violence. The Ace of Spades near both the Eight and Nine of Spades gives a gloomy reading, suggesting that the future will be heavy with disappointments — friends will betray, business will falter or even fail, deals and arrangements will threaten to collapse.

The Eight of Diamonds raises promises of travel — near any Heart the journey will be short, but near any Club it will be prolonged. If the Seven of Diamonds lies near any Club, the indications are that money will cause problems. A Nine of Diamonds near the client card suggests a path strewn with obstacles. While if the client card is near the Nine of Spades — traditionally a sinister card — there will be bad news and the possibility of illness.

Pairs, triplets, quartets

It is of particular significance when cards of the same value are laid down in pairs, threes, or — most powerfully — fours. These should be looked for first, since the message given by the cards as a whole will be influenced by their meanings.

These meanings have been subject to traditional variations, but the following are the ones most favoured:

Aces
Two Forthcoming marriage.
Three Minor love affair, or flirtation. According to some, excessive credulity.
Four Success.

Kings
Two The portents are good.
Three Considerable success, especially commercial.
Four Great success in all endeavours.

Queens
Two Friendship, but gossip threatens.
Three A visit, but there is jealousy and back-biting.
Four Menace of scandal and slander.

Jacks
Two Bickering will break out.
Three Disharmony, especially within the family.
According to some, laziness.
Four Vicious and upsetting quarrels. According to some, success.

Tens
Two Receipt of an unexpected, but probably small, sum of money.
Three Financial and/or legal problems.
Four Good fortune, particularly perhaps in a career.

Nines
Two Limited success, particularly financial.
According to some, obstacles.
Three Success.
According to some, boredom.
Four A fortunate surprise.

Eights
Two Trouble and argument.

Three Family problems.
Four An anxious, frustrating time.

Sevens
Two An old enemy appears — or perhaps a new lover.
Three A baby will be born.
Four Enemies encircle.

Laying out the cards

Now that you have some idea of what to look for in the cards, what are the forms or shapes in which they should be laid out?

Over the years there have probably been hundreds of ways, as seers and experts frequently devise their own variations. But to start with it is best to use a few methods, each simple to follow, which provide clear readings. These readings must always be supplemented by your own intuition. In order to aid this elusive faculty, the readings must be done in an atmosphere of intense concentration, in itself an aid to belief.

It is always a good idea to ask your subject to shuffle the pack before cutting it because this directs his or her attention closely on to the cards and creates a feeling of expectancy.

Cutting the pack

Cutting is traditionally done with the left hand, because the mystic forces which add to the divinatory power of the cards are supposed to flow through the left, or sinister, hand. The subject should certainly always cut the cards, even if he or she does not shuffle them.

Reading your own cards

By and large, it is not advisable to use the following methods of laying out cards for trying to divine your own fortune. Traditionally they are intended to answer the questions of others, using powers and energies for which you are supposed to be the neutral channel.

There are, however, a number of games of patience (solitaire) whose object is to give answers to one's own questions. Usually these work on the basis that if they do not come out, the answer is 'No', and circumstances are not propitious.

The wizard
One method which seems to demand a fair amount of co-operation from Fate is known as the Wizard. You take the thirty-two card pack and begin laying down the cards face upward. As

you lay down the first card, you say out loud "Seven". Then as you lay down the next card you say "Eight", and so on until you have called "Ace", when you start again with "Seven". Whenever you actually lay down a card which corresponds to the value you have called, put it to one side. Keep going through the pack until it is exhausted — or until you are.

The more swiftly you and Fate discard the cards, the better augury it is. If the cards and your calling do not coincide at all, or only at very long intervals, you may assume that your project is, for the time being, unlikely to prove successful.

Reading other people's cards

Some of the methods of laying out cards for divination for a client follow. The one thing that they all have in common is that you need to use your imagination and intuition to interpret the messages they have to offer.

It is for this reason, as well as to foster confidence, that you should learn the meanings of the cards by heart. Only when you have them immediately available will you be able to string them together into coherent and evocative predictions.

Cartomancers have a saying that the cards get tired, and this may be true if they are really under some external influence. Many people believe in the existence of psychic powers, and cartomancy is one way to concentrate them if you have any. But it seems they should never be abused by too much use, or by a shallow approach.

Limit your card readings, therfore, to one session an evening, or at most two, divided by a period of rest. Only do some half-dozen readings at each session. If the other people present want to hear what you see in their cards, let them wait for a future occasion.

Finally, one small warning. People take predictions of this sort more seriously that they themselves may realize. If you find yourself faced with what seems a very gloomy forecast, reflect if a little diplomacy might not be in order. Illness or bankruptcy are serious subjects. And while warnings are not threats, predictions have a way of influencing behaviour, If, therefore, you are faced with a row of cards heavy with Spades, you might be well-advised to make a compromise between honesty and optimism. A little consideration for your friends' peace of mind cannot come amiss.

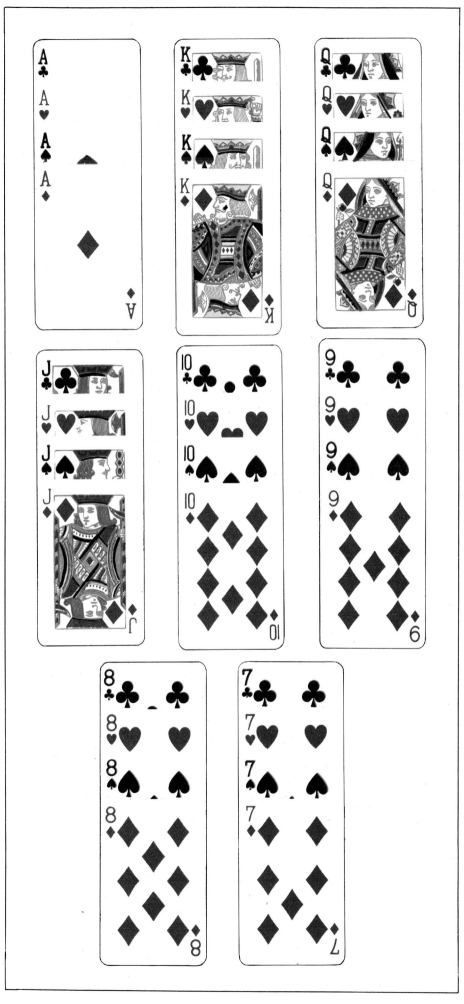

The fan

For this method, spread the cards face down on the table, and ask the subject to draw thirteen at random.

Take these thirteen cards and spread them face upward, in a fan shape.

Look to see if the client card which represents your subject is there, or the seven of the same suit which may act as its substitute. If neither appears, you can either begin again or take it as an indication that the moment is not propitious for divination.

Taking the client card first, count the cards off in fives, from left to right, reading every fifth card, and always using the card you have just read as the first of the next five. (Naturally you do not read the client card, but continue until you have read all the other twelve.)

Next ask the inquirer to pick five more cards from what remains of the pack left face down on the table. Spread these out face upward in a separate fan. These cards are read in pairs. The first and fifth together, then the second and the third. The middle card is read by itself.

Reading

Here is a reading of the cards which appear in the photograph opposite, top. The inquirer is a fair-haired girl, so the client card will be the Queen of Hearts.

First consider the cards as a whole. Clubs predominate — although only slightly. Bear in mind that money may be important in the reading. There is a pair of Sevens, and these might indicate a new lover — or an old enemy — erupting into her life.

Beginning with the client card, and counting off the cards in sets of five, the first card to be read is the Seven of Diamonds, indicating a gift, and this is followed by the treacherous but darkly handsome Jack of Spades. Then the bait of an advantageous marriage is dangled by the Nine of Clubs. The Seven of Hearts indicates contentment in marriage — a trait not normally connected with the Jack of Spades.

The Seven of Clubs gives a child associated with money. This may be involved with a legacy, for it is followed by news about money indicated by the Nine of Diamonds.

From here on, the marriage signs become clearer, for in the Jack of Clubs a new suitor appears, honest and sincere. He is more the type to lead to the contented marriage already indicated and he may well be the lover indicated by the adjacent pair of Sevens.

The Nine of Hearts suggests that hopes will be fulfilled, a suggestion reinforced by the Eight of Hearts with its hint of domestic felicity.

The Ace of Clubs offers financial success, probably by way of the Ace of Spade's new proposition. This could possibly be made by the affectionate, although widowed, Queen of Clubs. (She could be understood to be the new lover's mother.)

All this is confirmed by the first pair of the supplementary five cards, the Ten of Clubs suggesting unexpected money, and the Ace of Diamonds an important letter.

But now there is bad news. The money may have to do with someone's illness, perhaps even the death of someone close because the Ten and the Eight of Spades in juxtaposition make a formidably unpleasant pair. But the King of Diamonds is a man of power, a tower of strength. If your subject trusts in his ability, she will come through this final crisis.

To summarize this information:

First, the client is being pressed to marry a young man whom she does not trust because it would be financially advantageous for both of them to do so. She should resist, for a new and truly loving suitor will appear through whom both happiness and money may be hers. Nevertheless, a crisis is brewing. Someone close to her is likely to be very ill, and an anxious time will follow. She should trust the strong man, friend or relation, who will appear at that time to help her bear the strain.

The seven cards

After your client has shuffled and cut the pack, draw out each seventh card, putting the six cards in between to the bottom of the pack each time.

When you have twelve cards, spread them out from left to right in the order in which you draw them.

Select the client card. If it is not there, take it from the remainder of the pack. If it is there, draw a thirteenth card at random from the pack and lay it with the others.

Beginning with the client card, count off seven cards, reading the last one. Continue in this way, reading every seventh card. When you have read all the cards, shuffle the thirteen cards again, and ask the client to cut them (with the left hand, of course). Spread the top six cards face upwards in a line. On the first five of these, place one additional card, leaving the sixth by itself. Then on the first two, lay down

two cards which you have left.

The first little stack of three cards represents the subject as a person. The second stack of three cards stands for the house or apartment he or she lives in. The next stack of two cards shows what is expected to happen. The fourth stack represents what is not expected, the fifth stands for the real surprises that are lying in wait. The final, single, card will tell your subject's thoughts or wishes.

Reading

Opposite (below) is the second stage, the 'seventh cards' having already been drawn. The client is a man, well-set-up, middle-aged (his client card was the King of Clubs), who is married.

Begin with the three cards on the left, which relate to him directly, and they tell us that he made a financially helpful marriage (Nine of Clubs) with a warm, affectionate lady as dark-haired as himself (Queen of Clubs) and that he either likes travel and change or has very recently come back from a significant voyage (Ten of Diamonds).

Next, his house: it is a source of worry, sometimes feels like a prison (Ten of Spades), he has a neighbour who makes him feel uneasy (Jack of Hearts), but his house has accommodation for a child, probably a nursery.

He nevertheless expects, the next column shows, to remain contented in his marriage (Seven of Hearts) and anticipates seeing someone close to him in uniform (Jack of Diamonds).

There are shocks in store, coming by way of an unreliable lawyer (King of Spades) — but the outcome will be unexpectedly happy (Six of Hearts).

A relationship, perhaps a marriage, between two mature friends of his, both with a great capacity for affection (King of Clubs and Queen of Hearts) will be the real surprise the next few weeks will bring.

Then, his wish. Here the Eight of Hearts echoes the Ten of Diamonds in the first column: what he really wants is the chance to travel.

The mystic star

From the thirty-two cards, pick out the client card and lay it face up in the middle of the table.

Your client, having shuffled the rest of the pack, cuts it twice, placing the resulting three piles face downward. You then turn each pile the right way up, and read the top cards thus revealed, first one by one, then in combination. This is called a general

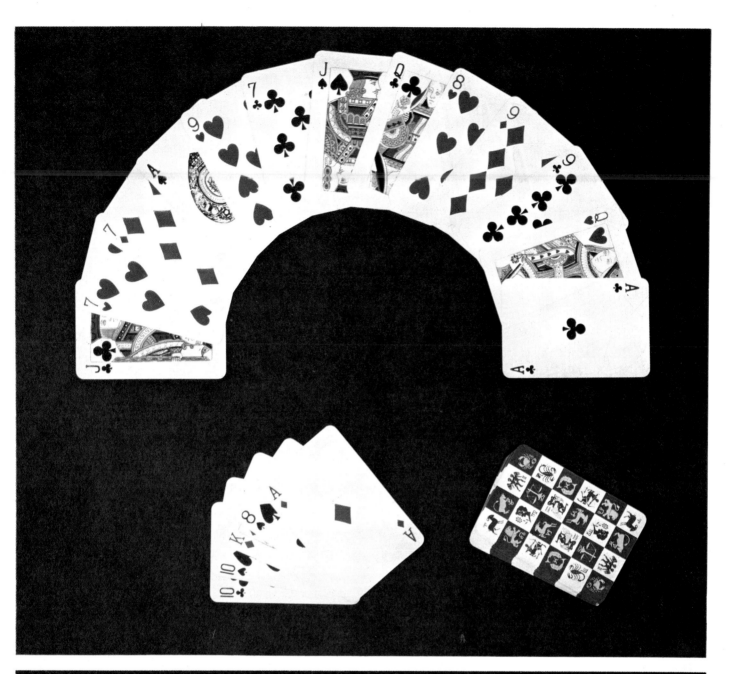

indication and will give you an overall idea of the way fortune is running for your subject. The client now reshuffles the pack.

You take the top eight cards and, in an anti-clockwise direction, lay them face downward at regular intervals around the client card, which still remains in the centre of the table. It is in this way that you form the mystic, eight-pointed star.

Your client now takes the rest of the pack, and on each of the eight cards lays two more, working round the circle twice and setting the cards face down one at a time.

One by one, still working anti-clock-wise, turn each little stack of three face upward. Read the information all three cards provide in conjunction.

Reading

The client card, the Queen of Spades, shows that we are considering the fortune of a dark, middle-aged, married lady.

The general indication, which was gleaned from the Nine of Spades, was of changes, with some steep ups and downs likely.

The first column, directly above the client card, certainly suggests a down-turn in fortune: a shady lawyer (King of Spades) and a man of power (King

of Diamonds) combine to bring about the client's failure (Nine of Spades). Moving leftward, we discover news (Nine of Diamonds) of a romance (Ace of Hearts) involving a very dear friend, probably blonde (Queen of Hearts). Since she is known for her generosity, it is probably her gift (Seven of Diamonds) which leads to a journey (Ten of Diamonds), almost certainly to visit her and discuss the financially advisable marriage (Nine of Clubs) which is in the offing.

But what of the client's own life? A new proposition (Ace of Spades) leads to an unexpected success (Ten of Hearts), one of the sudden ups in her

fortunes, which in turn gives her the chance of another journey (Eight of Hearts).

Can it be this which leads to domestic quarrels (Seven of Spades)? If so, financial success, already indicated above, now appears again (Ace of Clubs) and married happiness results for her (Seven of Hearts).

Yet now a new worry will appear, which seems to involve her daughter, the dark girl (Eight of Clubs). A letter arrives (Ten of Spades) concerning a dark young man (Jack of Clubs) who loves the girl. Correspondence ensues, for the Ace of Diamonds points to a very important letter — probably from the dark, friendly man (King of Clubs) who appears to be the young man's father. And the King of Hearts, a generous, affectionate friend, takes a hand in the affair. Despite the intervention of the spiteful and gossipy Queen of Diamonds, the arrival of the young man's mother, warm and likeable (Queen of Clubs), leads on to a short, happy and joyful journey (Eight of Diamonds) which one can only suppose will be taken to the sound of wedding bells.

To summarize, despite an initial setback in a legal matter, a new venture will lead to financial success and domestic contentment. A friend will seek advice about a proposed marriage, and the client's own daughter, after a short period of anxiety, will go happily to the altar with the approval of almost everyone concerned.

Single question

There are a number of systems for answering one question at a time. Let the client ask his or her question. There are then several methods of seeing how the cards will answer it.

Four Aces

One involves the four Aces. After your client has shuffled the thirty-two card pack, lay the top thirteen cards face up on the table, putting aside any Aces. Gather up all the cards again, having shuffled them as before, lay out another thirteen from the top, and again pick out any Aces. Repeat this a third time. Be careful to keep the Aces in the order in which they have appeared. The sooner the Aces do appear, the better for your client. The order in which they appear is very significant, the early cards having greater power than the later.

Thus the Ace of Spades, if picked out first, overshadows the other three, meaning nothing will be achieved without difficulty.

First seven cards

An even shorter method of answering a particular question consists of laying the first seven cards of the pack face down in a row, then turning up the first, fourth and seventh cards. These will provide the information you need for your answer. But here, of course, you need to remember the meanings of individual cards, as well as the significance of each suit.

Sometimes, of course, the answers given by the cards seem to make no sense at all. If this happens, you must remember that the information they are offering has to do with the future, in which there may well be other factors involved which will give the cards an unexpected relevance. So it is always a good idea to note down which cards have appeared, for they may yet become important.

However, if they do seem to be jumbled and meaningless, it is permissible to lay them down a second time, but no more. If on the second occasion too they reveal nothing, that must in itself be taken as a message. Like any other oracle, the cards reserve the right to keep their silence.

Reading

The commonest single question, of course, concerns love and its ramifications.

With the layout below a young lady asked the plainest question of all: 'Does he love me?' The Ace of Hearts, telling of warmth, domestic happiness and affection, seems to give the answer she is hoping for. But who is the dark lady, helpful and friendly, for which the Queen of Clubs must stand? 'Oh, his mother — she likes me', the girl says, at once. The Seven of Diamonds stands for an unexpected gift. In this context, almost certainly an indication that the young man will himself, quite suddenly and quite soon, indicate how he feels.

The weekly forecast

For this it is not necessary to learn the individual meanings of cards. All that is needed is an awareness of what the four suits as a whole represent.

Ask your subject to shuffle and then cut the pack into three piles. Take the top card of each pile, and lay it face down on the table in front of you. Begin with the left-hand pile, and end with the right.

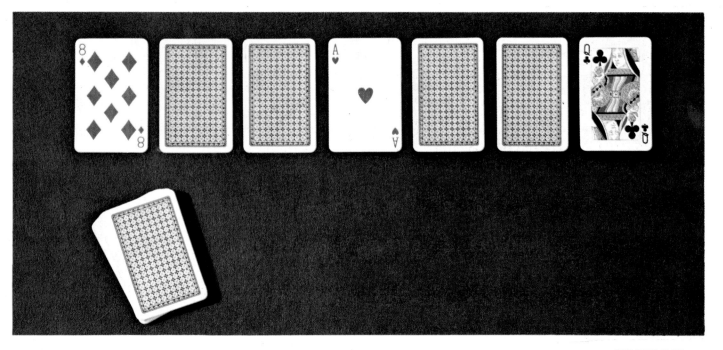

Take the remaining cards in the three piles, ask the client to shuffle and cut as before, and once again place the top card from each pile face down on the table. These should be placed alongside the original three, so that there is now a row of six.

Repeat this operation three times more, so that you end up with a row of fifteen cards.

Turn over the two cards at either end of the row. These will give you the general fortune for the following day, determined by the symbols and colours revealed. The right-hand card relates to the morning, the left-hand card to later in the day. (If you had Spades on the right and Hearts on the left, it might suggest early disaster, followed by affection or comfort later on.)

Working inwards, two by two, gradually turn up fourteen cards. These will give the seven day sequence of the week's fortune. The points value of each card may be important, for if the suit is unlucky, as Spades tend to be, the numbers revealed should be avoided on the day in question. Equally, numbers in a lucky suit should be followed up.

This leaves the central, fifteenth card still face down on the table. Use it to answer a question — the suit of the card will give you the reply. If your subject is anxious about some action to be taken in a love affair, a Heart would be an encouraging card to turn up. While for someone with a business query a Club would be preferable. For all questions, a Spade suggests that postponement of any plans might be the safest course.

Reading

A forecast of this kind was done every Sunday for the manager of a small factory. In this instance the Diamonds show for the next two mornings that conditions for business during these first days of the week remain equable. The evenings, meanwhile, display Hearts, which suggests that affection, perhaps love, will flower then.

The third day, Wednesday, has Clubs all day: a worrying day with some money problems seems likely. The next morning, Clubs persist — perhaps there is also a question of loyalty to a friend and a colleague, probably a woman, which must be decided. By the afternoon, however, the King of Hearts indicates that their friendship is restored. Saturday morning is a good time, with Diamonds back on display, to catch up on work lost during the midweek crisis; the afternoon, however, produces more problems, perhaps at home or with a neighbour. This is, if anything, intensified on Sunday morning when there is scandal in the offing, double-dealing, possibly domestic strife. By the afternoon, however, things seem on an even keel once more, and the client can relax and prepare to start work the following week.

The central card remains, answer to a single important question. On this occasion the man asked whether he should employ a particular young man. Clubs indicate steadfastness and loyalty, so the answer here is affirmative: the man should be taken on.

Temple of fortune

This more elaborate method was invented by a famous cartomancer in pre-Revolution Paris, when the glories of the mid-eighteenth century were collapsing in the uncertainty which preceded the storming of the Bastille. Ask the client to shuffle and cut the pack as usual, then lay it out, each card face upward, in the following manner.

Starting at the bottom of the column, lay six cards sideways, one above the other, on the right-hand side of the table. Similarly, lay six cards sideways, one above the other and starting at the bottom, on the left-hand side of the table.

Now place four cards sideways, again starting from the bottom, immediately to the left of the first column, in such a way that these four cards are opposite the spaces between the lower five cards of the column.

Now place five cards in the upright position, from right to left, in a row which is level with the top card of the right-hand column, thus making a connecting row with the top card of the left-hand column.

Now lay down another four cards, sideways again and working from the top, immediately to the right of the left-hand column, so that they lie opposite the spaces between the lower five cards of the right-hand column.

Finally, above the connecting row of upright cards, lay another upright row consisting of the last seven cards of the pack.

The two rows of sideways cards on the right reveal the past. The two rows of sideways cards on the left reveal the future. And the two rows of upright cards are concerned with the present. The three outer rows of cards give the primary indications in each case. The inner rows modify what the outer rows tell you. The order of the cards is, as always, of some significance. They should be read in the order in which you laid them down.

Below: The arrangement of cards which gives the weekly forecast discussed in the text. Above right: A temple of fortune — one of the more elaborate ways of reading the cards which is described in detail here.

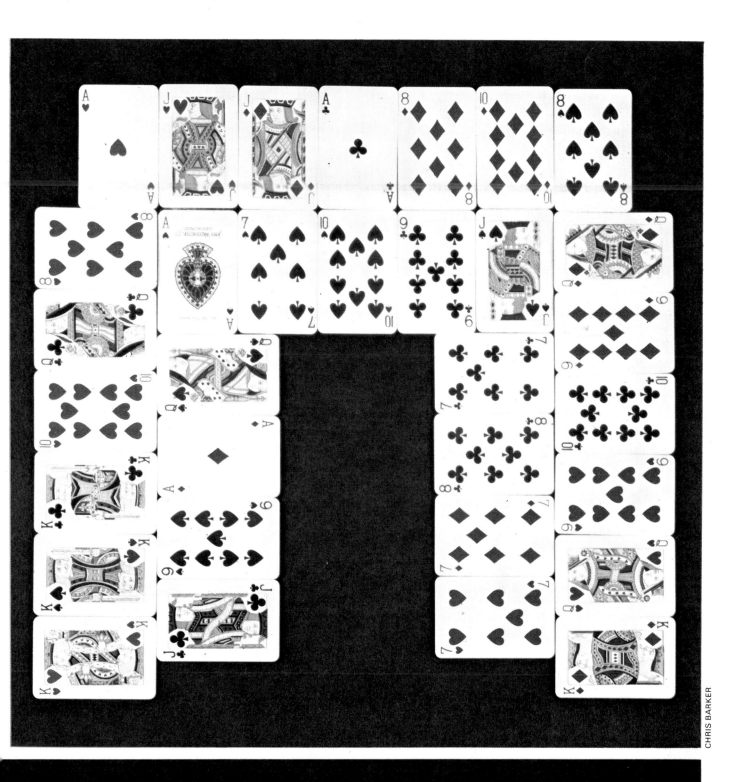

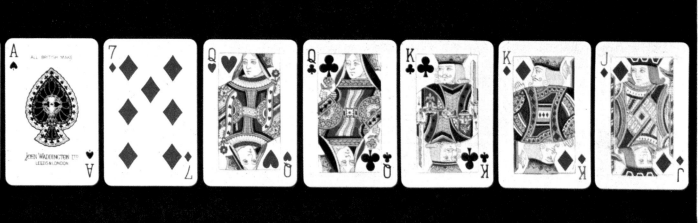

The mysterious Tarot pack

LE MAT.

LE BATELEUR

L'AMOUREUX.

LE CHARIOT

LA JUSTICE

L'ERMITE

TEMPERANCE

LE DIABLE.

LA MAISON DE DIEU

L'ÉTOILE

JUNON.

L'IMPERATRICE

L'EMPEREUR

JUPITER.

LA ROUE DE FORTUNE

LA FORCE

LE PENDU

LA MORT

LA LUNE

LE SOLEIL

LE JUGEMENT

LE MONDE

Most people regard Tarot cards with a degree of awe. Their age-old designs and symbols, their haunting figures, are deeply rooted in myths which remain mysteriously just beyond the boundaries of certain knowledge. It is easy to believe what these cards tell us and, involuntarily, to handle them with a feeling of solemnity, a sense of taking part in a very ancient ritual. Curious, and sometimes anxious, people have for many centuries consulted the Tarot. Partly because of their long history, and partly because of the power with which history has invested them, the Tarot cards are accepted by many people to whom no other system of fortune-telling makes the slightest appeal. It is, in a sense, the aristocrat of oracles.

Origins of Tarot

No one knows where these mysterious and potent cards were first devised. They have, however, consistently been linked with the Gypsies, who have long been regarded as the guardians of a secret branch of knowledge. This knowledge may have come from religious mysteries of pagan Greece, or the divine lore of the Chaldeans. What is true, is that both Tarot and Gypsies seem to have appeared in Europe during the period between the eleventh and fourteenth centuries.

Jacques Gringonneur, a fourteenth-century astrologer, sometimes credited with the invention of playing cards, almost certainly based the pack he devised for Charles VI of France on the Tarot.

The modern Tarot pack is based on the researches of an eighteenth-century French scholar named de Gebelin. His book *Le Monde Primitif* contained illustrations of the cards. It is this 'Marseilles pack' from which almost all the other Tarot packs used in the West have been derived.

The position of the Joker in the sequence has caused a certain amount of controversy. Many authorities have written works on the significance of the cards. But, untroubled by these discussions and differencies, Gypsies and others have used them to read the characters and fortunes of the thousands of people who have come to consult them.

Each pack of Tarot cards comes with instructions and interpretations. These are sometimes somewhat briefly or quaintly expressed, so below there is a simple explanation of the meanings of the cards.

Some people maintain that you should memorize all these meanings but you can, of course, refer back to the written word. And sceptics may be more inclined to believe your predictions if they see you referring to a text and interpreting it rather than apparently making the whole thing up as you go along! Belief depends a great deal on atmosphere.

The Major Arcana

The twenty-two cards of the Major Arcana, the Trumps, are subtle and complex symbols. They have a relation with the twenty-two letters of the Hebrew alphabet and the twenty-two branches of the Tree of Life which has a very prominent place in the Kabbala.

The Fool
Appearing anywhere, this card alters the meaning of the others. It is the free force in life, for it offers the inquirer a choice between good and evil, wisdom and folly.
Reversed: The choice may be bad and thoughtless.

1. Magician
Organization, control over natural forces, hence willpower. Suggests creative, perhaps artistic, ability.
Reversed: Weakness, force used destructively.

2. Priestess
The unseen, reached by divinatory power, thus an indication of unseen influences at work. Intuitive ability.
Reversed: Self-love, vanity, sensuality, superficiality.

3. Empress
The Earth Mother, thus fertility and marriage, wealth, the proper material rewards of endeavour.
Reversed: Barrenness, endeavour thwarted, resources dwindled.

4. Emperor
Determination, leadership, authority. The aid of powerful allies. A strong but well-controlled and directed sexuality.
Reversed: Immaturity, lack of control, subservience.

5. High Priest
Otherwise called the Hierophant or Pope. Stands for formal subjects: theology, ritual, law. Thus, acceptance of the conventions and hence social and material success.
Reversed: Inventiveness.

6. The Lovers
Harmony, balance between inner and outer, sacred and profane. Thus choice, based on attraction, hence success in love and — probably — marriage.
Reversed: Disharmony, unfaithfulness quarrels, perhaps divorce.

7. The Chariot
Triumph over financial difficulties, rivals and above all, over illness. Thus an indication of success in many areas.
Reversed: Ill health, undeserved success, restlessness.

8. Justice
Balance, legality, pedantry. Accountability for one's actions.
Reversed: Inequality, injustice. Merciful attitude to others.

9. Hermit
Meditation, prudence, receiving higher guidance. Thus a meeting with a wise counsellor who should be heeded.
Reversed: Immaturity, refusal to accept good advice.

10. Wheel of Fortune
Change, alteration — the endless highs and lows of life. Thus, unexpected change of fortune, sudden success.
Reversed: Failure and setbacks, demanding perseverance.

11. Strength
Courage, force of character, spiritual power triumphant over carnality. Thus the ability to overcome adversity, and hence any ill fortune shown in adjacent cards is modified.
Reversed: Materialism, lack of moral strength.

12. Hanged Man
To the spiritual — spiritual advancement. To the unaware — possible ill fortune. A pause in life, a withdrawal to develop inwardly. Thus, intuition, spirituality.
Reversed: Egotism, arrogance, false spirituality.

13. Death
Change, an ending — followed by a new beginning, perhaps in consciousness. Calm after a storm, reward after travail. But also, self-destructive fear.
Reversed: Inertia, stagnation. Revolution, perhaps assassination.

14. Temperance
Harmony with others, adaptation, successful timing.
Reversed: Quarrels, conflict of interests, separation.

15. Devil
Temptation, choice. Sometimes could

be inhumanity, carnality, illness.
Reversed: Dawn of spirituality and humility. Indecision.

16. Tower
Also known as the House of God. Catastrophe, undeserved disaster. Life style and ideas upset, permitting new enlightenment, but present material ambitions are likely to be thwarted.
Reversed: Oppression, perhaps false imprisonment. But through misfortune, freedom of body or spirit is gained.

17. Star
Hope, inspiration. Happiness-possibly fleeting. Spirituality glimpsed. Good health.
Reversed: Pessimism, obstinacy, gloom. Ill health.

18. Moon
Deception, secret enemies, unforeseen danger. Love misdirected or a loved one threatened. Intuitive powers increased.
Reversed: Practicality, avoidance of risk — but peace after storm.

19. Sun
Ambitions attained, material success, happy marriage, contentment — though none of these without proper labour.
Reversed: Plans unsettled. Loss, perhaps of job. Marriage problems.

20. Judgement
Awakening, new awareness. Strong influence of Fate. Spiritual union with the Absolute is near.
Reversed: Separation, disillusionment, loss of worldly goods.

21. World
Reward, success, fulfilment — not always in the way expected. State of cosmic consciousness and spiritual liberation.
Reversed: Fear of change, cramping of vision, success elusive.

The Minor Arcana

There are fifty-six cards in the Minor Arcana. They are divided into four suits: Cups, Swords, Pentacles and Wands (or Rods). These are the equivalents of Hearts, Spades. Diamonds and Clubs. There are fifty-six because each suit has an extra card, having four court cards instead of three: King, Queen, Knight and Knave.

The meanings of the suits

It is useful to remember that the suits have a significance of their own, and that a preponderance of one over the others slants the whole interpretation.
Cups Love, generosity, goodness.
Swords Disagreement, quarrels, strife.
Pentacles Intrigue. plots, politics.
Wands Change, travel, opportunity.
Upright or reversed, each of these fifty-six cards has a divinatory meaning and can alter the information which

the Tarot pack gives us. But the main significance always lies in the Major Arcana and in the evocative and almost frightening power of the figures it portrays. The Minor Arcana can do no more than modify the broad outlines of the analyses and forecasts these stronger figures give. It tells of people's abilities and manoeuvres while they are protected or threatened by the greater forces which the Major Arcana represents.

Of course, anyone who wants to practice Taromancy seriously will have to learn the significance of, say, the Six of Pentacles as carefully as that of the High Priest or the Chariot, for its evidence may prove vital in the end.

The appeal of Tarot

It is clear that the Tarot pack can reach down to deep levels of the subconscious mind. Some people, when they see you produce a deck of these cards and proceed to lay them out, will, despite themselves, feel the tiny shiver of apprehension, of delight mixed with fear, which most of us experience when faced by the unknown, the uncanny, or the supernatural.

If you have learned to master the complexities of reading the Tarot pack, you have one certain way of stirring people's curiosity and holding their interest which you will have undoubtedly earned. For, besides knowing the meanings of each of the seventy-eight

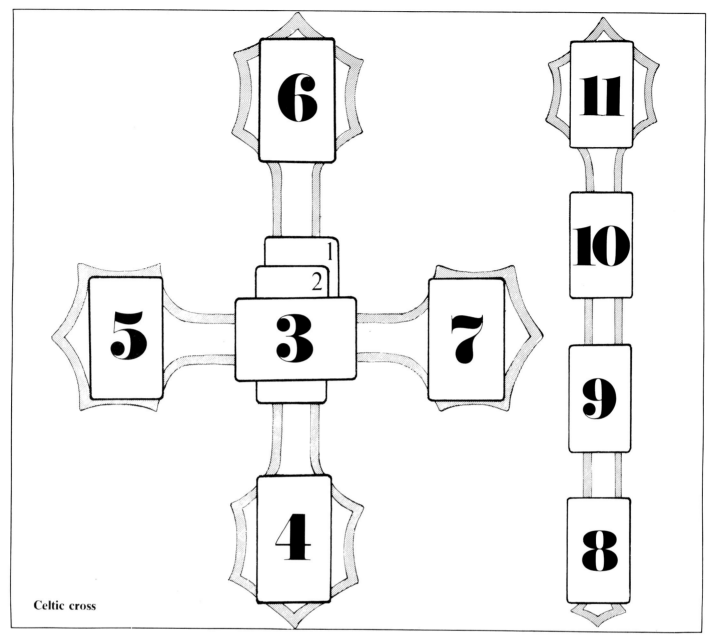

Celtic cross

cards, the reading calls for a high level of intuition, plus the intelligence to combine the individual meanings with the promptings of intuition into one coherent interpretation. If you do achieve this mastery, there is no question that you and your friends will have a new pastime — and perhaps something more.

Lay-out of the Tarot cards

First, as in simple Cartomancy, choose a 'client' card. How, or even whether, you use it, will vary from one lay-out to another. The subject should then shuffle the cards. If you do it yourself, it helps if, before cutting the pack, the client lays a hand on it. Ask the client to concentrate on the questions to be asked.

Using the left hand, the client then cuts the pack into three piles, setting each pile down to the left of the one

before. Pick up the first of the piles laid down, also with your left hand, and begin laying out the cards in the pattern you have chosen. There are dozens of these, as one might expect after so many centuries of practice. Here are two of the most common:

Celtic cross
Place the 'client' card in the centre of the table. Now, in sequence and face up, lay out ten cards as follows:
Covering Card placed over the 'client' card. This gives the influence at work around the client in question.
Crossing Card laid sideways across the 'client' and Covering cards (though read as if upright). This shows what the opposing forces are. Note that if the Covering card is unfavourable, these opposing forces may be good.
Beneath Laid directly below the central cards, to form the first arm of a cross. This points to a past experience

relevant to the matter in hand.
Behind Laid to the left of the central cards, to form the second arm of the cross. This shows an influence just passing.
Crowning The upper arm of the cross — a possible future event.
Before The right-hand arm of the cross. This points to events in the very near future.
Now to the right of the cross, four cards are laid in a vertical row, starting from the bottom:
Fears The bottom card. This reveals the outcome of which the client is most afraid.
Environment Second from bottom. This card sums up the opinions of family and friends on the matter.
Hopes What does the client hope will happen?
Outcome The top card, and the last. This includes in summary the message of all the other cards, as well as

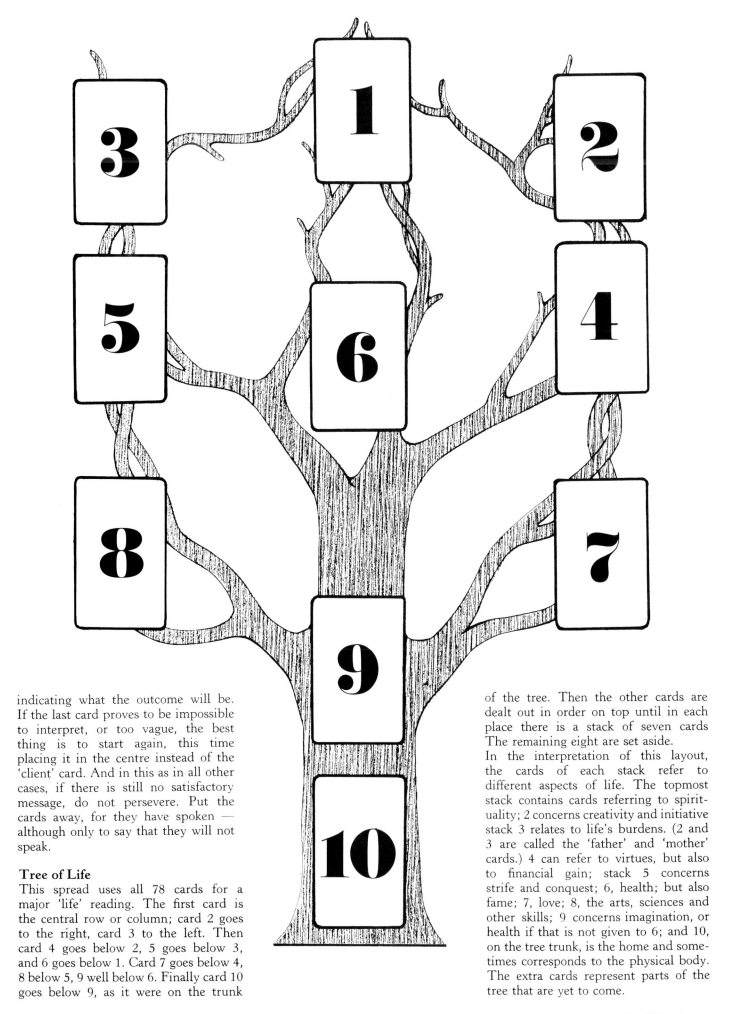

indicating what the outcome will be. If the last card proves to be impossible to interpret, or too vague, the best thing is to start again, this time placing it in the centre instead of the 'client' card. And in this as in all other cases, if there is still no satisfactory message, do not persevere. Put the cards away, for they have spoken — although only to say that they will not speak.

Tree of Life

This spread uses all 78 cards for a major 'life' reading. The first card is the central row or column; card 2 goes to the right, card 3 to the left. Then card 4 goes below 2, 5 goes below 3, and 6 goes below 1. Card 7 goes below 4, 8 below 5, 9 well below 6. Finally card 10 goes below 9, as it were on the trunk

of the tree. Then the other cards are dealt out in order on top until in each place there is a stack of seven cards The remaining eight are set aside.

In the interpretation of this layout, the cards of each stack refer to different aspects of life. The topmost stack contains cards referring to spirituality; 2 concerns creativity and initiative stack 3 relates to life's burdens. (2 and 3 are called the 'father' and 'mother' cards.) 4 can refer to virtues, but also to financial gain; stack 5 concerns strife and conquest; 6, health; but also fame; 7, love; 8, the arts, sciences and other skills; 9 concerns imagination, or health if that is not given to 6; and 10, on the tree trunk, is the home and sometimes corresponds to the physical body. The extra cards represent parts of the tree that are yet to come.

The ancient I Ching

The Book of Changes, which is I Ching in Chinese, is very old. Confucius and Lao Tse, founders of the two great streams of Chinese philosophy, turned to it for inspiration and information. It was regarded with such awe that in 213 BC, when the Emperor Ch'in Shih Huang Ti ordered a wholesale burning of books, it was one of the few which escaped. Its poetic teachings and symbolic commands, rich in metaphor, have had a great influence on the literature of China. Its intriguingly imprecise prophecies about the future were, until very recently, constantly referred to by the Chinese people, and those experienced in the interpretation of the I Ching were to be found in every village, almost in every street.

The philosophy

It is hard to say whether the I Ching reflected an already existing body of Chinese thought, or whether Chinese philosophy has been influenced by it to such an extent that it has almost derived from it. Certainly it is concerned with the duality of Yin and Yang, which is, very roughly, the opposition of the male — Yin — and the female — Yang — principles. Yin and Yang also stands for the tension between light and dark, the firm and the yielding, the sky and the earth. What is important for consideration of the Book of Changes is that such a state of universal tension means that the world is not static or inert. The ancient Chinese thinkers always rejected the notion of a motionless universe. They considered that events on this earth only mirrored the real events, which occured in a very different sphere, out of reach of all but a handful of the most highly developed human beings. So, what the I Ching offers is information about a world in flux — as its name implies, it is concerned with changes, with the driving forces which constantly modify life.

Since the book is concerned with action, rather than with a static picture of an unalterable state, it is also concerned with morality, with ideas of right and wrong. These are dealt with in the Judgements which accompany the pre-

The traditional Chinese way to cast hexagrams was with yarrow sticks.

dictions. They give the I Ching a dimension which no other method of scanning the future has. It not only predicts courses of action, it also gives some indication of whether their outcome will be beneficial or harmful. Consequently, people who consult the I Ching have an element of choice in their actions.

The role of fate

Underlying the morality of the I Ching is a belief in the prime importance of Fate. Changes happen all the time and everywhere, and this perpetual dynamic process depends upon the operation of Fate. The Chinese believed that God and Creation must get their energy from the workings of Fate. But these workings may be influenced and changed if anyone can put himself, as it were, in the place of a god and survey the future. The oracle in the I Ching allows that to be done. It does so by using the totality of every event, by treating nothing that occurs as being without meaning. Fate, or the mysterious supernatural forces through which it works, are everywhere and unceasingly active. The problem is to understand what their activity means.

Using the I Ching

First you need the book itself. This is freely available both in hardback and in paperback editions. Next you need either three coins or yarrow sticks. The latter are available from Chinese or fortune-telling shops. (Or you could, of course, find them growing wild and dry them yourself.) The book gives clear instructions on how to proceed from there — how to toss the coins or select the yarrow sticks, arrive at a hexagram and interpret it — to obtain a full reading.

The hexagrams

Of the two ways in which the I Ching may be consulted the first, using sticks, is rather complex and the other, using coins, is much simpler. Both methods, however, permit you to pick out the particular oracular statement which answers your question. Basically, these statements are an arrangement of six complete or broken lines,

forming a Hexagram.

In time past, it was believed that the oracle worked with the utmost simplicity, so that a complete line meant 'Yes', a broken one 'No'. But this came to seem inadequate, and the unbroken and the broken lines were joined in four combinations, and a third line was added to them. This gave the possibility of eight arrangements, or trigrams, to each of which a particular meaning was given. These symbols were again combined, and the arrangements changed from three to six lines. This achieved two results: each symbol became far richer in meaning, and the number of symbols was at once increased from eight to sixty-four. The I Ching had, in its essence, been created.

Method of consultation

The hexagram which answers a particular question is built up line by line.

The yarrow sticks

The Chinese sages used yarrow sticks and a complicated formula to arrive at the hexagram they wanted. This is described in detail in the book.

Coins

The alternative method, using coins, is much more practical today. In ancient times, the Chinese themselves used brass coins with a hollow in the middle, but ordinary coins will do as well. Three of these are used, with heads being given the value of three, tails that of two.

The three coins are tossed and the value they make together, once they come to rest, will be six, seven, eight or nine. The first two stand for broken lines, the last two for unbroken lines. Thus, each throw of the coins gives a line of one sort or the other and when you have thrown six times, you will have the hexagram you need. In the key with which each copy of the Book of Changes is provided you now look up the hexagram's number, and in this way find the page which tells you its meaning.

Interpretation

At this point, however, things become both more complicated and more interesting.

	Name	Attribute	Image	Family Relationship
☰	Chi'en the Creative	strong	heaven	father
☷	K'un the Receptive	devoted, yielding	earth	mother
☳	Chên the Arousing	inciting movement	thunder	first son
☵	K'an the Abysmal	dangerous	water	second son
☶	Kên Keeping Still	resting	mountain	third son
☴	Sun the Gentle	penetrating	wind. wood	first daughter
☲	Li the Clinging	light–giving	fire	second daughter
☱	Tui the Joyous	joyful	lake	third daughter

Lower Trigram ▼ / Upper Trigram ►	Ch'ien ☰	Chên ☳	K'an ☵	Kên ☶	K'un ☷	Sun ☴	Li ☲	Tui ☱
Ch'ien ☰	1	4	5	26	11	9	14	43
Chên ☳	25	51	3	27	24	42	21	17
K'an ☵	6	40	29	4	7	59	64	47
Kên ☶	33	62	39	52	15	53	56	31
K'un ☷	12	16	8	23	2	20	35	45
Sun ☴	44	32	48	18	46	57	50	28
Li ☲	13	55	63	22	36	37	30	49
Tui ☱	10	54	60	41	19	61	38	58

Key to the construction of the hexagrams

The world to which the hexagram's advice seems to apply, and the language in which it is given, make much of what is written in the I Ching strange at first glance. It is like trying to make sense of a fragment of poetry which has been translated from another language and another time. You will read of kings and princes, of lakes and mountains, of wanderers and sages, and wonder whether this can really apply to you. Sometimes. the very vagueness of the text allows it to have what seems to be a suitable meaning. It is possible to read into the words more than they actually hold. At other times, however, the advice can be very explicit.

Imagine that you are going to meet a man of slightly doubtful commercial reputation. You decide to ask of the I Ching whether he is to be trusted. The coins give Hexagram 13, 'Fellowship with Men'. Under the heading 'Judgement', are the following words:
'Fellowship with men in the open
Success
It furthers one to cross the great water
The perseverance of the superior man furthers'
The interpretation of this tells you, among other things, 'It is not the private interests of the individual that create lasting fellowship among men, but rather the goals of humanity. That is why it is said that fellowship with men in the open succeeds. If unity of this kind prevails, even difficult and dangerous tasks, such as crossing the great water, can be accomplished'.

Selection of lines

At this stage, another element enters the interpretation. Each line of the hexagram has a meaning, but you select only those lines for which you have thrown coins totalling either nine or six — in other words, all heads or all tails. These are the strong yang or yin lines and modify the general meaning of the oracle. When the coins total seven or eight, the lines have no individual meaning, but only help to build the hexagram. With a nine in the third line (reading, as one must, from the bottom up) this gives a new text:
'He hides weapons in the thicket
He climbs the high hill in front of it
For three years he does not rise up'
The interpretation of this (again in

Bottom left: In this engraving of a scene set in ancient China, yarrow sticks are being used. Above right: coins are a substitute for yarrow sticks in the casting of the hexagrams.

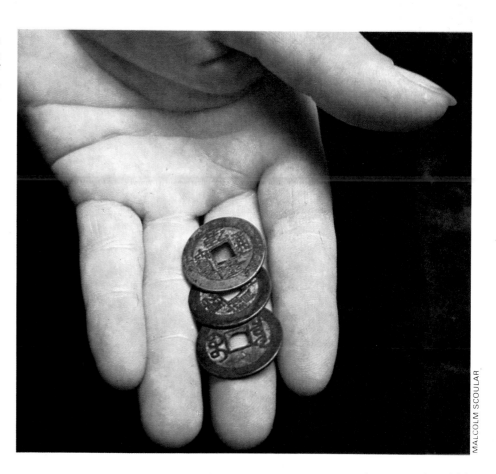

MALCOLM SCOULAR

part) is 'Obstacles standing in the way of fellowship with others are shown here. One has mental reservations for one's own part and seeks to take one's opponent by surprise. This very fact makes one mistrustful . . The result is that one departs further and further from true fellowship.'

All this seems to suggest that suspicions about the man you are to meet are unworthy and liable to do more harm than good. By not trusting him you will bring about the very situation which you fear. But the interpretation still needs one more phase.

Line reversal

When a strong yin or yang line, a line with the value nine or six, appears in a hexagram it has to be reversed, thus making a new hexagram which must in its turn be interpreted. Thus, the yang line, the unbroken line third from the bottom, was now changed to a broken yin line, and that gives Hexagram 25, Innocence (The Unexpected).
'Innocence. Supreme success.
Perseverance furthers.
If someone is not as he should be,
He has misfortune,
And it does not further him
To undertake anything.'
That is the Judgement, and its interpretation begins 'Man has received from heaven a nature innately good, to guide him in all his movements. By

devotion to this divine spirit within himself, he attains an unsullied innocence that leads him to do right with instinctive sureness and without any ulterior thought of reward and personal advantage.' So it would appear, finally, that as long as you are honest in your intentions and do not allow suspicion of this person to cloud your attitudes, everything will go very well.

The I Ching is a very seductive oracle. The very fact that it is not easy to grasp, that one has to work to make its messages clear, also makes it attractive.

However as the detailed example of interpretation shows, it can be practical, and it does seem to address itself to the problems raised. Of course, this is partly because the language of the I Ching is vague enough to apply to almost anything. Yet there are sixty-three other hexagrams which the coins might have chosen, many of which are much less well-adapted to answer a question dealing with suspicions about another person. Perhaps the ancient Chinese knew a thing or two about what makes coins fall in particular sequences, or why yarrow sticks should make patterns which are not really random at all. In any case, they have left us the I Ching, and whatever else its value may be, it certainly makes an unusual and absorbing game for agile-minded people who have an imaginative love of words.

The protection of amulets

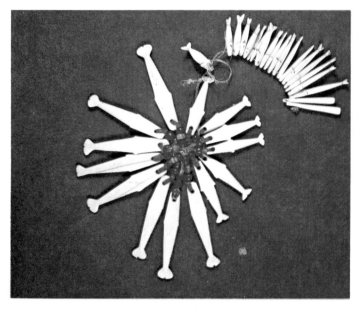

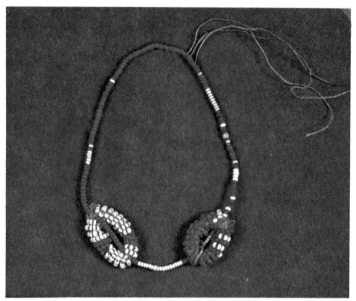

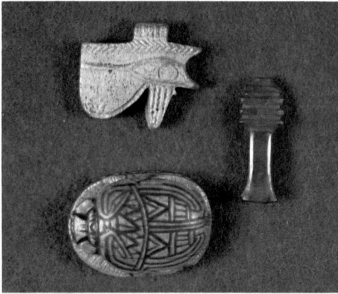

Amulets, talismans and lucky charms have been used since prehistoric times to ward off the evil effects of malignant forces, or as a sign of gratitude and devotion to benevolent ones. Lucky charms are still sold in great numbers, although charm bracelets now have a more or less decorative function. Most people have their own personal lucky charm — something they carry with them to examinations and important interviews, or always take on their journeys to help them arrive safely.

Nowadays, people are perhaps a little embarrassed about believing in charms. There is, however, still an element of 'just in case' about them, a feeling that they can help to protect one so it might be wiser not to discard them. In the past no such doubts existed; people were sure that they were vital insurance policies, to be discarded only at grave personal risk. Here are some amulets from different cultures and ages:

Above left: An Eskimo charm. The blue beads have mystical powers and the white whale — which the charm represents — was vital to the Eskimos' survival, so it, of course, often featured in their mythology.

Above right: A bead amulet worn by children of the Hadza tribe in Central Africa up until the middle of the twentieth century. This amulet was meant to protect the children from the evil and mystical effects associated with the calls of birds.

Below left: Egyptian funerary charms from the Pharaonic Middle Kingdom — 2133-1786 BC. These were supposed to help the deceased on the journey after death. Featured here: a scarab — the life symbol; a jet pillar of Osiris representing the backbone of the god and ensuring stability in the future life; and the eye of Horus: a symbol of health and happiness.

Below right: Northern Indian amulet of the early thirteenth century. This one, with the embossed figure, was worn by women who married widowers to protect them against the possibly malignant jealousy of the deceased wife.

Part 2
How to analyze your Handwriting

Manfred Lowengard

Introduction

It may be a formal thank-you letter, a scribbled postcard, even a note to the milkman – but what does it really tell you about the writer? Dr Manfred Lowengard, a professional graphologist, shows how you can get a grasp of the fundamental rules of handwriting analysis and find out about yourself, your friends and acquaintances. For instance, you could help a teenager who is confused and shy – look at her handwriting to find out what she might be good at, and help her choose a career. Or a note from a new boyfriend – might it show something that doesn't usually come to the surface? Even a strange signature at the bottom of an official letter can tell you whether the writer is kind, timid, aggressive or sexy. Graphology is a recognized aid to psychology in many countries and a highly specialized subject. But you don't have to be a professor to analyze a sample if you follow the simple step-by-step method devised for this book. Many samples from well-known personalities or just ordinary people are included as well, to help you to get an insight into the character of a writer by combining your findings with some intuition and a lot of common sense.

Contents

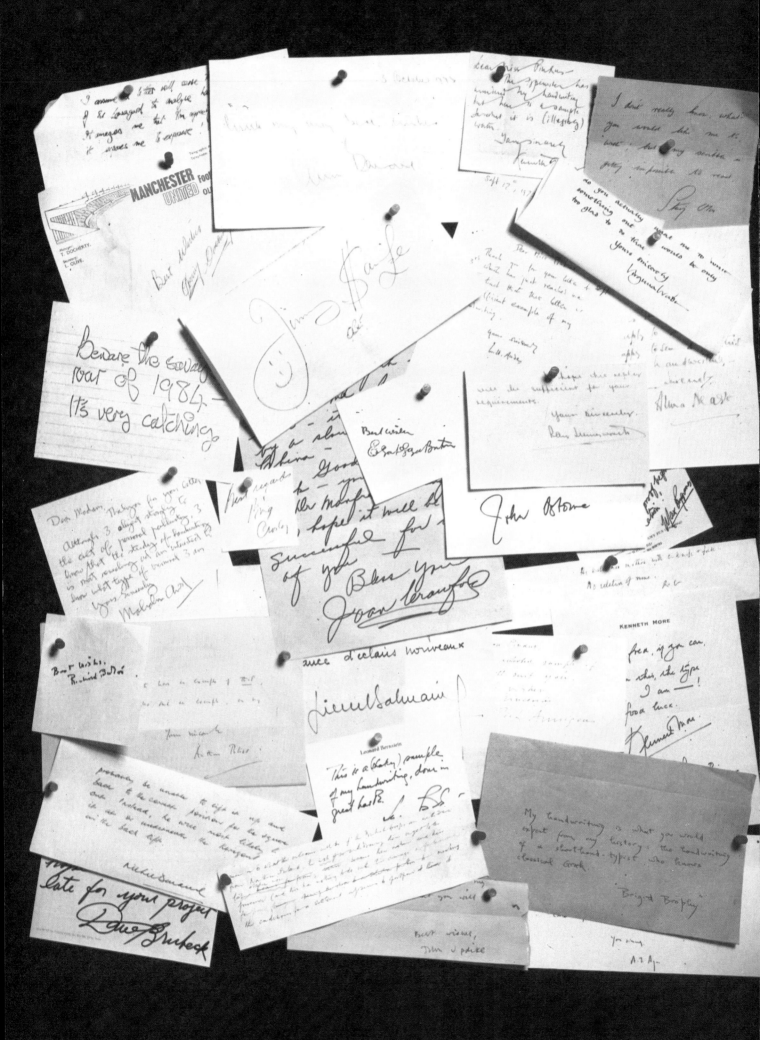

The meaning in writing

When you receive a letter, you probably cast an automatic glance at the writing on the envelope and instantly recognize whether the sender is a stranger or someone you know. Why is this so?

The answer is, of course, that everyone has his own individual way of writing. An American statistician has worked out that the possibility of finding two identical handwritings is 1:68 trillions, which is many times more than the population of our planet, to say nothing of the actual literate population.

What is writing?

Writing is a means of communication. Whether you look at Egyptian hieroglyphics, Nordic runes, Chinese characters, Gaelic scripts, Greek letters, Russian letters, or writings in our own alphabet, the marks are always for communication, to relay a message.

How does writing come into existence in the first place? Like all human activities, it has its first impulses in the brain, which sends the message through the arm to the hand of the writer. The hand is the most flexible extremity of the human frame and the most suitable to execute the art of writing. Experiments have shown, however, that when the pen is held between the toes, or even the lips, after a bit of practice people can write fluently,

Below: Letters, postcards, lists, bills . . .
whatever you write is revealing.

while maintaining their individual style. .
The term 'handwriting' is one of convenience. The activity could be called
'brainwriting'; but there's no need to
be too pedantic here—the main point
about writing is that it enables us to
understand each other.

The origins of graphology

It was in 1875 that the learned Abbé
Jean Hyppolite Michon first sat down
to list the deviations from the 'school
model' people learned to copy and,
being an imaginative and intelligent
man, he soon discovered that these
variations from the norm were related
to the writers' psychological make-up.
The result was an early textbook which
he called *Système de Graphologie*, with
observations so penetrating that a
slightly revised edition has been reissued quite recently.

How graphology can be useful

Graphology, the technical term for
hand-writing analysis, is now part of
the discipline of psychology, and can be
studied at university level in almost
every European country and in the
United States. England is one of the few
countries in Europe without a lecturer
on the subject. Many people believe
that the analysis of handwriting means
prying into someone's personality and
character without consent. This is
misinterpreting the role of graphology.
A professional graphologist must first
have a working knowledge of psychology, as graphology is used as an
additional aid by many psychologists. It
should be his aim to interpret not only
the facts he finds, but also the reasons
and the underlying causes. He should
try to find out why things are as they
are. If you want to be a successful
amateur graphologist, use your commonsense and your experience of
people's feelings and emotions.
Everyone can learn the basic rules of
handwriting analysis as they are set
down here. The step-by-step analysis
section has been arranged so that you
can analyze any handwriting without
previous knowledge. Combine a little
thoughtful insight into people's problems with considerable understanding
and you will have all the expertise you
need.
There are many practical applications
of the science of graphology, even for

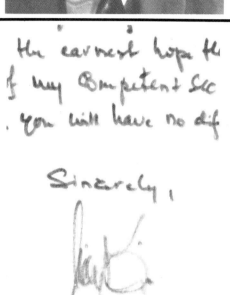

Victor Borge
The warm colour of the ink gives a
welcome, and the clever letter formations indicate an intelligent and quick-
witted man. The sharply placed i-dots,
slightly to the right of the stem signify
keen powers of observation.
The lines are extraordinarily straight,
as are the margins. Here is a well
organized and well mannered man
who enjoys whatever he is doing. The
large extensions into the upper zone,
with their unusual loop formations,
indicate a delightful imagination. This
originality does not stop when it
comes to his own assessment; the
delicately curved line into the upper
zone and the enormous circle of the 'o'
indicate a certain self-deception in
his personality. The long straight
line slanting through the middle of
the signature means that he can be
obstinate if he does not get his own
way.

Jean Shrimpton
This is a very natural writing. The
letter formations are intelligent, and
rather simplified than embellished,
showing that she has retained her
natural self. The lower zone loops show
there is no hint of vanity, while the
high t-bars indicate a refreshing degree
of independence.
In spite of considerable speed, the
i-dots and t-strokes are where they
belong, and this shows that she has
keen powers of observation and is very
capable of adjusting herself to new
surroundings or people or ways of life.
The pressure of the writing is firm, and
the spacing excellent, displaying organizing and planning abilities. Many final
strokes are clipped, which indicate that
she has suffered disappointments. The
many garlanded connections indicate
generosity almost to a fault. The small
carefully closed a's and o's show she is
not given to gossip and is a loyal friend.

6 HANDWRITING

Art Buchwald
Full of vitality with lots of end-clippings. His ambitions have been curtailed and disappointed at times. The signature has no underlining and no full-stop at the end, which indicates self awareness. This well balanced personality is further expressed in the neat formation of the individual letters, and the ascending lines indicate a consequent optimism. The light pressure denotes artistry and a wicked sense of humour. The impression is that he does not like the reality he has to face and that he tries to transform it into something nicer.

Lawrence Durrell
The felt-tipped pen gives the writing a warmth which it otherwise would lack, because this is a rather sharp script. It is fast, it is legible, and the lines are ascending. The connections vary, thereby achieving the fastest route of progress. There is, however, a syllable-impulse rather than a word-impulse, pointing to a man who thinks before he acts. The lower and middle zones are emphasized, indicating not only sincerity, modesty but also a love of good things. The overall roundness specifies good-naturedness and a feeling for humanity. The open 'a's' and 'o's', together with the underlining of the signature, show us a man who is not afraid to speak the truth and who can thus be trusted.

Gary Player
This large, neat, legible script shows an exacting, precise man who does nothing without careful consideration. The predominant upper zone and firm pressure indicate that he thoroughly enjoys positive action. His round, almost school-model hand means he is kind, but no fool either. This is confirmed by the absence of end-garlands and the firm, down-stroke word endings. The firm t-bars indicate good powers of observation. This is the writing of a man who uses his considerable common sense to sum things up.
The whole script has an unassuming air. The upper zone formations imply ambition, and the capitals in his signature indicate personal pride. But nothing is overdone. He is happy with his status in society and a very slight wavyness in his otherwise straight lines show a sensitivity he does not show in public.

the amateur. From a quick study of the writing of a friend, you can discover traits in his personality which will lead you to greater understanding and compassion. Clues to the make-up of an applicant for a job can be gained from a sample of his handwriting. Is he reliable and conscientious? A hard worker? Has he managerial potential? Is he frank or secretive?

The psychiatrist or psychologist who does a quick graphological study can find immediate clues to the personality of a patient which he will want to pursue, saving hours delving for subconscious traits of which the analyst is unaware. Marriage guidance counsellors can help couples by looking at samples of writing from each.

Some professional graphologists even claim to be able to detect physical ailments such as poor circulation, heart disease or digestive disorders. For instance, heart disease can show itself in fraying line formations in the upper part of letters. You will probably need a magnifying glass to see them clearly. However as often as not, these are signs of fatigue—and you will probably be able to tell from other signs in the writing whether the writer is the sort of person who would overwork or stay up late every night at discos and parties!

Signs of illness can often be detected long before the writer is aware of them himself, so handwriting analysis can act as a useful early warning system. Of course, a graphologist would never attempt a diagnosis, but would certainly suggest a visit to the doctor for a check up.

Only adults have a fully developed writing but less experienced writings do point out developing personality trends. Teachers find handwriting analysis helpful in detecting and following the development of intellect and personality in children, particularly in overcrowded classrooms where truly individual attention to each child is impossible. Handwriting analysis is particularly useful in adolescence when vocational guidance is needed but the child has not yet shown in which direction his potential lies.

A toddler not yet of school age copies letters from posters or television and forms his own delightful variations. Even if he only draws pictures, the way he uses the drawing paper and the themes he picks provide clues about his evolving psyche to concerned and objective parents.

Florence Nightingale

The delightful flourish of the letter 'F' in the signature gives away the gentle sweetness of this intelligent and determined personality; it hooks to the spiritual sphere and anchors soundly to the down-stroke, showing her earthiness and realism. All letter-formations are original without being distorted or illegible; and the straightness of the lines, combined with the firm pressure, show the determination and energy she put into her plans. All three zones are well formed, and when simplification was possible, she took the shortest route. There was no unnecessary delay, false politeness or idle chatter in her, but a will to succeed and a superior ability to organize and get things done. The endgarlands show her sincere desire to help. This letter could have been written today, so modern and contemporary does it look.

Mendelssohn

Considering that this writing is over 150 years old, it looks extraordinarily contemporary. A neat writing, executed with delicate pressure using a writing instrument infinitely more difficult to control than our ballpens, shows the depth of his feelings and the fluctuating middle zone in the notes shows his sensitivity. The endgarlands tell how gentle and warmhearted he must have been. The rhythm and the upright style of the writing and the rhythmical distribution of pressure indicate a healthy control of his emotions.

Open 'a's and 'o's show his frankness and openness with just a hint of tactlessness. The firmness of the underlining of his signature shows that he knew what he wanted, and the originality of his letter formations indicate that he was intellectually advanced.

Dr. Samuel Johnson
This sample, written with a quill, shows energy and intelligence. Some letter formations—'I', 'D', 'M'—show good flow, speed, and intelligent simplification which increases the speed without impairing legibility. Any lack of legibility is due to bad ink flow. The upright script, with letters going straight from upper to lower zone, indicates a methodical way of thinking and working. Wit, if not sarcasm, and absolute frankness are shown in the open 'a's and 'o's and the sharp pressure. I-dots are exact or slightly ahead and accentuated, confirming a far-sighted wit and critical ability. Distribution is clear with a decreasing left-hand margin—an attempt to control the generosity exhibited in the frequent end-garlands. Arcades in the upper zone show respect for tradition and convention.

The Duke of Marlborough
A very speedy writing, large and rich in pressure. The word connections are poor, and occasionally he tries to connect letters by a kind of welding method. Letter formations are delicate. The 'd' in particular shows culture, intelligence and interest and pleasure in beautiful things, whilst ink-filled loops in the lower zone confirm his sensuality and love of beauty. The name is larger than the rest of the script—he was aware of his status and of his abilities. However note that there is no underlining and no full-stop at the end of his signature. In a large writing, this indicates that he was open to advice, and in this respect was indeed the "humble servant", he calls himself. The i-dots are exactly placed, and occasionally ahead of their stems, suggesting good powers of observation, a keen memory and a speedy reaction to stimuli.

Benjamin Franklin
Here we have delightfully old-fashioned American writing. Every movement and line is carefully and deliberately designed and formed. The writing proceeds in straight lines to and from straight margins, on both sides. The even rhythm ends with the final flourish of the signature. The many leftward movements and arcades show intense loyalty to tradition. His manual skill is shown in the simple letter formations which he has delicately transformed into pieces of illustrative art. The exact, slightly high i-dots indicate fine powers of observation and a good factual memory. This is the writing of a diversified craftsman, absolutely sincere and honest. The large, slightly enriched signature shows pride and vanity, but this is overshadowed by the good rhythm, pressure and general layout.

Learning to write

Everybody learns to write at school by copying from a book or from the shapes the teacher puts on the blackboard. Every child eventually develops his own style, thereby forming a writing which is uniquely his own, but the letters will follow the general pattern of his school model. In the English-speaking countries, even though the basic alphabet is the same, this school model is subtly different, as the illustrations show.

This is why a graphologist always asks for the nationality of the writer under analysis. He need not actually read the text of the writing he analyzes, but, since graphology assesses the deviation from the norm, it is essential to know the origin of the school model. This is especially true in analyzing a passage written in a language other than that of the original school model. For example, a Swedish national makes i-dots like little circles, as in his school model. This feature has a quite different interpretation if it is used by a writer educated in Britain.

Generally, the size of the school model is relative to the country it represents. Australian writing is a little larger than English writing. The handwriting of Swiss people is smaller. But psychology can also come into play and some inhabitants of a small country will write a very large hand, as if trying to compensate for a kind of national inferiority complex. Since English is spoken and written all over the world, and a writing style is as difficult to lose as a spoken accent, it is necessary to study the various school models. When odd letter formations appear, they must be compared to the school model of the country where the subject learned to write.

Below: Ten-year-old Lee has already formed his own unique style of writing.

> Dear Granma,
>
> Thankyou for the loveley holiday
>
> We drove home ~~into~~ safely and
>
> mummy did not crash this time.
>
> I liked the picnic best and
>
> When we went ~~of~~ to see the
>
> gliders.
>
> Love from,
>
> Lee

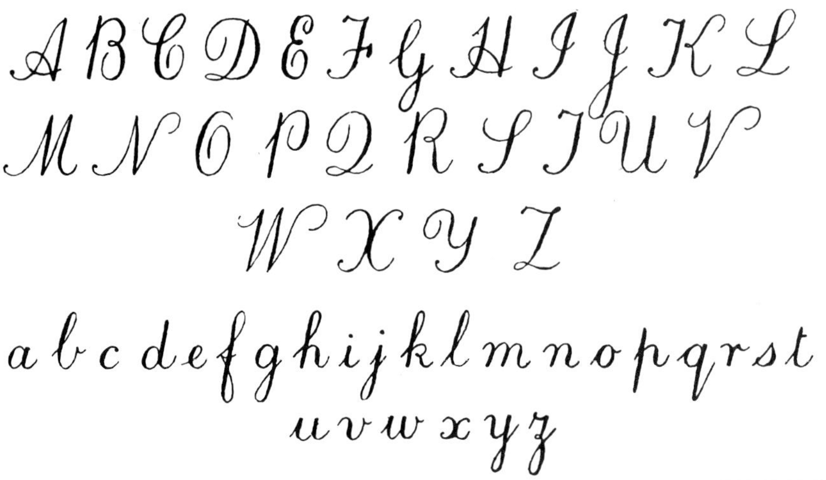

A B C D E F G H I J K L M N O P Q R S T U V W X Y Z

a b c d e f g h i j k l m n o p q r s t u v w x y z

Australia The size is large, as is the country itself. Pressure is good, the loops are full, and the capitals are more elaborate. The writing is well connected, and the d's and t's are smaller than the other letters of the upper zone. T-bars are on the right of the stems, and do not cross them.

New Zealand's school model (not shown) leans forward to a much greater degree than the Australian one (about 70°). The p's and q's are shorter than other lower zone letters. A variety of shapes exist for capitals.

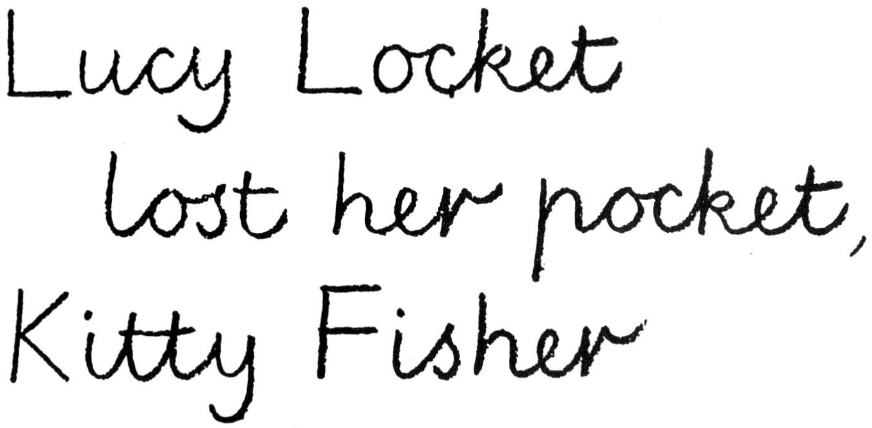

Lucy Locket
lost her pocket,
Kitty Fisher

England This school model gives a slow, rhythmic script with garlanded connections and a large middle zone. It is mostly upright, but has a slight forward leaning trend. Pressure is firm and unexaggerated, and the words are well connected. The t's are lower than other upper zone letters. Nowadays small children are taught to print first, not usually connecting the letters until 7 or 8 years. Many schools teach italic script at a later stage, which includes careful thick and thin strokes and angular connections.

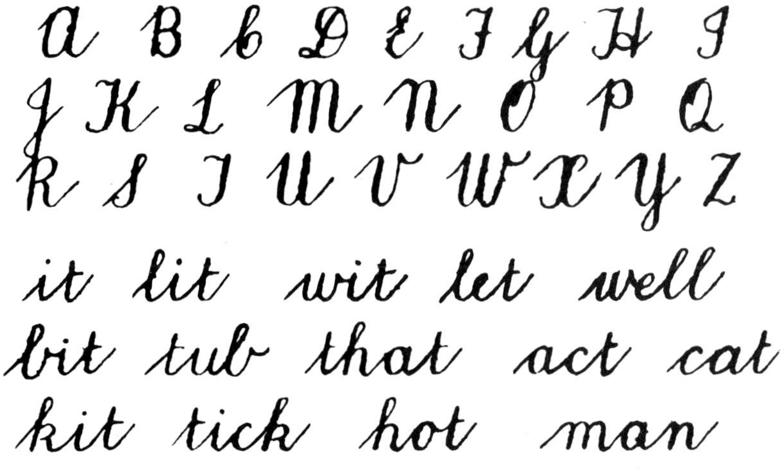

A B C D E F G H I J K L M N O P Q R S T U V W X Y Z

*it lit wit let well
bit tub that act cat
kit tick hot man*

South Africa The school model shows heavy pressure. It is comparatively narrow, but leans forward a little. The capitals are slightly embellished, and the writing well connected. The bars are to the right of the stem, not crossing it, and the t's and d's are slightly smaller than other letters in the upper zone. First and last letters have long flourishes.

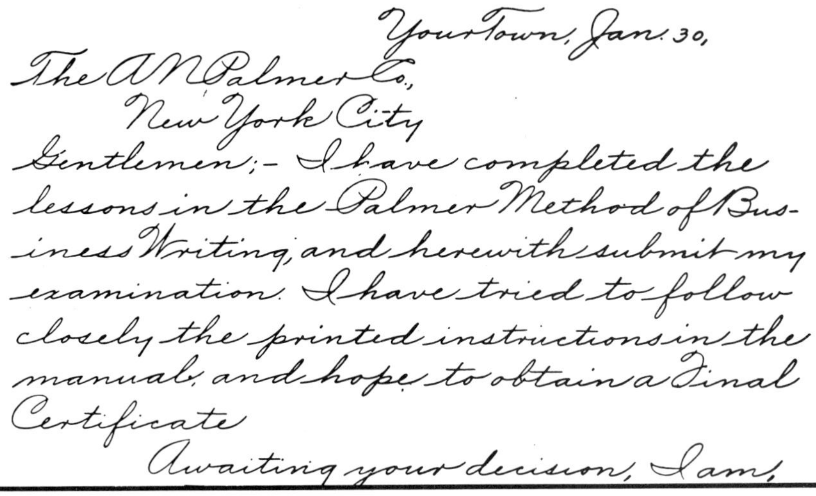

Your Town, Jan. 30,
The A.N. Palmer Co.,
New York City
Gentlemen;– I have completed the lessons in the Palmer Method of Business Writing, and herewith submit my examination. I have tried to follow closely the printed instructions in the manual, and hope to obtain a Final Certificate
Awaiting your decision, I am,

The United States and Canada This model shows a marked lack of pressure. The lower zone is large. The writing leans forward, the formations are simple, the loops are large, and the writing is well connected. The capitals are, in spite of being somewhat simple, enriched or embellished. The first and last strokes are large and often curved. Models vary from state to state, but retain the same fundamental characteristics.

These children are learning how to write. If they have any problems which they are unable to communicate, a trained graphologist could probably detect them.

How you write

The way we write is determined by three impulses—'motor', 'formative' and 'spatial'—all of which stem from the brain. Though writing may change superficially according to mood or method (the writing you use for a formal letter probably seems very different from a scribbled shopping list), the fundamental characteristics are the same.

The motor impulse

When you need to write, a message is sent from the brain to the muscles of the hand. It is therefore easy to understand that the graphologist talks of the 'motor impulse' as the basis of all writing. All that is needed for it to operate is an able-bodied human being with normal reflexes, reasonably good eyesight and a memory for the shapes of the alphabet used as means of communication.

The formative impulse

With the 'formative impulse', we can actually begin to analyze writing because this second impulse is the result of the writer's individuality and makes writing differ from the school model. As a result, the letters are shaped in a fashion entirely of each person's own making and design.

The spatial impulse

People write on a variety of surfaces: paper, cards, blackboards—even walls —and it is significant to note how writing is organized according to the space available. This is known as the 'spatial impulse'. The formation of lines and margins play an important part in handwriting analyses.

Left-handed writing

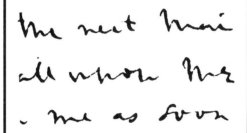

Lord Nelson, who was naturally right-handed, taught himself to write with his left hand after he lost his right arm in a battle. Compare the two here: top, his right-hand script; bottom, left-handed.

It is not as easy as it may seem to find out if a writer is left-handed. People seem to believe that left-handed writing must slant to the left. In fact this is rarely the case. Here the use of an orange stick or toothpick is very handy. Take the instrument and try to copy the way the letters were formed. If you find the task awkward with the right hand, try to use your left one. Very often you will find that the movement comes more naturally.

Left-handedness is not important to the graphologist, since it gives no indication as to the writer's character or personality. However, until quite recently, children who were left-handed by nature were often forced to use their right hands, and this sometimes resulted in a nervous disturbance. Nowadays, left-handedness is considered quite natural—merely rarer than right-handedness. Needless to say, among left-handers there are as many shades or degrees of intelligence, decency, honesty and so on as there are among right-handers, and the same rules of graphology apply to both.

Does writing change with age?

Since handwriting reflects the writer's state of mind and the degree of wisdom acquired by living, making mistakes and coping with difficult situations, it would be strange if signs of psychological development did not appear in the writing as well. If you look at a letter written by a child or teenager and compare it with one written by the same person in mature age, you are bound to find marked differences. These differences depend not only on the manual skill and dexterity developed over the years, but even more on the degree of adaptability that the writer has acquired. Everyone has moments of happiness, times of despair and disaster or emotional upsets. We are all forced to make decisions which may affect the rest of our lives. If people fail to respond to such challenges in a positive manner, if they try to avoid responsibility out of laziness, their lives are bound to develop quite differently from the way they would had they accepted all challenges as natural and positive forces.

Writing can reflect changes like these over a lifetime, and it is interesting to see if potentials seen in adolescent handwriting are reflected in the same person's writing in later life.

Some psychiatrists use the information derived from handwriting from many different periods of a patient's life for diagnosis and consequent treatment, watching, of course, to see if their patients' writing improves as treatment proceeds.

Sir Winston Churchill's writing in public life

1910

At this time, Churchill was already Home Secretary, having 'crossed the floor' to join the Liberal Party.

This well-spaced and well-shaped script, showing many Greek 'e' formations, indicates leadership and clear thinking. Pressure is strong, becoming a little smudgy in places, which may indicate that enjoyment of the good things in life was always present at this period of his life.
At the same time the simplicity of letter formations and the neat connections show that the writer was capable of adjusting himself to circumstances.

1936

Churchill was now a vociferous Conservative backbencher — bitterly opposed to the official policy of appeasement.

The writing is faster, and in a way more simplified, which means, of course, that concentration on essentials was greatly increased.
The dagger-like 't'-stroke, placed on top of the letter, indicates his directness, and since the degree of connection is very good indeed, probably this was a time of forceful argument and discussion. Again, one does not find a trace of vanity, but only determination to get things done.

1946

After the triumphs of the Second World War, Churchill and his party were voted out of office. During this year he made a famous speech in which he coined for the first time the phrase, 'the Iron Curtain'.

This writing is much smaller. This is mainly due to the fact that concentration on essentials had increased, and wisdom and experience ruled his thoughts and actions. The increased pressure indicates how successfully he coped with slight physical fatigue, shown in some cracks in his down-strokes.

The three zones

The three zones

The alphabet consists of two kinds of letters: capitals and small letters, or in graphological jargon: Majuscles and Minuscles. They represent the foundation of all writing.

The diagram shows that letters can be divided into three 'zones'—the upper, middle and lower. These three zones are the most important part in graphology, for they provide the cornerstone of the whole analysis. If you follow the way the pen moves over the surface during the act of writing, you will find that it is a constant movement from the top to the bottom of the line, and at the same time from the left towards the right. It also will become obvious that all movement entering the lower zone is directed more or less towards the writer while movement up into the upper zone goes away from it.

The meaning of the zones

The English language speaks of people who 'get *down* to business', or 'live *up* to ideals'. This division is also seen in graphological analysis.

The lower zone The lower zone contains the loops or 'descenders' of

Pronounced loops in the lower zone
the 'g', 'y', 'q' and, in some cases 'z'. Since all lines which enter the lower zone are drawn towards the writer's body, it appears that all matters which have any connection with the writer's material wellbeing are expressed in this zone. Attitudes towards food, sex, conventions and traditions, money and possessions are all indicated here.

The upper zone The upper zone contains the top of all capitals and the loops or 'ascenders' of 'f', 'l', 'h', etc. Here the writer's attitude towards

A strong upper zone
higher matters like ideals, moral values, or religion, are expressed.

The middle zone The middle zone contains all small letters. It is the most

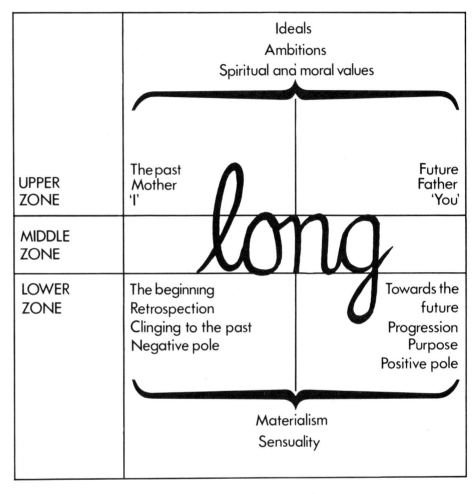

important of the three zones since some part of every letter must go through it, no matter which zone it develops into ultimately. The middle zone stands in between the entirely materialistic and the absolutely idealistic spheres. It is

Emphasis on the middle zone
particularly significant in that it expresses the writer's attitude ,towards everyday matters—friends, family, work and immediate environment.

When one zone is over-emphasized, the whole balance is, of course, upset. Where there is too much on one side, there must be too little on the other. A warning is necessary here: it is dangerous to jump to conclusions. If, for example, a writing shows a greatly emphasized upper zone, do not think that the writer is necessarily an idealist.

This assessment could be entirely wrong: it may only indicate great ambition. Always try to fit the meaning of each part into an all-round analysis. It is not an over-simplification to say that greatness cannot be indicated by imbalance—unless, of course, we consider ruthless dictators or successful crooks as great.

The three zones represent the writer's attitudes towards life and indicate the degree to which the writing style and movement have become habitual — in other words, unconscious or subconscious actions. It is not easy to define a subconscious action—there is a constant intermingling with conscious action. If you try to analyze your everyday activities, you will find that there are lots of things which you do without really thinking about them. This applies particularly to the way you write, unless, or course, you use 'copperplate' or 'italic' script.

The angle of lines

The zones deal with the vertical movement in writing. The next point to investigate is the left-to-right movement. Writing moves from the left towards the right hand side of the paper, as if symbolizing the 'reaching out' of the writer towards the receiver, or the 'I' towards the 'You'. Movement towards the left represents the writer's attitudes towards the past. Movement towards the right indicates attitudes towards the future. The centre is symbolic of the present, the very moment at which the pen performs the act of writing.

Delving still deeper, the left represents a subconscious attitude towards the mother-figure, since birth is, of course, the first thing in anyone's past. The left also denotes the female element within the writer's surroundings. The right expresses the attitude towards the male element, or the father. This may account for the tendency among young people suddenly to develop writing which slants towards the left during puberty. The psychological diagnosis could be that they begin to feel the growth of sexual forces which may frighten them. Consequently they shrink away from an unknown future (the right) and take refuge in the past (the left), perhaps even subconsciously wish-wishing that they were back on their mother's protective lap.

Lines

As you proceed from the left hand side of the paper to the right you produce lines of writing. The most direct way from point A to point B is the straight line. But unless you use ruled paper, you will probably waver a little, or your lines may go up, down, curve or go in steps.

Straight lines on unlined paper are a sign of steadfastness and purposefulness. In addition, this characteristic can confirm the trait of aloofness.
Wavy lines, particularly on lined paper, suggest degrees of unsteadiness, excitability, or lack of inner stability.
Curved lines indicate that the writer was tired, but pulled himself together to reach the end.
Arched lines may indicate depression or mental or physical fatigue.
Stepped lines occur very seldom; they are produced by hesitating after every syllable, or word. If the steps go up, the writer probably has doubts about the success of the purpose in mind but has sufficient pluck to try again. If the steps descend, the writer is a pessimist, expecting no positive response from anything he does.
Ascending straight lines, or even wavy ones, show energy, optimism, and self-assertion.
Descending straight lines probably show temporary depression or fatigue.

Straight lines

pe, man approaches more to the seni
treme variational tendency of man
xpresses itself in a larger percenta
genius, insanity and idiocy; wor

Sagging lines

re art of putting 30 words togethe
xke reasonable sense is purely a
vocabulary. Even a moron can t

Arched lines

very glad that you are in
to project as discussed
d to hearing from you

Descending lines

World you please let me has
findings in the enclosed.

Ascending lines

landed in a gooseberry bush —
thus proving that sleeping dogs are
best let lie.

Margins

Margins follow logically from the investigation of the left-to-right movement. They are dictated by the spatial impulse and are particularly important as part of the general positive or negative impression of a page of writing. A careful, methodical writer always tries to produce a straight margin, neither too near nor too far from the paper's edge.

What margins can mean

Wide margins If the margins are wide the writer is rather extravagant, or perhaps a snob who wishes to make a good impression on the recipient.

Narrow margins If both the left and the right hand margins are narrow, the writer is economical and wants to use the page to the fullest, probably squeezing in his signature at the very bottom of the page.

Decreasing margins If a margin is reasonably wide at first and decreases as the writer fills the page — quite a common feature — it means the writer gradually withdraws from his original wish to make contact with the recipient. This may arise from modesty or a feeling of inadequacy and inferiority; or it could be because he has had unpleasant emotional experiences in the past.

Increasing margins When both margins increase towards the bottom of the page, the writer begins with generous intentions but wishes to remain distant enough to be free from influences. However, his emotions can get the better of him in spite of himself.

Irregular margins Irregular margins, particularly on the left, are relatively rare. They indicate a person who neither plans nor organizes his life carefully, is always muddled, often talks too much. This is particularly true when one line droops down at the end and interferes with the line below so that it becomes illegible.

Slanting margins Lefthand margins slanting to the right show an extrovert and optimistic personality, while the opposite indicates retreat, and a fear of the future.

Wavy or irregular margins A jerky, irregular margin indicates a restless, talkative person who is probably a bad organizer with an untidy mind. If the margins are wavy rather than jerky they show absent mindedness.

Letter slants

The next step is to assess the meaning of the angle of writing. You need to know the nationality of the writer before assessing the meaning of the angle. Most writing is taught with a slight forward slant, though British school children generally learn an upright script. Use a protractor to measure the degree of slant and find the average throughout the writing, since it is inclined to vary.

If the writing is very upright it can be considered as a slight leftward movement if the school model slants rightwards. If an upright school model is adhered to it indicates self-control and reticence.

Upright writing

The forward slope

It seems natural that a writer who wishes to convey something to someone should instinctively lean towards the right, as if trying to get close to the

A positive forward slope

person to whom he is writing. This feeling for contact is particularly strong when a British person's writing slopes to the right. But if the slope is exaggerated, and the writing almost falls on to the line, an obsessive nature is indicated.

The backward slope

When the slope is backward, the writer is shy and afraid to show his real

feelings, but he may also be hesitant to face the consequences of his statements.

Left-sloping writing

The Left-or-right significance

You should also apply the findings which relate to left and right, remembering that the left is the female element or past, the right the male or

Extreme rightward slope

future—the negative and positive poles. In backward sloping writing this could show an unwillingness to face the reality of the present; in forward sloping writing, a dominant personality is indicated—ambitious, forward-looking but possibly also domineering.

I don't believe in graphology of course. If I did I would certainly not enter this sample the results might come as a nasty shock. Now palmistry is quite another matter. Both the past and the future are there for all to see.

I am very glad that you are interested in the project as discussed and I look forward to hearing from you shortly.

Yours sincerely

Increasing margins

time my work has been interrupted by requests for graphology samples, I sure hope it is the last! I am very glad that you are interested in the project as discussed and I look

Very narrow margins

We are still living under the reign of logic, but the logical processes of our time apply only to the solution of problems of secondary interest. The absolute rationalism which remains in fashion allows for the consideration of only those facts which are narrowly relevant to our experience.

I am very glad that you are interested in the project as discussed and I

Irregular, wide margin

I was surprised to see his hair close-clipped in a popular Rajasthani style. Always before he had worn it in the old Kotar way - a four inch strip shaved from forehead to crown, leaving long thick bunches of hair to hang over his ears and the back of his head and neck. This was used as a disguise to hide them from the conquering Muslim armies. I am very glad that you are interested

Decreasing margins

Addressing envelopes

The purpose of the address on an envelope is of course to ensure that a letter reaches its destination without difficulty. It is natural therefore to write envelopes more clearly and distinctly than the letters inside — some people even use capital letters to make quite sure. However, a surprising percentage of people address their envelopes so indistinctly that it would need an expert in codes to decipher them. The way the envelope is written is a useful confirmation of findings arrived at through analysis of other writing.

The position of the address

To interpret envelopes graphologically, the same techniques apply as for general writing analysis — the zonal arrangements, and the left-right aspects, together with the assessment of the whole writing. A reasonable, well-balanced person arranges his envelope neatly, placing the name and address in the centre, or slightly to the left, leaving ample margins all round.

Some people write the address at the top of the envelope, too close to the postage stamp, making the envelope practically useless. These people are constantly losing the ground under foot and lack a firm grasp of reality.

The writer who places the address near the bottom of the envelope is too dependent upon the material world, and will be easily depressed by business or financial affairs which he has difficulty in managing well.

Some writers place the address too far left. The left is symbolic of the past, the 'mother' attachment, and it is not surprising that these writers are not confident about the future. They shy away from the right, from contact with society. They prefer to arrange matters in their own way, not asking for help. They are unforthcoming and not particularly friendly. The past has more meaning for them than the future, and they treat the present suspiciously.

When the address is placed too far right, the writer is anxious to make contact with society. He is an extrovert, anxious and eager to find someone he can rely on to assist him in managing life. He may indeed rely more on others than on himself, hoping others will pick his chestnuts out of the fire for him.

The size of writing

Most people make an extra effort to write clearly on envelopes, even printing the address in capitals, to be sure the letter arrives safely. However, if the writing on the envelope is smaller than that used in the actual letter, the writer loses self-confidence when confronted with strangers and unfamiliar situations, particularly in his social life. On the other hand, he may prefer to keep his real feelings to himself. When the address is larger, the writer may be overbearing, vain and excitable, keeping up an insincere pose of self-assurance.

How letters are joined

Most textbooks of graphology agree that one of the most important features in handwriting analysis is the form of connection that links the individual letters into words. These connections usually occur in the middle zone and are made with curves or angles.

Once again, a knowledge of nationality is essential. For example, the German school model until the late nineteen-thirties was angular. Therefore a German national born in the first half of the twentieth century would still use this form of connection, even when writing in a foreign language. Italic script demands angular connections as well, whereas the sort of copperplate script taught in most North American schools relies on garlands. Connections are revealing because they occur in the middle zone. The way they are shaped, the forms they assume, are most revealing. From them you can analyze the writer's degree of adaptation to his environment, his partners, his profession and life in general.

Types of connection

The garland This is the most frequent, allowing the down-stroke to connect the following up-stroke in a flowing, rhythmical movement from left to right. The garland suggests the receptiveness of a bowl; its curve towards the upper zone suggests that the writer is open to the influence of ideals. It is also a fluent left-to-right movement, and a pure garland writing shows openness to spiritual, emotional and social influences. Garlands vary a great deal and should be interpreted accordingly; they can be firm or loose, looped or sharp, narrow or wide.

Garland writers have a natural relationship with the world around them and are open to influences from outside. Impressionable and adaptable, they try to avoid unnecessary conflict.

The arcade This is the opposite of the garland. Its curves are closed towards the upper zone and open towards the lower zone. The arcade writer tries to close himself off from the outside world. He has his own way of adapting himself to the world around him, but never discloses his inner self. The writer of arcades places more importance on form and behaviour — aesthe-

Angles

Threads

Garlands

Arcades

tic as well as social — than on the contents of his letter. Members of the aristocracy, royalty and high clergy often use arcades. Many criminals use them because they have reasons for not disclosing their private lives. Artists, particularly craftsmen and designers, are often arcade writers.

It is difficult to establish emotional contact with someone whose writing contains arcades, no matter which of the many variations of them he uses. Such people often feel embarrassed by personal questions and will answer with reticence or overdone politeness, giving the impression that the questioner is prying.

Angled connections These differ from garlands and arcades, both of which are curved movements that flow naturally from the pen. The angular connection impedes the even flow, because the hand has to stop for a moment to turn the nib and make the angular spike. Garlands and arcades represent forms of adaptation, while angles express a refusal to adapt, an element of opposition or an inability to react to stimuli as expected. Angular writers have little sense of obligation to the world; they oppose it by their very angularity. But these writers make no attempt to shirk obstacles — they often look for hindrances for the fun of overcoming them and they prefer difficulty to smoothness. People of great will-power use this form of connection, requiring the world to adapt to them.

The threaded connection This is neither angular or flowing, and if the whole script shows nothing but threads, it becomes illegible. Threads increase the speed of the writing, and are used by people for whom time is precious. If threads occur at the end of words instead of the last syllable or final letters, the writer expects the reader to be intelligent enough to grasp the meaning of a word by its context and may be paying him a compliment. However, a writer who uses threads can also be an opportunist with few convictions, someone who wants to better himself at any cost.

Connection and disconnection

A writer who sits down to send a letter lets his pen flow from left to right without thinking of anything but the

message he wishes to convey. The act of writing is quite automatic. If his thoughts flow freely, his writing will also and he will produce a well-connected script. If he is a cautious, pedantic person, a perfectionist or someone who is afraid that his image may suffer if he puts down his thoughts freely, some of the letters will be disconnected.

Within the same writing some words are fully connected and others seem to consist of disconnected syllables or letters. Establish to what degree the writing is connected, remembering that some people have a 'word-impulse' and others a 'syllable-impulse'. This means that the motor impulse moves the pen through whole words, or through one syllable at a time. In addition, ascertain the width of the distances between words. These gaps are as important as the spaces between lines.

Partially-connected writing If a writing shows a good flow, but the letters are only partially connected, the writer thinks before he acts; he takes a deep breath between thoughts. A writer with a 'syllable-impulse' is an intelligent person who pauses to think and wishes to make himself clear by choosing the right words. This may indicate thoroughness, or he may be a calculating person who plans his impression on others with care.

Disconnected writing If a writing is completely disconnected you have a shy, idealistic person who does not find it easy to have free relationships, especially intimate ones. You rarely find a disconnected script with a large lower zonal development: this is quite logical, since the lower zone indicates the degree of material pleasure hoped for. Disconnected writers often have very wide spaces between their lines: they actually try to avoid any social contact at all and place a vacuum around themselves. Disconnection slows the writing flow as well.

Connected writing A social person who likes to talk and meet others will have well-connected writing, with some breathing spaces which do not affect its legibility.

Space between words Wide spaces between words in which letters are only partly connected indicate reserve, shyness and perhaps caution, as well as thoughtfulness. Narrow spaces may show lack of reserve, impatience, self-confidence and action. If the words are actually joined by an extra stroke, so that the pen never actually leaves the paper, it shows a talkative person, who could be a busybody. It certainly shows someone who has much to communicate.

Fully connected writing

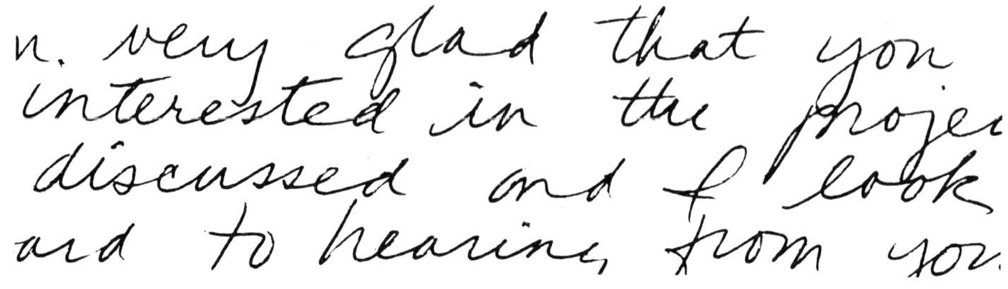

Partially connected writing

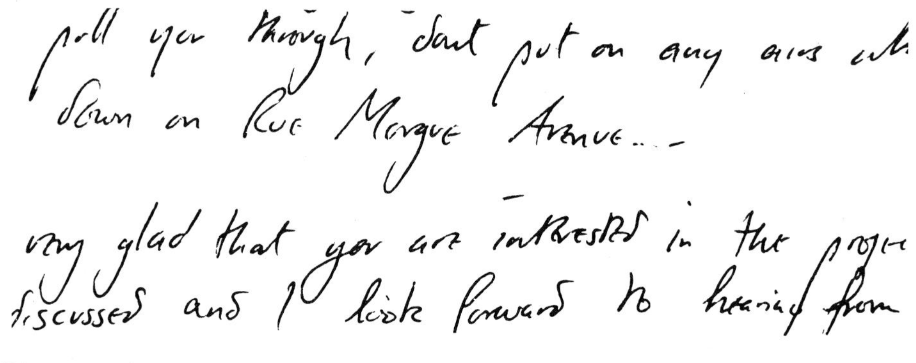

Disconnected writing

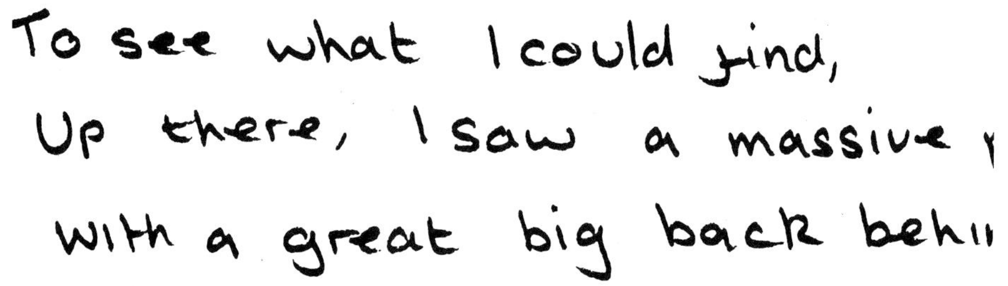

Narrow word spacing

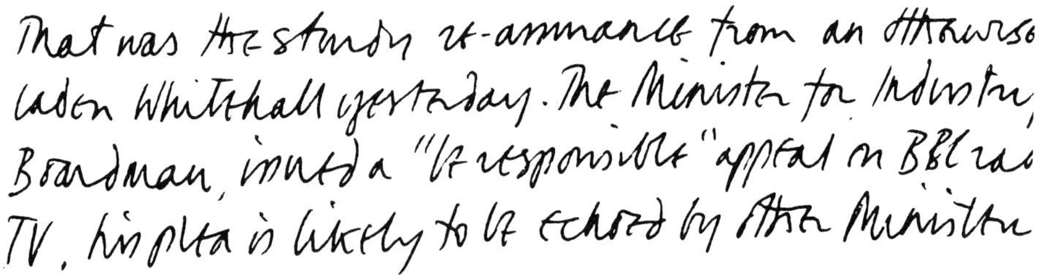

Connected words

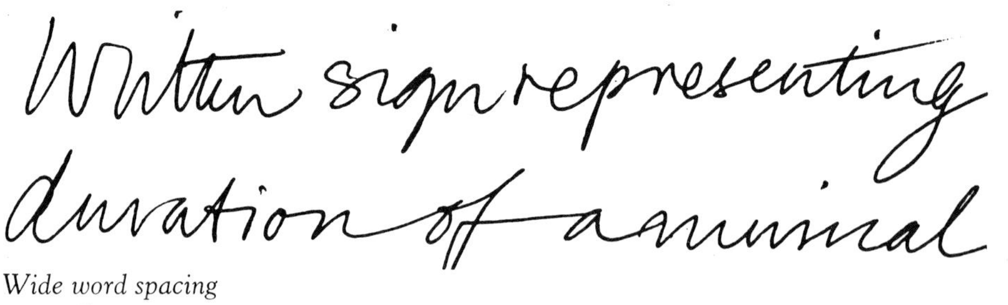

Wide word spacing

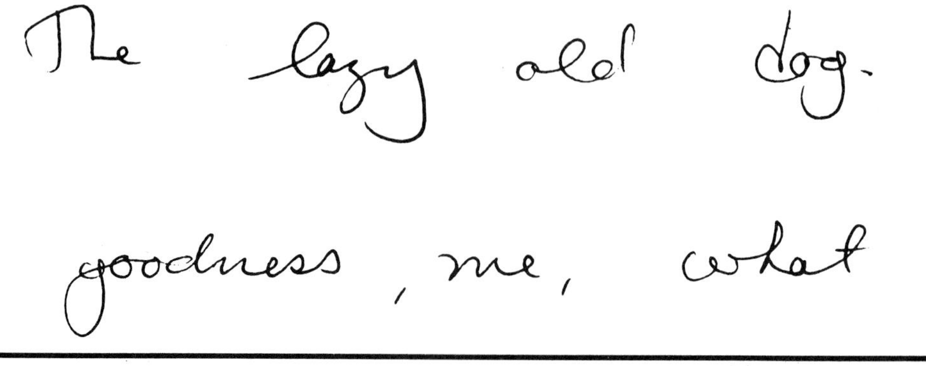

> *I would be grateful if you could just*

Anthony Last
Age: 26
Occupation: Printer

Specific features:
Small, but speedy writing.
Letter formations intelligently simplified.
Sharp angles, mixed with arcades and garlands.
Small left-hand margin.

Analysis:
This is a highly strung man with ambitions. He is a fine organizer and visual planner. This means he possesses a visual imagination which he tries to put into practice, constantly fighting against his enemy, time. He is the type who is fun to work with – but not so funny to work under, because he expects others to be as quick on the uptake as he is himself. He does not suffer fools gladly. (He himself hates to work under anybody).

He can be rather obstreperous when interfered with because he is sensitive and intuitive and hates it when someone interferes with his free-flowing imagination. At the same time one will find him to be a realist and a very practical person – one who works best when under stress or pressure. Very honest and sincere, he is also discreet and capable of keeping a secret – as good a friend as he can be a fierce enemy.

> *affairs sufficiently to be able to attend the next function.*

Désirée Swain
Age: 21
Occupation: Secretary

Specific features:
Lower Zone neglected. Hesitant connections.
Bent 'f' formations. Indistinct forms of connection.

Analysis:
The writer is a shy, but very sincere person who as yet has not found the strength of self conviction necessary to fulfil all her aspirations. She is basically a sincere idealist, but because she has not yet the courage of her own convictions she is usually a little on the defensive. And her defensive remarks are at times a little too blunt and outspoken. One will find that she is somewhat jealous of people who seem to be more adequate to cope with the complexities of life. This will change as she gains experience and confidence. She is conscientious, prepared to work hard, and eager to please her superiors – even if she somehow hates them for being superiors. She may be a little moody but she is at heart decent, a little naive and a very nice, honest young lady.

> *let me know as quickly as possible whether you can organize your affairs sufficiently*

Elizabeth Walker
Age: 28
Occupation: Managing Editor

Specific features:
Threaded forms of connection.
Right-hand margin irregular.
Lower zone emphasized.
Some disconnections.
Fast.

Analysis:
The writer is a delightful, highly intelligent, scatterbrain who is capable of talking the hindlegs off a donkey. Her mind is a quick and perceptive one. It is not easy to fool her, but one is much more likely to be fooled by her, or at least roped in to assist her in completing one of her schemes which she has no time to complete herself. She always seems to have a variety of plans in hand, and a combination of her drive and her charm enable her to complete most of them with the help of others. Free and easy going as she may be, she knows very well what she wants, and when it comes to assessing the monetary rewards due to her, one will find that she knows very well what she is worth. In other words she has excellent common sense and her attitudes to work and people around her are the result of experience and, perhaps, clever scheming.

She may be vague, but never dishonest. If she occasionally seems a little forgetful this is not intentional, but the result of having just a little too much on her plate.

Width

The width or extension of the writing is expressed in the middle zone, and from it one analyzes the writer's generosity, emotional equilibrium and, if the pressure of the pen is firm, energy and willpower.

Wide writing

played his han
xing the annexat

If the writing is wide, but the letter-formations are neglected, its rhythm weak, and large margins are thrown in for good measure, the writer is wasteful and extravagant. If width is combined with genuine garland connections, generosity and self-sacrifice are indicated. When the ending of the last stroke of a word or line is elongated, sociability and determination are shown. On the other hand, if individual letters are unduly wide and large, arrogance and pretension are indicated. But when the writing is fluent, the connections easy, and the i-dots or t-strokes part of the connection, it means versatility.

Narrow writing

scientist cried out in the law
that the earth cannot possibly be
never half would fall into it

Narrowness is also expressed in the middle zone. When fast, rhythmic writing with angular connections is narrow, the writer is determined and self-controlled.
If narrowness occurs in an upright script with low placed i-dots slightly ahead of the stem, the writer will be distrustful. A tight slow writing with a leftward slant or movement, shows narrow-mindedness and probably selfishness. The writer may also bear grudges. When many end-strokes are missing and the whole script looks disjointed, avarice and miserliness can be expected. Narrowness combined with weak pressure indicate shyness.

Speed

The speed of writing can be deduced from a combination of many of the individual writing characteristics already discussed. Of course, most quick writing shows signs of hesitation and even the slowest writers have a certain rhythm to keep their writing at a steady pace. However, there are general points which can differentiate between fast and slow writing.

Quick writing

Quick writing usually shows many of the following characteristics. Smooth, unbroken strokes and rounded forms connected by garlands, arcades or — more especially — threads, show speed and a good flowing rhythm. Frequent signs of rightward movement obviously indicate speed, since the writer is anxious to get to the end of one line and carry his ideas on to the next. This can also be combined with a slight leftward movement at the end of a line when the end of the sentence is on the next line. Letters which are joined by t-bars, and words joined by light strokes (showing that the pen has not even left the paper) are also signs of speed. Any simplification of letter forms speeds up the writing process — and this often manifests itself as a complete curtailing of letters at the ends of words, almost to the point of illegibility. Other characteristics of quick writing are widening of the left hand margin; no initial or final embellishments; rising lines — even though the writing remains at a constant angle — and wide distances between letters, especially if the script itself is narrow. It is unusual to find writing which shows all these points; in fact, it would indicate a hasty, agitated person who is nervous almost to the point of being unbalanced. But if the writing is legible as well as quick it shows that the writer has some control over his natural exuberance, is generally well-balanced and socially adjusted.

Slow writing

Anything which stops the natural movement of the pen across the pages could be considered a sign of slow writing, though the way in which letters are formed in our alphabet often necessitates certain stops, hesitations and leftward movements. For instance, i-dots and t-bars have to be indicated even if only in the most rudimentary way, since illegibility and confusion can occur if they are absent. If i-dots and t-bars are habitually missing, the writer is either thoughtless or scatter-brained. Other signs in the handwriting will establish which is the case. However, very carefully placed i-dots and t-bars are two of the many things which can slow writing down. Wavering forms and broken strokes indicate slow writing and suggest inhibition and lack of co-ordination. Frequent leftward movements and frequent pauses indicated by meaningless blobs, angles, and divided or touched-up letters are further indications of slow handwriting. Embellishments and enrichments of all kinds obviously slow the writing though creative embellishments often do not actually impair the rhythm. Signs of slowness are indicated by sinking lines, light pressure and pasty writing. If some of these signs are incorporated into an otherwise quick hand, the writer is moody and changeable, restless or impatient. Slow writing without embellishment indicates a person who is slow-thinking but thorough — not wanting to be hurried and using logic rather than impulse to make decisions. He has an even temperament and is reliable.

that you are interes
discussed and I
ing from you she
in the win st e
they are continull
ples of yur tale

Above: Two examples of fast and slow writing. Top: a typical slow script, carefully formed, very legible, but with some enriched letters — note the 'n' and 'h' formations. Bottom: fast writing with threaded connections and strong rightward trends.

Letter sizes

To examine the size and width of writing, you need a ruler, a compass and a good magnifying glass, without which some finer points may escape you. It is not only the size which is important, but also the relative sizes of the zones. Most school models show the relationship between the middle zone and the upper and lower zones as about 1:3; that is, middle zone letters should be roughly one third the size of the ascenders and descenders. In England, the ratio is usually 1:2.

Sometimes a writer shows a large middle zone with a small lower or upper zone. This can give the impression of a generally small writing. In this case, return to the interpretation of the three zones, and work out how they apply specifically to that writer. Generally speaking, considerable difference in zonal size shows an element of unrest.

There are also two kinds of large writing: relative and absolute. Relative largeness occurs when the middle zone is disproportionately large, absolute largeness refers to writing which is big in all three zones.

In a normal-sized writing, the relationship between the zones is harmonious and spacing is good; margins and lines are well-formed and straight, and the impression is that the writer is realistic and positive. The writing appears neither large nor small.

Large or small?

It is not surprising that the size of the writing indicates the writer's sense of self-importance. Often a writer makes up for the lack of acknowledgement from society by producing large writing. If the lower zone letters are badly formed or neglected, and loops are absent in the upper zone, this means that the writer is unhappy, and that his aims and ambitions have remained unfulfilled. Whether this is mainly his fault or due to other circumstances can often be established by other factors in the writing.

'Absolute' small writing

Small middle zone writing

Large middle zone writing

'Absolute' large writing

A small, well-shaped middle zone which is well-organized in its space, indicates an intelligent, critical person, with some specialized knowledge. He is modest, but knows what he wants and is prepared to work for it. On the other hand, small writing may indicate a modest, introverted character, who does not stand out in a crowd. Or, when other indications confirm it, a writer who suffers from fears, shows a lack of self-respect and has a subordinate attitude towards society.

Space between lines

A well-organized page of writing is obviously the work of a well-organized mind. The lines should be sufficiently spaced to give the page an orderly and pleasing appearance. The descenders of one line should not interfere with the ascenders of the line below it.

If the lines are too close the zones become interwoven and illegibility follows. This often happens when people use a large, extravagant hand — people who write like this often talk too much and are uneconomical in many ways.

If the lines are very far apart, they indicate isolation, detachment and a degree of reserve which could become anti-social. This could be caused by shyness, bad conscience or mental disorientation, but whatever the case may be, it spells difficulty in coming to grips with reality. It also implies some extravagance or mismanagement of affairs.

Very close lines are illegible.

Sometimes the zones intermingle.

This is clear line spacing.

The colour of the ink

Most people use blue-black ink to write a letter, but now and then a letter arrives in the post written in red, blue, green or brown ink. No doubt an odd colour ink gives writing a special face, and the colour chosen gives another clue to the kind of person who is writing.

Light blue ink indicates that the writer has spiritual rather than material interests. He may be religious and have a deep understanding of people's problems.

Blue-black ink is preferred by rational, conservative people, who are probably in business and adher to conventions and traditions. They do not want to be different from others, so they use the universal colour.

Black ink contrasts strongly with most notepapers, especially white, and writers who use it are making sure that their statements are noted.

Red is symbolic of strength, vitality and energy. It also represents affection; hence red roses to a lady-love. Certainly a person who uses red ink wants to be different, to stand out. In a bold script this may indicate some pomposity, but if a business executive uses red ink, he likes action and has an original approach.

Green is connected with harmony, adaptability and versatility. People with extra-sensory powers often choose green as their favourite shade. Young people frequently have a phase when they write in green ink, sometimes indicating an inferiority complex. Usually it is women who use green ink, or slightly effeminate men. One needs to try to understand why such a writer needs to stand out from the crowd.

Brown ink is rare, but the writer who uses it is often a man who has 'arrived'. He is likely to be an aristocrat or at the top of his profession. Brown ink leaves the impression of authority; but beware. Shrewd, professional men know how to impress, and a letter from a businessman in brown ink may be a bluff.

PETER ANDERSON

Pressure

Pressure is another important aspect of handwriting analysis since it shows much about the writer's will and vitality — in psychological terms his 'libido'. If pressure is very heavy, it indicates strength or will. It shows irritability or alternatively a slow, heavy-going personality. Sudden, dagger-like pressure formations indicate a tendency towards violence. Random and unnecessary heavy pressure which disturbs the harmony of the writing as a whole indicates maliciousness, or at least pretentiousness.

It is sometimes hard to distinguish the degree of pressure. When a pen is correctly held, there is a difference in shading between the up-strokes and the down-strokes, because the pressure is naturally stronger in the down-strokes. It is a good idea to find out how

not mean that pop stars do not find pleasure in reading poetry. It is a question of sensitivity rather than adherence to tradition, and adds weight to the point made already that the graphologist must not pre-judge, but analyze letter-formations as he finds them. No one is completely without prejudices, but everyone should try to be objective when the task is to understand other people. You may disagree with their outlook to life, but if you understand something of why and how they arrive at their views it helps towards a more tolerant view of life, and you may be able to help the other chap when he finds himself at loggerheads with the world.

Pens and pressure

The degree of pressure can be affected by the writing instrument. In script written with a felt-tip pen, it is very difficult to detect light and heavy strokes, though use of a magnifying glass will help to show the difference of thicks and thins. But ask yourself what

Thick and pasty: this shows sensuality
Fine and sharp: a very sensitive writer

the various characteristics have been formed. Follow the movement and flow of the writing with an orange stick or toothpick. This is especially useful when assessing writing in felt-tip — you will be able to feel the emphasis depending on the relative weights of the ascenders and descenders.

'Pasty' writing — in which both the up-stroke and the down-stroke are equal in weight, looks somewhat smeary and lacks shading. It is a sign of heavy, even pressure. Look carefully at the originality of the deviations from the school model. Such writers may be greedy, perverted in some way, or un-inhibited.

'Sharp' script which is fine and spidery, an indication of light pressure, shows a hypersensitive person — an inhibited writer who may have moral prejudices, a mystic or ascetic.

Pasty writing indicates sensuality, while sharpness denotes aestheticism. Of course, this doesn't mean a gourmet cannot be an aesthete, on the contrary, but both will find pleasure in quite a different way and for entirely different reasons. Aestheticism is difficult to define. A poet may find pop music anything but enjoyable, but this does

sort of person might prefer to use a felt-tip pen rather than any other. The choice of pen provides immediate clues to the writer's make-up. If the writing is by ballpoint pen, turn the paper over and feel the impression with your fingertips.

Many people still prefer to write personal letters with a fountain pen. They feel that the instrument, and the ink flowing from it, give the letter a more personal note, and the feel of pen pressing into paper, producing light- and shadow-strokes, is a pleasurable experience. People who prefer to write with an ink pen are likely to be more fastidious than the down-to-earth types who write with ball-point pens, which are easier to use.

Simple or ornate

It is obvious that embellishments or enrichments will cause writing delays, because any movement which adds unnecessary curves or spirals to the formation of letters contributes to a slowing-down of the writing flow. Simplifications have the opposite effect. An intelligent person will try to reach his goal by the quickest route. Over-simplification — to the point of illegibility — may point to someone who needs to show off, trying anything to get attention. Someone who is competent and well-balanced has no need to embellish his ego.

The kind of impression that an embellished writing makes depends, of

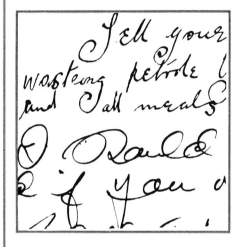

Top: These embellishments show a fussy character. Below: These show someone who needs to boost his ego.

course, on the recipient, and on whether the enrichments are executed with skill and taste. Embellishments could indicate an important person who likes ceremony and fuss, a writer with a personal fantasy for which he has not found the right outlet, or someone who needs to boost his ego or social position. Sometimes a few letters in an otherwise well-shaped script are written differently within a word. A versatile and intelligent person probably uses this common form of enrichment. Capable of tackling complex problems efficiently, he is inventive and original, attacking every project with zest. This phenomenon, usually involves 'e', 'a', 'd', and 't', especially the Greek 'eta' and 'delta'.

Legibility

Writing must be legible otherwise it ceases to communicate its message. If it is written in haste or is malformed, it goes against its own purpose by being illegible. To establish the degree of legibility of a specimen of writing, you must take the words apart and see if you can decipher every syllable when they are taken out of context. If you can read every part of a word quite clearly, you have an absolutely legible writing. However, it is not enough to examine just one word — you must look at a interpretation applies, find out how the upper and lower zones were formed by following the flow of the writing with an orange-stick or toothpick.

When legible writing shows delicately-formed loops and arcaded connections of high standard, the writer is a thoughtful person, unlikely to say anything tactless or hurtful. If the middle-zone letters increase in size, and the writing has a forward slant combined with a wide first letter, we find a writer who is zealous about morality, likes to play 'first fiddle', and may put moral values before his other duties. When the first letter is very high, and the i-dots very weak, we find a shy person who suffers from self-deception. If, however, intelligent simplifications are used which do not interfere with message they can give to the world is so involved that nobody will comprehend its esoteric meaning anyway, and so they do not bother to write clearly in the first place.

More often than not it is the speed of the writing that renders it hard to decipher. Speed creates threadlike formations — a sort of shorthand if you like — and thus an awkward deviation from the norm. A small hand with many threadlike formations indicates a hypersensitive person. However, if only the endings of words are neglected, the writer lacks perseverance and needs outside pressure to fulfil the tasks he sets out to do. If the first and last letter or words are emphasized, combined with sharp pressure and illegible formations, beware! Such a writer is

Illegibility comes in all shapes and sizes!

Legible writing will always communicate its message.

number of multi-syllable words. Illegibility can occur in any of the three zones, and it is not good enough to examine just the middle zone, even though it is here that most evidence comes to light. Legibility shows natural consideration and balance. Most people have an acceptable degree of illegibility arising from simplification of letter forms. We all expect anyone reading our writing to have sufficient common sense to understand the message through its context to some extent. Absolute legibility need not necessarily be a recommendation — the writer may simply be conventional, pedantic, fussy or slow. But it is also a sign of reliability. Double rolled 'a' and 'o' formations, combined with arcaded forms of connection in legible writing, may be signs of dishonesty. A writer may only be dishonest in his emotional reactions, due to personal disappointments and setbacks. He may be perfectly reliable in practical matters. To establish which legibility, we find a writer who sets aside personal interests for the common good.

Illegibility

There are definite degrees of illegibility in writing — from one or two words which are difficult to decipher to totally incomprehensible scribble. It is irrational to write a message which cannot be clearly understood. We must investigate what kind of person produces an illegible script and why. The illegible writer is just as anxious that his letter should arrive at its destination as the legible writer. Illegibility is caused by an unconscious action and indicates difficulty in observing ordinary social conventions. The writer shows reluctance to adapt to people and situations, and may be tactless or clumsy as well.

There are also people who, for deep and complex reasons, believe that the thoughtless, ungrateful and tactless.

A compass is a handy gadget to help establish the variation of sizes within a writing. Measure the size of letters with a compass and ruler. If your findings vary greatly and the writing is uneven, this means the writer is not very stable. He is a moody sort, someone who doesn't find it easy to steer an even course.

If illegibility occurs in a large writing, a sense of detail will be lacking. Unrhythmical changes of slant and wavy lines indicate a person who has been thrown out of gear by adverse circumstances. If other findings confirm this, the illegibility may also indicate insincerity or deceit, or at the very least a wish to conceal the truth. Someone who changes his letter formation frequently within whatever he is writing is either very versatile — if the writing is of a generally high standard — or else if the writing is of a low standard, lacking in principles.

Positive/ negative

It is important when assessing personal qualities and characteristics from handwriting to decide whether the writing is positive or negative. This comes from an overall impression rather than individual items. The first impression is important, since other items you investigate may also fall into a more negative or positive place as you go along. It rarely happens that the first impression is not confirmed in further analysis.

Positive or negative assessment makes a great difference to your interpretation — for instance, narrow writing with

Positive writing

Negative writing

firm pressure can mean initiative, ambition and self-possession, all very positive qualities. On the other hand, a negative script will turn the interpretation towards 'negative' traits, in this case recklessness, lack of self-control or

impatience. Strictly speaking there is no such thing as absolutely positive or negative writing: but since one needs some standard or ruling from which to work, the following is a useful guideline.

Positive writing

Positive writing fulfils its purpose first of all as a means of communication by being legible. It uses the writing space neatly. The margins and the spaces between lines are such that they form a pattern which is easy to read. The deviations from the school model mean that legibility is not impaired, and the writing is speeded up. The zones are harmoniously proportioned and the whole script is a pleasure to see and read.

Negative writing

On the other hand a negative script shows odd discrepancies at first glance. The lines probably intermingle and letter formations are badly shaped, leaving one in doubt as to which letter they actually represent. The size of letters is often exaggerated — either extremely large or small, making comprehension difficult, if not impossible. Margins and spacings are disorderly, and the whole document has an unpleasing appearance.

Capitals

Capital letters are of special interest to a graphologist because they form the size and shape of the upper zone. They are based, of course, on the line which forms the middle zone, but they should only go up into the upper zone. Since we are concerned mainly with writing in English, we must consider the fact that capitals are more rare than they are in other languages. On the other hand English is the only language in which the first person 'I' — the writer, the self, or ego — has a capital letter at all times, not only at the beginning of a sentence.

First person 'I'

It is possible to tell quite a lot about a writer from the way the 'I' is shaped, both in size and formation. If the 'I' is much larger than any other capital letter, you can assume that the writer has — or at least pretends to have — a high opinion of himself. If it is markedly

smaller, the opposite is the case. A well-adjusted, harmonious person who is content with his role within society writes a letter which is in equal proportion to the rest of the writing.

Illegible capitals

If intelligent writers speed up the

Capitals can tell you how a writer sees himself.

writing progress they try to streamline their capital letters. This can go too far, of course, and the writing becomes difficult to read.

It is also possible to enrich capital letters beyond recognition. This may not render the script unreadable, but it slows the speed of writing down, because any unnecessary movement

must cause delay.

Anything which seriously reduces the speed of writing means that the writer is either inefficient or hesitant or lacking good judgement and taste. He may be suffering from all these things. He may also need to underline his difference from others or to make an impact on the society within which he lives.

Whether this is a clever, efficient or even effective way of doing so is another matter. It is necessary to find out what makes people write in the way they do and why may they feel the need to make a particular impression on their society? These things will become clear after other features are analyzed.

i-dots and t-bars

The letters 'i' and 't' are the only two letters which are the same in every school model, regardless of nationality. This is a great help to any graphologist who is asked to analyze a manuscript written in a language he cannot understand.

i-dots

The dot over the 'i' can be low or high, ahead of the letter or just a little to the left. The slant of the writing and its interpretation are important here.

Backward-slanting script A low-placed dot to the left of the stem shows a very cautious person. If the dot is where it belongs exactly above the stem, we still find caution, but also a good retentive memory and attention to detail. If the dot is placed low and to the right, caution is combined with desire for action, an urge to get things moving. Dots placed in a relatively high position combine caution with an enquiring mind. When the dot is placed exactly on top, but high — which is quite a difficult thing to do — it spells accuracy, imagination and a more constructive degree of caution and inquisitiveness. When the dot is high, and in advance of the letter, discretion is shown. With this goes an enquiring mind and a measure of imagination and vision.

Upright script A low dot slightly to the left shows a writer who is a little cautious, but independent in judgement; he may be a practical realist. If the dot is placed on top of the letter, one finds an accurate person, who has good, practical judgement. If the dot is far to the right, it shows an active mind with vision and realism. If the dot is high to the left, the writer will reserve his final decision. When the dot is correctly placed on top of the stem, a shrewd combination of planning, movement and action exists, and all unnecessary reserve has been overcome.

Forward-slanting script A low-placed dot to the left of the stem indicates a writer who has learned to brake a little before he rushes into action. If the dot is on top, a positive, realistic and well-balanced writer is at work. A low dot ahead of the letter comes from an impatient person of extreme action. He is a realist with constructive vision;

he may be in a top position in industry. High dots on the left are a positive sign, since the dot's cautionary position indicates that this writer is someone who takes note of everything that is going on without hindering progress. If it is high and forward, the writer has forward vision and imagination.

t-bars

The t-bar can be just as informative as the i-dot. What is even more interest-

Some i-dots

Different t-bars

ing is that a t-bar may occur in a capital T, as well as in a small 't'. Strong long bars are always indicative of leadership of some sort, and short ones show a tendency toward subordination.

The position of t-bars is interpreted

in the same way as i-dots, but it is no longer necessary to point out what each slant of the writing indicates.

Left-hand placing A low-placed bar indicates uncertainty and possibly feelings of inferiority. If the bar is raised to the middle of the stem caution is shown. If the stroke is on the top, the writer has leadership potential but is too cautious to exercise his ability.

Central placing If the bar crosses the stem at the very bottom, the writer tries to overcome his feelings of inferiority by patiently and thoroughly following his duties. The correctly placed and shaped bar may come from a reliable and conscientious worker. A stroke which balances on top of the stem comes from a writer of leadership quality, who wishes to be in command or control, or to be recognized, but who may seek something outside his reach.

Right-hand placing A low short bar shows lack of confidence and reluctance to assume responsibility — the typical subordinate. A similar bar half way up still indicates lack of originality, but shows sufficient sense of responsibility to fulfil given duties carefully. If the stroke is at the top, but still short, the writer has limited leadership abilities.

A longish, but low-placed, bar shows a conscientious person who will be able to look after people working with, or under him. A long-bar at the correct height shows an increased degree of responsibility. The writer is probably in a 'middle management' position. A high bar is a positive symbol of a writer who can control and supervise others correctly and fairly.

If the t-bar is woven into the first letter of the next word, forming a protective arm, we find a firm leader and manager, someone who likes problems to solve. He is quick in his decisions, does not waste time or energy, shows fine co-ordination and is meticulous. A zigzag bar shows an argumentative, quarrelsome person who likes to be right.

If the writer forgets to make any i-dots or t-strokes, he impairs the legibility of the writing. This may mean that he is not capable of accepting responsibility, since he lacks real purpose. Alternatively he may believe himself different from others and in this way demonstrates his refusal to conform to tradition and convention.

U.S. Presidents and their assassins

The assassination of President Garfield of the United States in 1881: his signature is frank and pleasant in contrast to the spiteful script of Guiteau's confession.

Compare the sincere, practical signature of President McKinley with the unbalanced script of Leon Czolgosz, who assassinated him in 1901.

Signatures

Like envelopes, signatures can also be strikingly different from the rest of the writing, both in size and letter formation. The signature is, in a manner of speaking, the visiting card of the writer, and the way it is written shows the impression that he wishes to make on the person he writes to, or on the world at large.

Legibility

Since writing in general should be legible if it is not to negate its purpose—communication—the signature should be legible too. But it rarely is. What can be deduced from this? Can it be that, for example, when someone signs a document which may contain a commitment in some form or other, he unconsciously hopes to 'leave the backdoor open' as an escape route? He could say, 'That doesn't say John Smith — it's just a scribble or doodle.' It may well be just that, but it is also a trade-mark of sorts, because nobody else can produce the same 'scribble or doodle'. Even if 'John Smith' hoped to get away with it, he certainly would not succeed, because handwriting experts would easily be able to identify the producer of the scribbles.

Types of signature

A large upper zone is often produced by people in business, particularly on the sales side, together with odd shapes in the lower zone.

Underlining, often combined with two dots underneath or one above and below the line, indicate that the signatory will stick to a bargain, making sure that every item of a contract is strictly kept. Lawyers, bankers, civil servants and people in similar professions often have this characteristic which is a sign of reliability and sincerity — provided the rest of their writing bears out the existence of these qualities.

Small signatures, smaller, that is, than the rest of the writing show modesty and even understatement.

Large signatures, on the other hand show that the writer is proud of his descent, position or success — or at least makes himself believe that he is.

Surnames and Christian names may be given different emphases. The surname is representative of the social element, and forms the nucleus of the signature, the whole Christian name or initials represent the private and intimate part of it. Children are exclusively called by their first names and the Christian name is therefore a symbol of 'childlikeness'. Wherever there is a harmonious balance and relationship between Christian-name and surname you can assume that there is no discord between private and public life. If the Christian name or initials are very much smaller than the rest of the signature, this is a sign that the writer is sacrificing his private life at the cost of position, power, success, and so on. If the first name is larger than the rest of the signature, this indicates that the importance of the writer's private life is so great to him that it over-rides all social considerations. If the Christian name slants to the left, in an otherwise differently directed signature, this shows an acute conflict between private and social life.

Signatures of married women are of special interest. A woman when she marries consents to take not only the man of her choice, but also his name, and her signature is a useful guide to her happiness, contentment, and satisfaction in married life. When she writes her Christian name or initial larger than the rest of the signature, it indicates that she was happier when unmarried. When her first name or initial is smaller than the next of the signature, the opposite is true. If surname and Christian name are the same size, the writer is well balanced and content. It must be pointed out in fairness that a husband's writing can be analyzed in a similar way; a man keeps his own surname of course, but if he writes his first name or initial, larger than his surname, he unconsciously feels that he was happier as a child or a bachelor. Bear this in mind if you ever find yourself in the position of marriage counsellor.

Opposite: All these signatures are from original specimens and are reproduced actual size. The majority are people who are, or have been, in the public eye, but four are ordinary people with quite different backgrounds. Two are British, one is from New Zealand, one from the United States. See if you can identify which is which!

Prince Rainier of Monaco A light-hearted, delightful hand. Humour, determination and an aloofness used to keep bores away. Pressure indicates determination, discipline and a high working capacity. I-dots are all-seeing eyes; he is firmly anchored to reality and material values. Strong powers of observation and well-disciplined.

Frank Harris Good pressure, combined with the size of the signature, indicate a man who knew his worth. He delivered the goods and did not mince words. He had a firm grasp of reality. He took no chances; everything was organized and down-to-earth. Self-loving and vain, but unashamedly honest about it.

George Bernard Shaw Small, cramped, legible. A man who had something to say, but who kept the public at arm's length. Upper zone is better developed than the lower, not in size but in loop-formation — intellect, not emotion inspired him. Size and crowding indicate a calculated generosity based on economic principles.

A very large, hasty signature with a long end-line putting a safe distance between him and the outside world. Here is a thoughtful but active man who knows what he wants and how to keep it when he gets it. The large loops show his imagination and depth of feeling. (John Ruck).

Here is an emotional person trying to find a way of life which promises fulfilment. Some letter formations indicate artistic discrimination. The neatly placed i-dots indicate a fine power of observation and a reliable factual memory. Some 'a' and 'o' formations are open, indicating that the writer is sincere, if a little blunt.

The writer is a fast worker and an imaginative thinker. The initial capitals intermingle and form a complex piece of abstract sculpture, which illustrates the complexity of his visions and his proclivity for doing more than one job at a time. (P. Edwards).

This signature shows a down-to-earth attitude to life. The slow, well-formed writing indicates reliability. Arcades and some disconnection show she thinks carefully over every step she takes. She is dependable, and intelligent, with common sense. (Jennifer T. Down).

[Signatures shown: A. Einstein, Theodore Roosevelt, Frank Harris, G. Bernard Shaw, Lloyd George, John Gielgud, Wendy Martenson, Tony Jacklin, Benjamin Spock, Jennifer T. Down, Longford]

Albert Einstein Simple and childlike at first glance; but beautifully simplified. The garlanded capital 'E' in Einstein shows kindness and gentleness; angular connections indicate hard, concentrated work confirmed by the first low i-dot. The high t-bar indicates that he knew his degree of authority, but innate modesty held him in check.

Theodore Roosevelt Sensitive, well-shaped writing with pressure, indicating energy and mental prowess. Letter formations are unassuming, clear and legible. The wide space between Christian name and surname indicates the breathing space he needed to formulate his thoughts. Honest and sincere, free from vanity.

Lloyd George Highly intelligent, well underlined to boost his self-respect, but with delicate line-connection. Speed and pressure show intuition and intellectual shrewdness. Everything is brought to bare essentials. The downstroke and pressure indicate his ability to get things done, with time for thought and meditation.

John Gielgud A highly intelligent man with great powers of concentration. I-dots indicate reliable memory. His signature is larger than the rest of his writing, showing modest pride in his success. He likes to impress his fellow men.

Tony Jácklin The letter 'J' aims for a hole in one! Slight, firm pressure indicates discipline and concentration; lines over and under show that he is aware of his obligations. A hook at the first t-bar — and right hand underlining — show an ability to cope with reality. He is well-balanced and confident.

Dr. Benjamin Spock A man who makes an impact. An idealist; honest; no-one interferes with his ideas. Well educated. 'j' and 'i' dots indicate a quick mind that thinks ahead. The capital 'S' and small 'p' show ability to plan and organize. Copes with reality cautiously — note the closed 'a' and 'o'. Angular connections show conviction.

Lord Longford Well-shaped, large, intelligently simplified and legible. A man whose superior intelligence concentrates on basics. The end curve of his signature indicates a gentle man who does not bear grudges. A rational pride is shown in the large 'L', and the 'g'. Personal matters take second place to public life.

How to analyze a sample

By this time you have a foundation and understanding of the theory of graphology. Now you can apply this knowledge to the analysis of any sample of handwriting, using the step-by-step analysis section which follows. Carefully evaluate every aspect of the writing according to the questions, writing down the number and letter which applies (i.e. if the writing slopes slightly backwards, the key will be 11a). If the question does not apply, leave it out. It will not make any difference to the final analysis.

Equipment

Certain equipment is necessary to begin a thorough analysis. It is always easier to do the job — be it woodworking, dressmaking or sheep-shearing — if the proper tools are at hand. You will need the following:
a pad and pencil for note taking; a compass; a protractor; a ruler; an orange stick, toothpick or sharpened matchstick; tracing paper. (You may find it easier to trace the diagrams and place them directly on to the sample when assessing angles, zones, space between lines, etc.)

Before you start

There are certain facts to ascertain before you begin.
Nationality As we have seen, school models vary widely and must be taken into account immediately.
Age Characteristics of aging can appear in the writing of younger people with various illnesses.
Sex We are all bi-polar rather than bi-sexual, which means that men have some feminine characteristics and women are masculine to some degree. Make sure the characteristics you find are really indicative or just appear occasionally. Some writing is fairly standard so try not to read eccentricities into it! Many letters can be made in a variety of ways in a single piece of writing so look for the majority and interpret from that.
When you have completed the questions, key all the numbers to the relevant answers. Do not be tempted to look at the answers until you have completed the full analysis — it may influence your final interpretation. Check that you have not missed any combined characteristics which will add further points to your analysis.

Intuition

Do however play any hunch that may occur to you, based on prior knowledge of the writer or simply by putting clues together in a variety of ways. Although intuition is an un-scientific quality in a systematic method, it can be combined with knowledge and training. Intuition is a decisive factor in differentiating between a good technician and a brilliant one. The expert who clings to his textbook knowledge will never be outstanding.

The angle of lines

1 *Lay a ruler under the line of writing*
Is it straight and at right angles to the edge of the page?

2 **a)** Does it slope upwards—a little?
b) A lot?

a

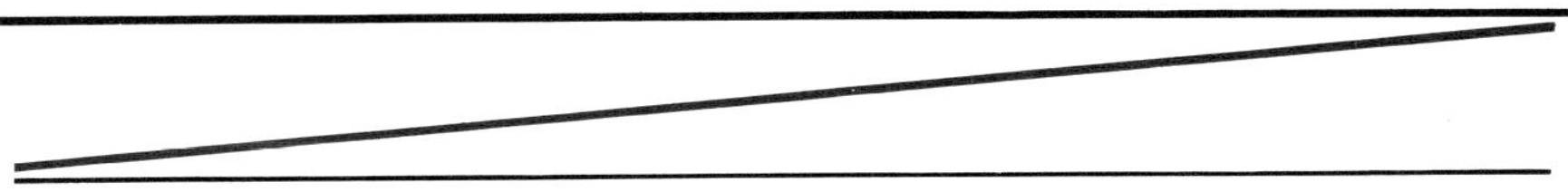

b

3 **a)** Does it slope downwards—a little?
b) A lot?

a

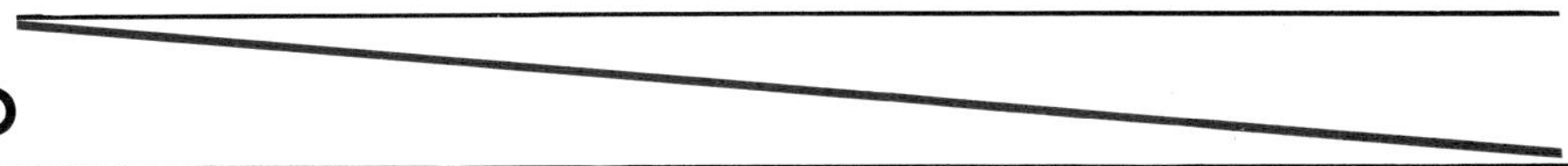

b

4 Does the line of writing wave up and down?

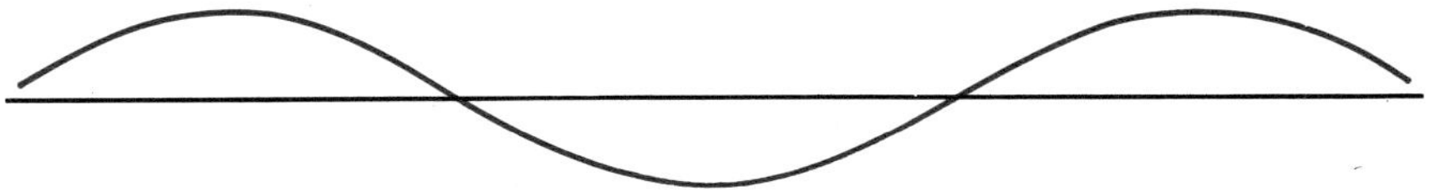

5 **a)** Does the line progress in steps up?
b) Or steps down?

a

b

6 **a)** Does the writing arch in the middle?
b) Does it sag in the middle?

a

b

The three zones

7 How big is the middle zone?
  a) Is it like this?
  b) Or like this?
  c) Or like this?
  (Samples shown are twice life size.)

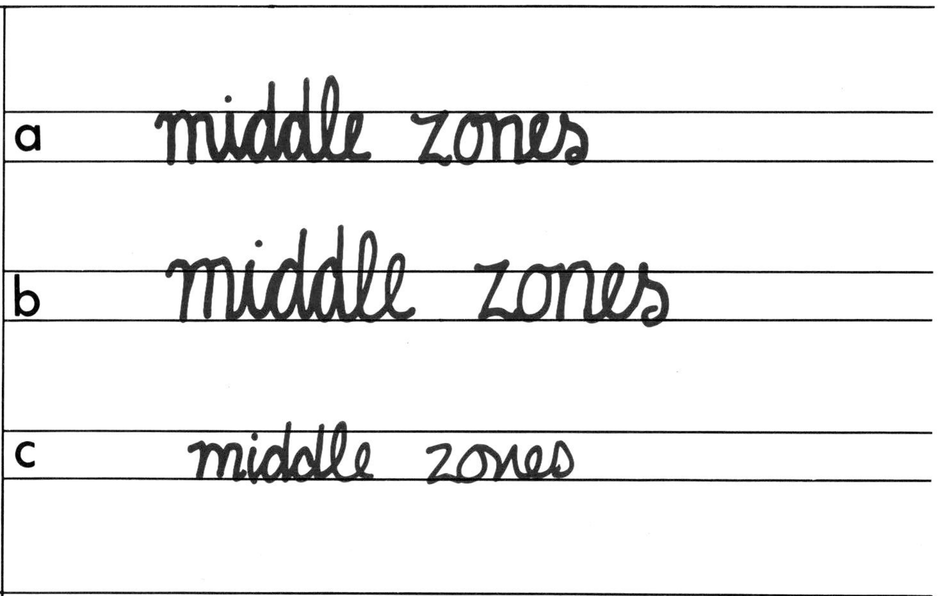

a *middle zones*

b *middle zones*

c *middle zones*

8 **a)** Are the middle zone letters evenly sized?
  b) Do they start smaller and get larger?
  c) Do they taper towards the end?
  d) Are they uneven throughout?

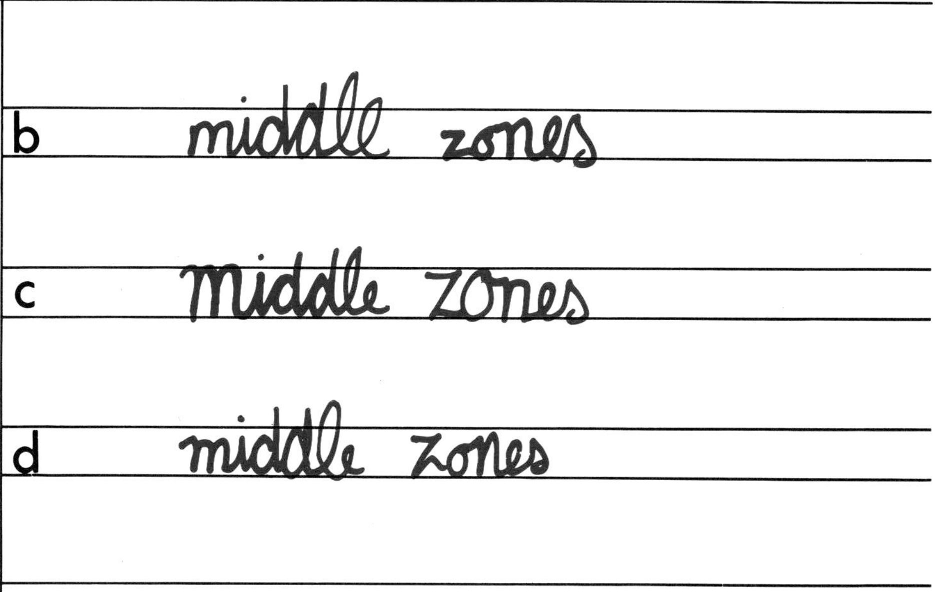

b *middle zones*

c *middle zones*

d *middle zones*

9 **a)** Is the emphasis on the ascenders?
  b) On the descenders?
  c) Does the middle zone take precedence over both?

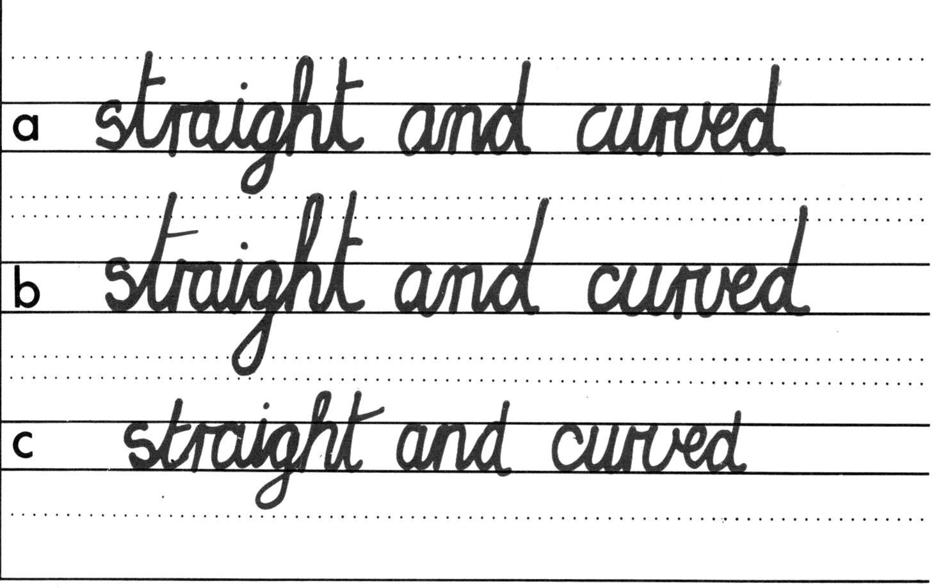

a *straight and curved*

b *straight and curved*

c *straight and curved*

The slant of the letters

10 Does the writing slope to the right?
a) A little?
b) A lot?

a

b

11 Does the writing slope to the left?
a) A little?
b) A lot?

a

b

12 Is the writing upright?

Margins

13 If the margin is straight, how wide is it?
  a) Narrow?
  b) Medium, well-proportioned?
  c) Wide?

a b c

14 **a)** Does the left hand margin get wider towards the bottom?
  b) Or narrower?

15 Is the left hand margin missing altogether?

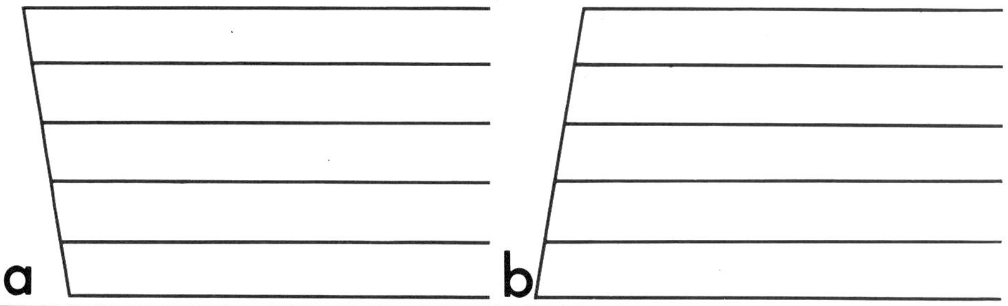

a   b

16 Is the left hand margin uneven?
  a) Jerky, in steps?
  b) Wavy?

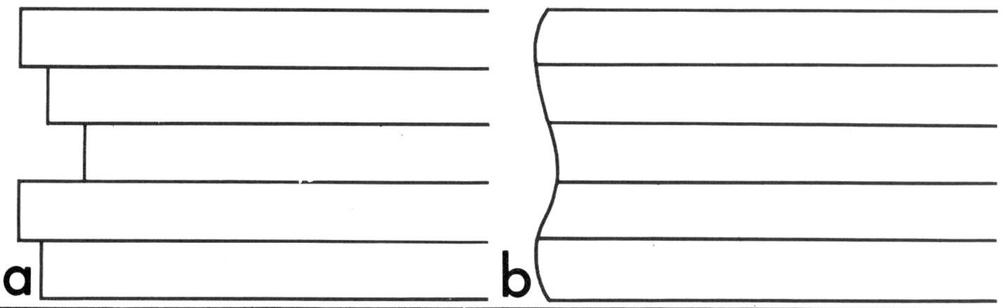

a   b

17 Is the right hand margin
  a) Unnaturally regular?
  b) Naturally uneven, but well spaced to indicate a margin?
  c) Or do words 'drop over the edge' or have to be squeezed in?

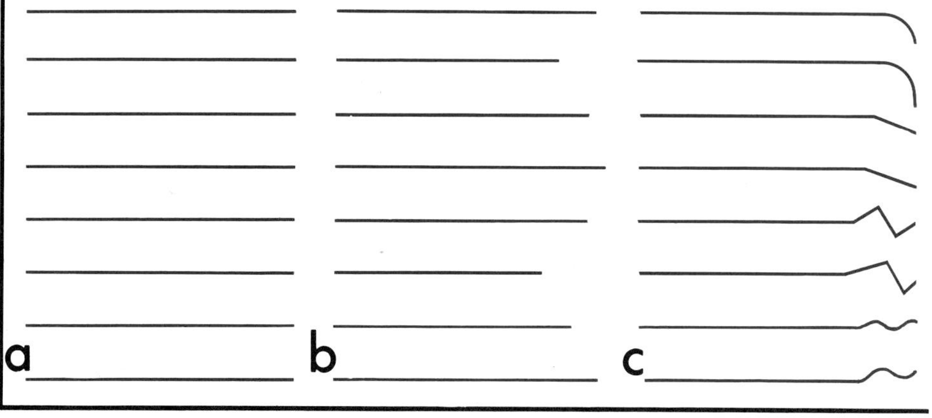

a   b   c

Space between lines

18 How well spaced are the lines?
a) Are they so close together that letters touch or mix?
b) Quite close but not touching?
c) Clearly spaced?
d) Very widely spaced?

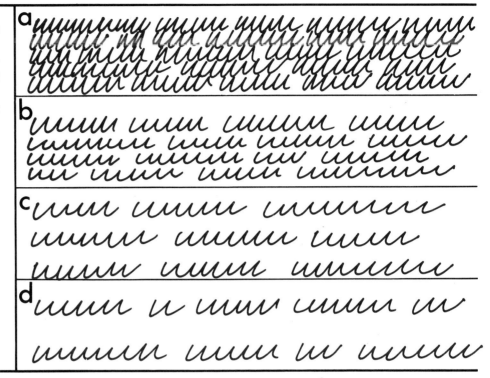

Envelopes

19 *If the writing you are analyzing came in an envelope written at the same time, apply these questions to the envelopes.*
a) Is the address positioned in the centre?
b) Very high?
c) Very low?
d) Far left?
e) Far right?

20 a) Is the writing the same as the main script?
b) Is it illegible?
c) Is it larger than the main script?
d) Is it smaller?

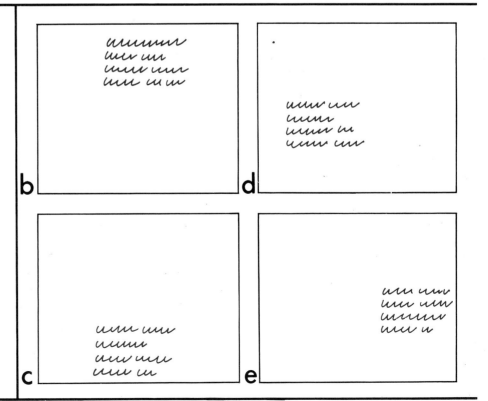

How letters are joined

21 *Work out which type of connection predominates.*
a) Are the connections garlanded like this?
b) Or arcades like this?
c) Angular like this?
d) Or threads like this?

a garlands

b arcades

c angular

d threads

22 a) Are the connections spread out like this?
b) Close together like this?

a wide apart

b close together

23 a) Are some of the letters disconnected, like this?
b) Are they all disconnected?

a some disconnected

b all disconnected

The width of the writing

24 *Measure the extension of the letters, using only the middle zone.*
a) Are the letters very close and cramped like this?
b) Are they wide like this?
c) Are they quite regular like this?

a close and cramped

b wide like this

c regular

Pressure

25 How much pressure does the writing show?
  a) Is it fine and spidery?
  b) Is it firm and even?
  c) Is it heavy?

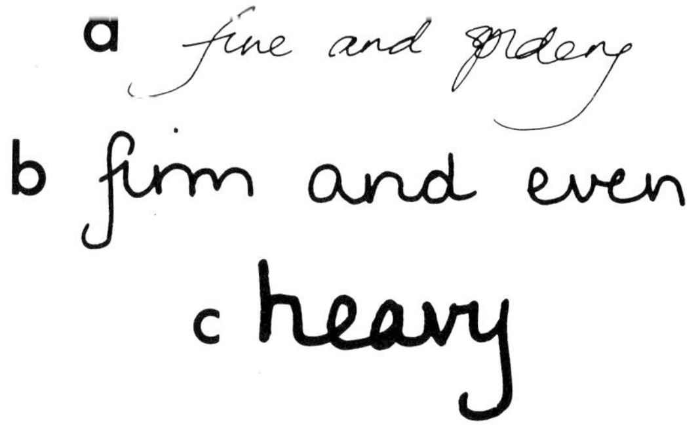

a *fine and spidery*

b firm and even

c heavy

26
  a) Does the writing have conscious thick and thin lines, done for effect?
  b) Is it irregularly thick and thin?
  c) Is it consistently thick and pasty?

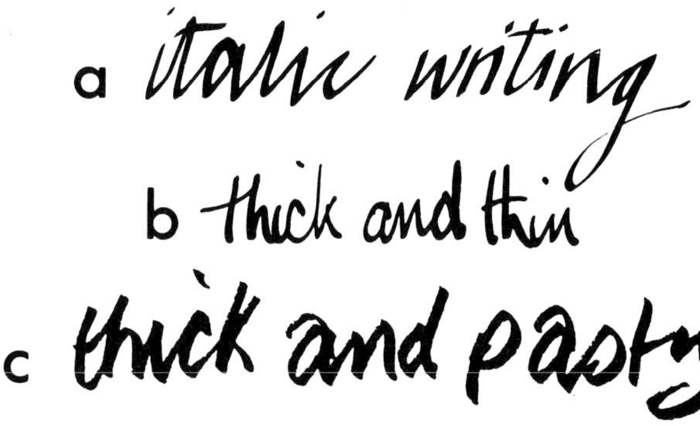

a *italic writing*

b thick and thin

c thick and pasty

Speed and rhythm

27 *Follow the writing with an orange stick to feel the flow and rhythm.*
  a) Is the rhythm very smooth and quick?
  b) Is it slow and careful?
  c) Is it jerky or disjointed?
  d) Is it hasty so that some words are illegible?

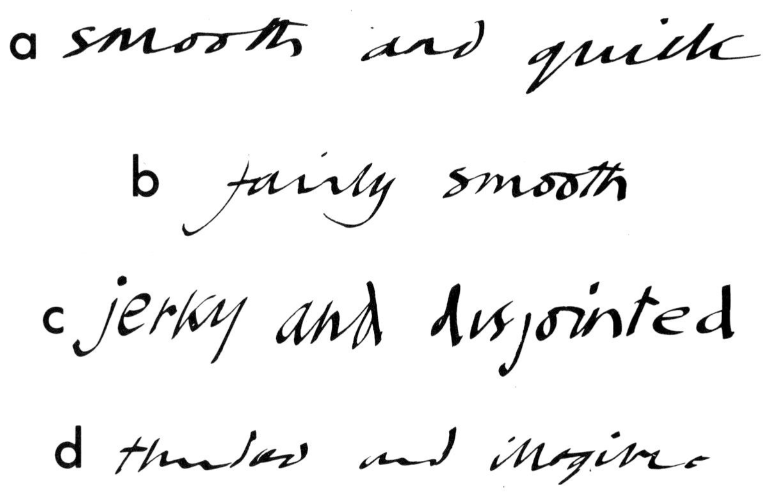

a smooth and quick

b fairly smooth

c jerky and disjointed

d hasty and illegible

Initials and finals

28
a) Do words begin with long straight strokes like these?
b) With a garlanded first stroke?
c) An arcaded first stroke?
d) Do they start with enrichments like these?

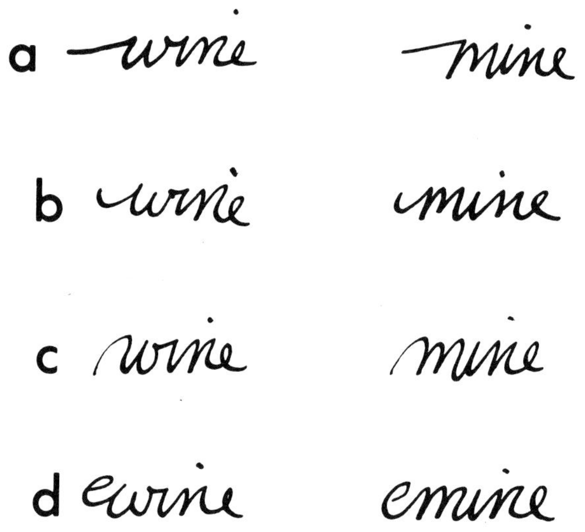

a — *wine*   *mine*

b *wine*   *mine*

c *wine*   *mine*

d *wine*   *mine*

29
a) Do end-strokes point to the right like these?
b) Are they clipped like these?
c) Do they go up in arcades like these?
d) Do words finish with garlands like these?

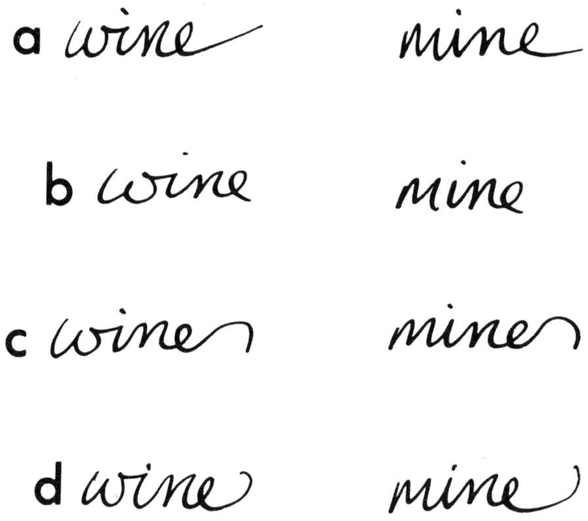

a *wine*   *mine*

b *wine*   *mine*

c *wine*   *mine*

d *wine*   *mine*

Words joined by finals

30 Are words joined together?
a) Never
b) Occasionally
c) Nearly every word

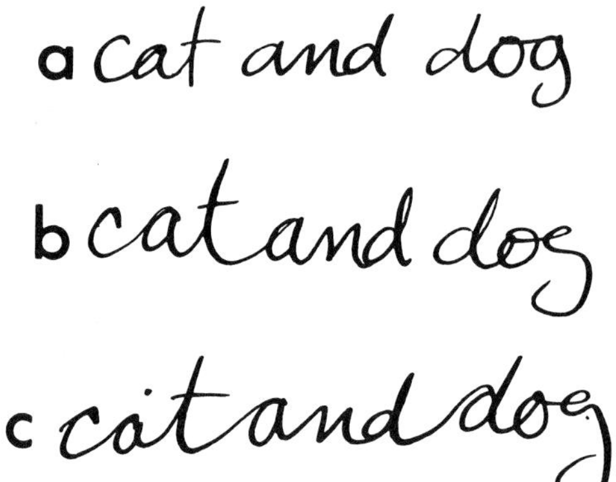

a *cat and dog*

b *cat and dog*

c *cat and dog*

Dr Manfred Lowengard, the author of this book, likes to spend many hours poring over a specimen of writing. To him a magnifying glass is vitally important, so that he can catch the minute changes of emphasis in every single stroke of the pen.

Capital letters

31 How do capitals relate to the middle zone?
  a) Are they low?
  b) Quite standard?
  c) Are they high like this?
  d) Are they embellished?

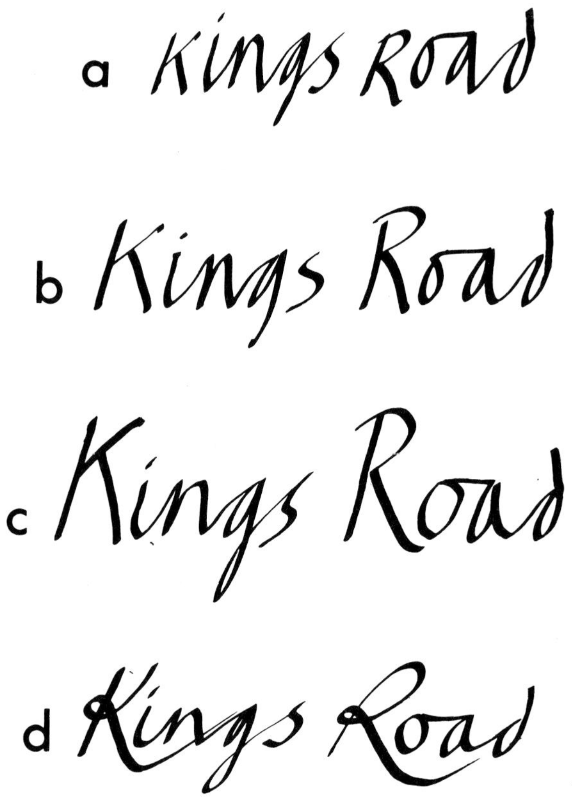

a *Kings Road*

b *Kings Road*

c *Kings Road*

d *Kings Road*

First person 'I'

32 Are the first person 'I's like any of the following? (Remember to look for the majority if the formations vary.)

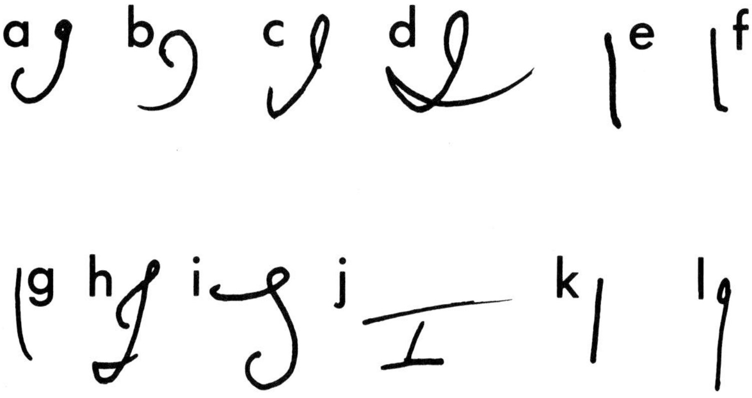

a b c d e f

g h i j k l

Simple and ornate

33
a) Does the writing include awkward embellishments like this?
b) No embellishments at all?
c) Creative embellishments which add style to the writing?

a

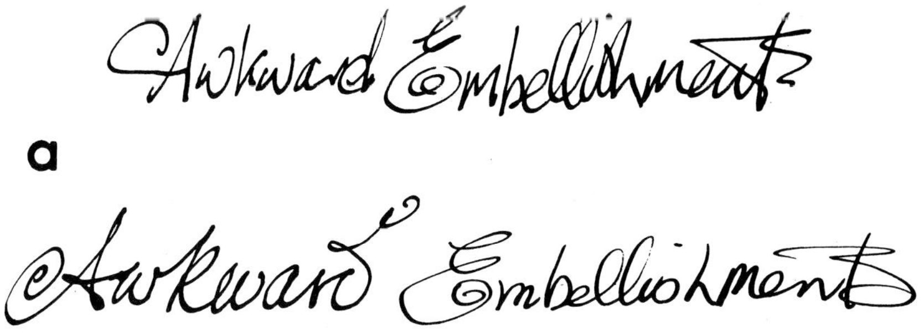

Awkward Embellishments

Awkward Embellishments

Creative Embellishments

c

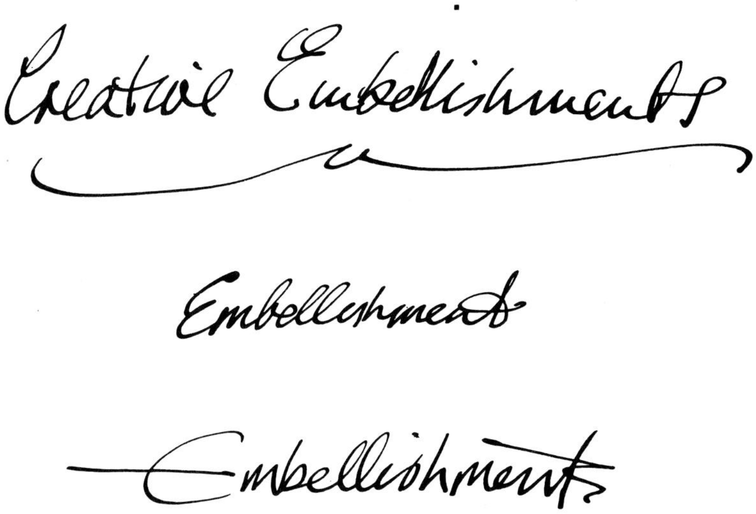

Embellishments

Embellishments

34
a) Do simplifications help the speed and clarity of the writing?
b) Are all letters simplified so much that their meaning is not always clear?

a

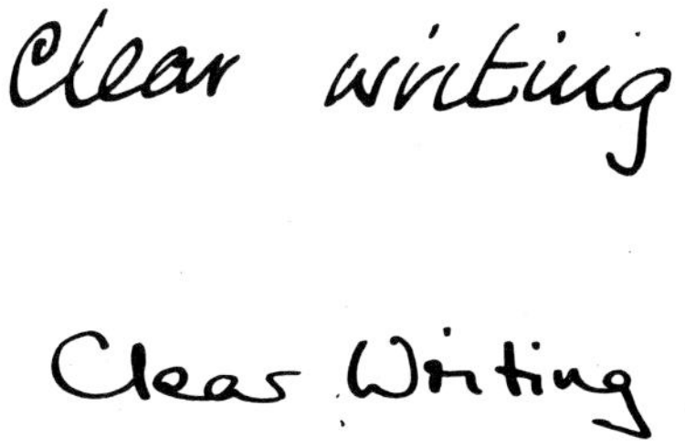

Clear writing

Clear Writing

Simplified Writing

b

meaning writing

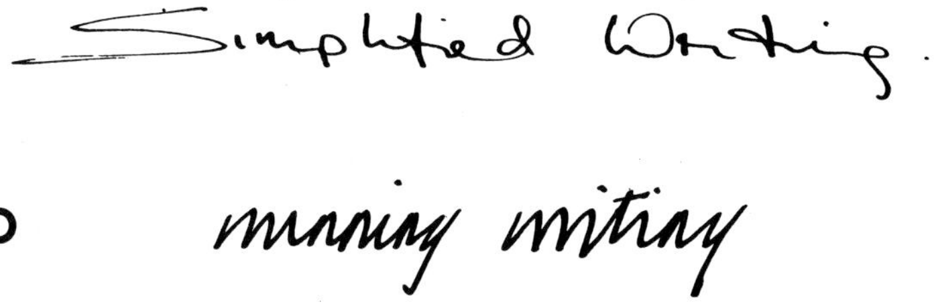

Signatures

35 Does the signature differ from the main writing in any of the following ways: **a)** Is it larger? **b)** Is it smaller? **c)** Is it less legible? **d)** Is it just as legible? **e)** Is it more embellished?	**a** *Yours sincerely, Arthur Jones.* **b** *Yours sincerely John Smith* **c** *Yours Sincerely ...* **d** *Yours sincerely Albert Ross* **e** *Yours sincerely Edward Briggs*	
36 **a)** Is there a full stop at the end? **b)** Is it underlined?	**a** *John Smith.* **b** *Bertram Peters*	
37 **a)** Is the first (Christian) name or initial more emphasized than the surname? **b)** Is it less emphasized? **c)** Is there an equal emphasis?	**a** *Elizabeth Jones* **b** *Susan Peters* **c** *Arthur Jones.*	

Letter formations

38	a) Are the 'a' and 'o' letters open at the top? b) Are some of them open? c) Are they open at the bottom? d) Are they all closed? e) Are the 'o's knotted at the top?	a *open* b *Some open* c *open* d *all closed* e *knotted*
39	Are the tails of letters open (i.e., made of 2 strokes)?	*a d f p q t y*
40	Bearing in mind questions 8, 26 and 29, are the ascenders a) Looped like this? b) Simplified like this?	a *b d h k l* b *b d h k l*
41	Are the 'd's and 'e's 'Greek' formations like this?	*ð ð ε Ɛ*
42	Are the descenders of these letters a) Looped like this (including 'z' in some school models)? b) Curved like this? c) With flourished loops like this? d) Or like this? e) Are the descenders straight, with neither loops nor curves?	a *gjyzp* b *gjyzp* c *gjyzp* d *gjzyp* e *gjyzp*
43	Are 'l' or 's' formations crossed through like pound or dollar signs?	*£ Live $ Sums*

44 *Note the position of the i-dots. Bear in mind questions 9, 10 and 11.*
a) Is the i-dot directly above the stem?
b) To the right?
c) To the left?
d) Is it heavy?
e) Faint?
f) A dash or tick?
g) A circle?
h) High?
i) Low?
j) Omitted altogether?

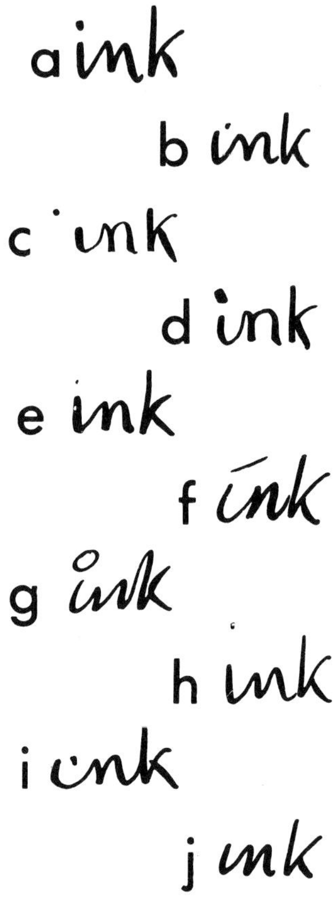

a ink

b ink

c ink

d ink

e ink

f ink

g ink

h ink

i ink

j ink

45 *Note the position of the t-bars. These are related closely to the position of the i-dots.*
a) Do the t-bars cross the stem like this?
b) Or like this?
c) Are they to the right like this?
d) Or like this?
e) Are they to the left?
f) Are they faint?
g) Or heavy?
h) Are they high?
i) Or low?
j) Do they slant up?
k) Or down?
l) Are they knotted?
m) Do the finals form the cross?
n) Are the t-bars above the stem?
o) Are they long enough to cover the whole word, or used as a connection?
p) Are they omitted?
q) Do they curve over the stem?
r) Do they curve over a very short stem?

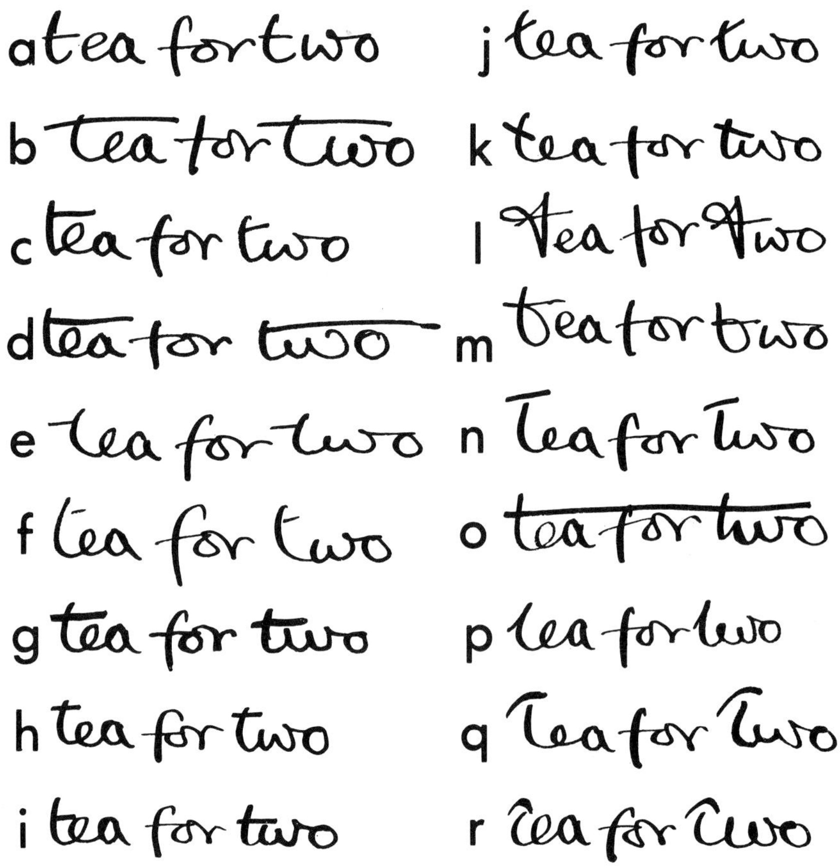

a tea for two   j tea for two

b tea for two   k tea for two

c tea for two   l tea for two

d tea for two   m tea for two

e tea for two   n tea for two

f tea for two   o tea for two

g tea for two   p tea for two

h tea for two   q tea for two

i tea for two   r tea for two

All the answers

1. Toeing the line. Conventional. Reliable.

2. a) Active, positive writer who knows his aims and ambitions.
b) Too anxious to succeed. Perhaps a little hasty in judgement. Optimistic.

3. a) Fatigue. Slight depression. Worry that problems are too much to cope with.
b) Depressive. Physical or mental fatigue. Pessimism.

4. Emotional. Slightly unstable.

5. a) and **b)** Writer is trying to control undue optimism or pessimism, depending on whether the lines go up in steps or down.

6. a) Enthusiasm held in check.
b) Either fatigue or depression held in check.
In other words both denote self-control.

7. a) This is the average size of most writing and means little on its own: it could mean thoroughness, convention, honesty, loyalty or even possessiveness.
b) Pride, vanity, ambition, pretention, enterprise, arrogance, self-esteem, en-thusiasm, excitability. Very large writing shows a tendency towards irritability.
c) Power to concentrate; conscientious-ness; critical, analytical mind: often an academic, whether literary or scientific.

8. a) Another sign of a conscientious nature.
b) Tactless.
c) Diplomacy, discretion, tact. A good businessman.
d) Keeps his feelings to himself, but can be moody. In a strong person-ality could be objective and observant.

9. a) Idealism; ambition; intuition.
b) Sensualist; exaggeration; materialist.
c) An over-developed ego — a tendency to throw his weight about and influence others.

10. a) Keenness, optimism, will to succeed.
b) Emotions may run away with the writer. Lack of self control.

11. a) The writer is not too keen to face the future.
b) Cautious, unapproachable. Could have something of a mother complex — or a hankering for the past.

12. This can be considered as a slight leftward movement when the writer's school model slopes to the right. If an upright school model was used and this is adhered to, it indicates self-control, reticence, or general lack of emotion. Poise, coolness and an ability to weigh up people and situations.

13. a) A sign of practical economy — not necessarily meanness, but the wish to get as much information on to the page as possible.
b) The normal margin which means nothing by itself.
c) A very wide left-hand margin show the writer's desire to put a safety mar-gin between himself and his objective. If both margins are wide it shows culture or good taste.

14. a) If the left-hand margin gets wider towards the bottom it shows an affectionate nature. It also shows some extravagance, especially with money — inability to save.
b) Margins getting narrower show practical money sense.

15. No margins at all show neurosis, self-obsession with no room for any-one else's feelings.

16. a) A bad organizer, talkative, a

Combined characteristics

Many of the answers given above and overleaf are modified when combined with others. For instance, even- sized middle zone letters [8a] *combined with i-dots directly over their stems* [44a] *show a painstaking nature.*

Double check your answers and see if any of these combinations apply to the writing you are analyzing.

4. Wavy lines in an otherwise quick, [27a] garlanded [21a] script with neat margins show willingness to try any-thing once and do the best he can. Wavy lines combined with several changes of slant show a person thrown out of step by adverse circumstances.

7. a) Average-sized writing combined with clearly spaced lines [18c], neat margins or angular connections [21c] means a good head for business.
c) Combined with hooked finals [29d] and narrow letters [24a] can indicate niggling or petty attention to detail.

Combined with drooping lines [3b] it indicates depression and a feeling of inferiority.

8. a) Combined with i-dots placed directly above [44a], painstaking.
b) Writing which increases in size in forward-sloping writing [10b] indicates moral zeal.

c) Combined with straight lines [1] or small writing [7c]: versatility.
Combined with leftward t-bars [45e]: or faint t-bars [45f]; a sign of chronic indecision.

9. c) Combined with large size [7b] this writer has problems in coping with everyday matters.

11. b) Combined with any of the follow-ing, it indicates brutality: a medium-sized middle zone [7a]; heavy pressure [25d]; uneven middle zone letters [8d]; heavy t-bars [45g].

12. Combined with angular connections [21c] this can show laziness or indolence. Combined with very small writing [7c] or hooked finals [29d]: avarice. Combined with thick t-bars [45g] or

All the answers

restless mind.
b) Absent-minded.

17. a) Another sign of neurosis: an obsessive love of order and self-control, even inhibition.
b) This is normal and shows a well-balanced, easy-going personality, with a sense of order and style.
c) A talkative person, with little feeling for time.

18. a) Confusion to the point of un-balance — it is very jumbled. Indifference to luxury.
b) This is normal and shows ability to sort out ideas.
c) Clear and logical.
d) Isolation.

19. a) This is normal.
b) This indicates a dreamer.
c) Clings to the material and practical side of relationships.
d) Shy, unforthcoming.
e) Extrovert, dependent on others.

20. a) An unaffected person who has no desire to appear other than he is.
b) Someone who finds it difficult to adapt, is tactless or clumsy socially.
c) Self-assurance which is a pose — lack of sincerity.
d) The writer's self-confidence is greater than his somewhat reserved outward behaviour might appear.

21. a) Impressionable, receptive nature.
b) Reserve, conservatism.
c) Resilience, strength, perseverance; possibly dogmatic attitudes.
d) Flexible, changeable, easily influenced; fast-thinking.

22. a) Spontaneity, expansiveness.
b) Restraint, moderation.

23. a) A good judge of character. A person who relies partly on logic, partly on intuition.
b) Another sign of isolation, probably due to absent-mindedness or an impractical nature.

24. a) Restraint, moderation.
b) Wasteful, careless.
c) Drive and spontaneity.

25. a) Sensitivity, refinement, spirituality, modesty.
b) Energy, elasticity. This is average.
c) A strong but rigid will, obstinate.

26. a) Affection and conventionality, especially if the writing is close to the school model.
b) An insistent character, with a forceful personality.

27. a) Spontaneity, drive, action, an ambitious personality.
b) Deliberate nature, thorough.
c) Inhibition, frustration, dissatisfaction.
d) Lack of method, rashness.

28. a) Obstinate, stubborn.
b) Genuine, open, welcoming nature.
c) Polite, conventional.
d) Hesitant, bad judgement.

29. a) Generous nature.
b) Selfishness or reticence; disappointment.
c) An open but spiritual nature.
d) Dogmatic attitudes.

30. a) This is normal and means little on its own.
b) Speed and quick thinking.
c) Talkative, a busybody.

31. a) Modesty, a humble nature, simplicity.
b) This is normal and means little on its own.
c) Self-respect, conceit. The higher the capitals the more conceited the writer.
d) Affection, vanity, an overblown idea of self-importance.

32. a) Well-balanced, humble.

Combined characteristics

embellished capital letters [31d]: arrogance.

13. a) Combined with small, narrow writing [7c, 24a] it is a sign of thrift.
c) Combined with large writing [7b], this shows wastefulness or extravagance.

15. Neurosis is especially confirmed if non-existent margins are combined with arcaded [21b] or angled connections [21c].

19. c) Combined with drooping lines [3b] this means that the writer is easily depressed by practical difficulties.

21. a) and b) Arcades combined with garlands denote secretiveness. If the garlands are obviously mechanical — following the school model very correctly — it shows reserve or hypocrisy.
d) Threads in small writing [7c] show hypersensitivity. If only the ends of the words deteriorate this shows lack of perseverance.

22. a) If the letters are very wide apart, with wide spaces between lines [18d], this can mean isolation and lack of spontaneity.
Wide writing with firm pressure [25c] can show initiative, ambition or recklessness and impatience. With light pressure [25a], it shows tolerance, imagination, adventurousness, superficiality. Look for other signs to decide which applies.
b) Narrow writing with firm pressure [25b], can show moderation, tact, discipline, reserve, or even jealousy, distrust, or deceit. With light pressure, [25a] it shows caution, timidity, anxiety, narrowmindness.

b) Sensitive, nervous.
c) Keen, ambitious.
d) Down-to-earth
e) Proud of social standing.
f) Intelligent, positive.
g) Highly intelligent, fast-thinking.
h) Musical, but weak.
i) Sensitive, engaging.
j) Ambitious, but needs security.
k) Wobbly self-esteem.
l) Determination, self-esteem.
m) Unsure of role in society.

33. a) Pretention, vulgarity.
b) This is normal in most school models. It shows balance and lack of pretention, a desire to stick to essentials.
c) Talkative, strong personality, a sense of style.

34. a) Someone who is purposeful, objective and wants to get straight to the point.
b) Indecision, ambiguity.

35. a) Overcompensating for lack of self-esteem; vanity; bravado.
b) Keen to understate one's own importance; modesty.
c) Of little significance; merely a sign that the writer signs his name many times a day.
d) Conscientiousness, fussiness.
e) Pride, self-respect.

36. a) A well-developed sense of self.
b) Shows reliability and sincerity.

37. a) More interested in himself than other people.
b) Private life is sacrificed to public life: business, or social contact.
c) Balance between private and public or social life.

38. a) Frank, open, perhaps indiscreet.
b) Sincerity.
c) Hypocritical, false.
d) Close, discreet.
e) Secretive.

39. The writer keeps people at arm's length, will go so far but no further.

40. a) Warm-hearted.
b) Sticks to essentials.

41. Scholarship or acquired intellectuality. A sense of style.

42. a) Healthy emotional appetite.
b) An interest in harmony — visual as well as emotional.
c) Vanity, sexuality.
d) Sensuality, exaggeration.
e) Sober down-to-earth personality.

43. Someone with money on his mind.

44. a) Perfectionist.
b) Thinking ahead.
c) Careful.
d) Pedantic, fussy.
e) Idealist.
f) Haste.
g) Over-emphasis on detail, eccentricity, dishonesty.
h) Spiritual, intuitive.
i) Down-to-earth, practical.
j) Unreliable.

45. a) Conventional, anxious to please.
b) Protective, warm-hearted.
c) Forward thinking.
d) Anxious to make social contact, but without emotional commitment.
e) Careful.
f) Sensitivity.
g) Determination, pig-headed.
h) Spiritual, intuitive.
i) Down-to-earth.
j) Ambitious, aggressive — especially if the stroke is sharp and pointed.
k) Pessimism.
l) Sensitivity, thought for others.
m) A good arguer, but jealous.
n) Self-protecting.
o) Protective towards others. A capacity to help others.
p) Unreliable.
q) Probably at loggerheads with a father-figure, or someone in authority.
r) Guilty conscience or inferiority.

25. b) Combined with long, final strokes, [29a] this shows a mild temperament. Combined with a high t-bar [45h] it shows someone with a nature which looks forward in hope.

27. d) Combined with badly formed letters this shows laziness.

29. a) If they are very long, it shows fixed opinions.

37. a) If this is combined with a leftward slant it shows a tendency to look back towards childhood. In a married woman emphasis on the Christian name shows a tendency to view herself as she was before marriage; her marriage is either not intrinsically important to her, or she is unhappy in it.

38. b) Especially sincere if the lines are straight [1].
d) and e) If either of these are combined with thick, pasty writing [26c], the writer is irritable, argumentative.

40. b) If simplified to the point of illegibility, this shows a thoughtless or snobbish personality.

42. e) Combined with very light pressure [25a] depression, dissatisfaction.

44. a) I-dots over the stem on left slanting writing indicate a good retentive memory.
c) Leftward i-dots on a left-slanting script indicate extreme caution.
e) Faint i-dots in a word which has a large first letter show shyness.
h) High i-dots with left-slanting writing [11b] indicate curiosity, even nosiness.

45. n) Combined with a weak stroke, lack of confidence.

The assessment of qualities

What to look for in writing— an index of characteristics

Accuracy
Very close to the school model, with some simplifications. Good rhythm. Good spacing and margins. Size of letters slightly increasing towards the end of words and lines.

Ambition
Lines sloping up. Long t-bars crossing through the stem or slanting slightly upwards.

Argumentativeness
Open 'o's and 'a's. Thick, pasty writing. Wide loops on the ascenders or t-bars slanting up.

Arrogance
Upright writing. Embellished capital letters and heavy t-bars. Embellishments in ordinary letters as well.

Brutality
Heavy pressure and thick pasty writing with emphasis on the middle zone. Left-ward trends with heavy, pointed i-dots and t-bars.

Bully
Large, impressive with heavy pressure. Narrow extension, with emphasis on the final strokes. Leftward trends, high t-bars and dagger-shaped i-dots. Triangular, sharp loops in the lower zone.

Business Ability
Small middle zone. Clearly spaced lines with neat margins. Angular or garlanded connections. Some letters like numbers.

Caution
Backward sloping writing. I-dots to the left of the stem.

Conscientiousness
Even middle zone. Straight margins and upright script. I-dots placed directly over the stems. Neat t-bars.

Cowardice
Slow, hesitant rhythm and light pressure. Narrow middle zone. Faint t-bars.

Cunning
Lines that slightly rise combined with angular connections. Uneven middle zone or a tapering middle zone. Arcaded end strokes and o's and a's open at the bottom.

Emilio Pucci
This is an elegant writing from a man who likes his riches. He is conscious of class, he is chic and he has enormous style. The 'E' in his Christian-name has two parallel lines in the centre, turning the letter into a £ sign and signifying his certainty about his aims and ambitions. The i's on their

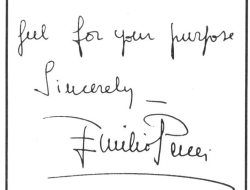

pedestals indicate pride.
This is a man who commands authority, but some of the middle zone letters spell modesty and humility. He bows to beauty.
Here, a knowledge of foreign, non-English school models is essential. This letter is typical of the Italian school model, even though it is written in English.

Deceit
Writing which slopes upwards quite steeply combined with uneven middle zone letters and a's and o's tightly knotted at the top.

Dignity
High, straight ascenders.

Dishonesty
Rising lines of small, narrow writing. Uneven middle zone letters with tight knotted a's and o's.
Slow writing. Some letters are made with several little strokes where one or two would do. 'a', 'o', 'g' and 'q' open at the bottom. A combination of arcaded and threaded connections.

Distrust
Slow but narrow writing with arcades and sometimes angled connections. Some words joined by the final strokes.

Eccentricity
Rising lines and upright writing. Small middle zone with garland connections. Embellished letters and i-dots drawn as a circle.

Egoism
Strong leftward slant. Middle zone letters larger at the beginning of words. Embellishments with angular connections in narrow writing. Tightly knotted o's and a's.

Emotional nature
Writing which slopes so far forward it almost seems to fall onto the line.

Enthusiasm
Large middle zone with writing sloping up. Heavy pressure. Emphasis on the upper zone with looped ascenders.

Exaggeration
Embellishments in large writing. Very wide margins and wide spaces between lines.

Friendliness
Garlanded connections in fully connected script. Medium sized middle zone with a definite forward movement.

Generosity
Quick, large writing with clear space between lines. Connections wide apart.

Many important qualities must be revealed in the signatures on the American Declaration of Independence!

SIGNING THE DECLARATION OF INDEPENDENCE.

A Declaration by the Representatives of the UNITED STATES
OF AMERICA, in General Congress assembled.

   When in the course of human events it becomes necessary for ~~a~~ ^one^ people to
dissolve the political bands which have connected them with another, and to
[~~advance from that subordination in which they have hitherto remained, & to~~] as-
-sume among the powers of the earth the ^separate and equal^ ~~equal & independant~~ station to
which the laws of nature & of nature's god entitle them, a decent respect
to the opinions of mankind requires that they should declare the causes
which impel them to ~~the change~~ ^the^ separation.

   We hold these truths to be ^self-evident^ ~~sacred & undeniable~~, that all men are
created equal, ~~& independant~~; that ~~from that equal creation they derive~~ ^they are endowed by their creator with equal^
~~rights~~ [inherent & inalienable ^rights; that^; among ~~which~~ ^these^ are ~~the preservation of^
life, & liberty, & the pursuit of happiness; that to secure these ^rights^, go-
-vernments are instituted among men, deriving their just powers from
the consent of the governed. that whenever any form of government

THE FIRST DRAFT OF THE DECLARATION OF INDEPENDENCE IN JEFFERSON'S HANDWRITING, AND WITH HIS
OWN CORRECTIONS.

(From the original, preserved in Washington.)

Gentleness
Garlanded connections and light, firm pressure. Emphasis on the upper zone.

Greed
Thick, pasty writing. Large loops in the lower zone.

Honesty
Quick writing with a tendency towards the right. Garlanded connections and fine, neat spacing. Well-proportioned, no exaggerations.

Hypocrisy
Slow script. Signature smaller than the preceding text. Small a's and o's open at the bottom.

Idealism
Large but natural writing. High placed i-dots and t-bars. Emphasized upper zone, light pressure and occasional irregularities in the spacing.

The Archbishop of Westminster John, Cardinal Heenan
An erudite signature, written with soft pressure and well controlled speed. There are many scholarly formations, especially the Greek 'E'. The last letter of the signature reaches out gently for the spiritual, whilst the wavy lines, slightly ascending, show sensitivity mixed with a sense of humour. The arcaded connection

between the 'o' and 'h' in 'John' indicates the love of and adherence to tradition. Many words are woven together by large arches, his symbol of faith. Connections between words are very good, indicating free flow of thought and speech.

Inconsiderate
Irregular in shape and direction. Erratic spacing. Various connections, but with threads which impair legibility. Irregular margins.

Inferiority complex
Small but hesitant. Threaded connections; narrow extension and little pressure. Wavy lines, which also droop at the right hand margin. Neat, but narrow margins.

Intellectual balance
Fast writing with legible simplifications. Greek 'e' and 'd' formations. Good spacing and signature the same size as the rest of the handwriting.

Intuition
Quick writing with light pressure. Variability of connection including some disconnection. I-dots and t-bars connected to other letters.

Irritability
Lines sloping downwards a little. Lines rather close together. Heavy, but irregular pressure. Some signs of speed, others of slow writing. T-bars to the right of the stem.

Jealousy
Writing sloping far to the right. Final stroke of the 't' curving back to form the bar. Light pressure with some missing i-dots. Slow writing.

Kindliness
Forward sloping writing, light pressure and looped descenders and ascenders.

Logic
Letters always connected. Straight lines, small writing.

Materialism
Untidy. Heavy pressure and uneven spacing. Some pastiness and leftward tendencies. Angular connections and emphasis on the lower zone, though unpleasantly shaped.

Modesty
Tendency towards the left, with left slanting lines. Capital letters lower than the ascenders. Simple letter forms.

Opportunism
Letters tapering in size towards the end of the word. Variety of connections. Wide, but light pressure. Increasing left-hand margins.

Optimism
Fast writing with rising lines and wide script. Good spacing and large writing, but well-proportioned.
Intelligent simplifications.

Organization
Neat margins with clear spacing. Middle zone in proportion to both upper and lower zone. Letter 'f' running from upper to lower zone.

Passion
Fast writing with extreme forward slope. Irregular pressure with pastiness. Large writing with a tendency to be narrow.

Pride
High capital letters. Embellishments. Signature larger and more embellished than normal handwriting.

Sadism
Pasty writing with emphasis on the lower zone and angular connections. Sharply pointed final strokes. Sudden stabs of heavy pressure.

Self-confidence
Fast writing with no inconsistencies. Medium sized script with regular, firm pressure. Heavy t-bars.

Self-control
I-dots to the left of the stem in upright or forward sloping script. Straight lines. Regularity of pressure, size and spacing.

Self-indulgence
Slow writing. Letters badly finished, tapering at the end. Capital letters slightly large.

Sensuality
Pasty writing with an extreme slant and emphasis on the lower zone. Lack of pressure in a woman, strong pressure in a man. Clipped final strokes indicate sensuality if the writing is slow.

Sincerity
Quick, rhythmic writing, Well-spaced lines, and the extension is standard. Some simplification, but not at the expense of legibility. No leftward movement.

Talkative
Very narrow margins, almost non existent. Large writing but written very quickly. Bad spacing. Garlanded connections combined with threads. Words joined by final strokes. Width of letters and connections and close spacing. Irregular righthand margins.

Vanity
Perfect spacing. Peculiar enrichments, but not impairing legibility. Well-proportioned middle zone but unnatural loop-formations in the lower zone. Very emphasized capital 'I'.

Religious texts were handwritten for centuries, as this medieval illumination of St Matthew indicates.

SCS MATTHEYS
EVANGELISTA.

Barbara Cartland
A full analysis

This delicately shaped writing, which shows an even finer, but firm pressure, comes from a woman who aspires to penetrate deeply into the mysteries of life. The high i-dots and ascending t-strokes show that she is determined to reach for the sky. The connection of the initial 'I' with the word 'hope' shows her determination not to let anything or anybody interfere with her plans and ideas. The letter shapes are simple — occasionally too simple in the middle zone. The threadlike formations which result show how fast she thinks and how well she is able to concentrate on essentials. The writing is upper-zone directed. The lower zone is insignificant in both size and formation, indicating that she pursued her causes and interests not for material gain, but for the sake of propagating the ideas and ideals which have occupied her interest and imagination. The pressure indicates her determination, which uses gentle persuasion rather than domination. This does not imply that she is easily persuaded to change her ideas, as the large signature and its ascending underlining indicates. She knows what she is doing and is convinced that her causes are fair.

There is a basic gentleness and artistic sensitivity here. Look at the way the word 'Yours' is shaped. The sample was obviously written in a hurry, and the flying i-dots and t-strokes indicate that everything she undertakes is executed speedily. The 'Yours' formation looks like a delicate flower, and people who make such shapes have a feeling for the arts. They enjoy beautiful countryside and good music.

The size of the writing contrasts sharply with the enormous signature— she feels the need to fill the page to prevent somebody else adding anything to her document. This is confirmed by her occasional over-connections, as in 'I hope' and 'my handwriting'. She is ensuring that no one else's thoughts obscure her message. After that the spacing is neat and wide, indicating that she thinks profoundly before putting her final thoughts on paper, a sign of methodical reasoning and intelligence. Some end-strokes are clipped, which is not surprising. A sensitive and intelligent person will have experienced disappointments and occasional grief, and these will have contributed to the formation of the personality which has emerged.

The size of the signature indicates pride and daring. She has to convince herself to do certain things, to try to hide her initial shyness. She hates to interfere with the privacy of others as much as she dislikes it if they meddle with her solitude.

This is a sincere, reliable and honest script from a person with ideals and ideas which she will defend with intelligent firmness and persuasion. The whole writing is intelligent rather than emotional. She has her emotions under control without suppressing them; everything is in its proper place, and in this aspect of the writing one finds a trace of old-fashioned values.

Biographical background

For most people, writing 150 books and novels, bringing up three children and running a 500 acre estate would be a full life. For Barbara Cartland these three demanding occupations are only a small part of her extraordinary life.

She embarked on her professional writing career 50 years ago as gossip columnist and soon published the first of more than one hundred romantic novels. Two years later, her first play, previously banned by the Lord Chamberlain, was performed. She was subsequently presented at Court, and, never wanting to miss the opportunity to help a friend, she wore a gown given to her by a struggling young Cambridge undergraduate, Norman Hartnell. She participated in the General Strike of 1926, and after the birth of her first child, she organized the first of her numerous large-scale charity efforts — a pageant which she designed, produced and presented at the Albert Hall and London Pavilion.

Her two brothers were killed at Dunkirk, and she sailed with her daughter and two sons for Canada to await the end of hostilities. But when she realized that the war would be a long one, she fought for, and finally received, permission to return home. By the end of the war she was regarded as one of the nation's greatest morale boosters. In 1955, she won the Hatfield seat on the Hertfordshire County Council and began running her 500 acre farm in a way that kept her in touch with her electorate.

Her charitable work is combined with a vigorous fight for a healthier Britain. She has campaigned, against bitter opposition, to better conditions for Nurses and Midwives and for gypsies and against fluoridation of water supplies. She has served as President of the National Health Association. She has written biographies, cookbooks, etiquette manuals and works of sociology. Now past 70, she is as energetic as ever. Her own autobiography consists of four volumes — so far. She appears on radio and television frequently and travels thousands of miles each year, writing, lecturing and giving interviews everywhere she goes.

Key to Barbara Cartland's handwriting

[1] Reliable, conventional.
[2a] Active, positive writer who knows her aims and ambitions.
[7c] Power to concentrate; conscientious.
[8a] Another sign of a conscientious nature.
[9a] Idealism, ambition, intuition

[12] Self-control, poise; an ability to weigh up people and situations.
[13a] Practical economy.
[14a] Affectionate nature.
[17b] Well-balanced, easy-going personality.
[18c] Clear and logical.
[21d] Flexible, fast-thinking.
[22a] Spontaneity, expansiveness.
[23a] A good judge of character. A person relying partly on logic, partly on intuition.
[24c] Drive and spontaneity.
[25c] Energy, elasticity.
[27a] Spontaneity, drive action.
[29b] Reticence; disappointment.
[30b] Speed and quick thinking.
[31c] Self-respect.

[32d] Down-to-earth.
[33b] Balance; lack of pretention; a desire to stick to essentials.
[34a] Purposeful; objective; someone who wants to get straight to the point.
[35a] Lack of self-esteem.
[36b] Reliability and sincerity.
[37b] Private life sacrificed to public life.
[38d] Close, discreet.
[40a] Warm-hearted.
[44b] Thinking ahead.
[44c] Careful.
[44h] Spiritual, intuitive.
[45j] Ambitious.
[8a] and [44a]: painstaking.
[21d] and [7c]: hypersensitivity.
[22a] and [25c]: intuitive, ambition.

John Wayne
A full analysis

This large, speedy writing reflects an immensely active and ambitious man (look at the capital D in 'dear'). The writing is obviously derived from an American school model, but he alters it by using considerable pressure in the down-strokes. This indicates his strong sense of purpose and will to succeed. The large t-strokes also confirm this strong will. They form a kind of connection between words, eliminating any gaps in his thoughts which may be taken advantage of by others. This implies that he sees his objective clearly and that he will not permit anyone to interfere with his actions. They also show a protective nature.

The pleasant curves or garlands at the end of many words indicate that he is basically kind and generous, but the triangular loops of his 'g' and 'y' formations indicate a shrewd assessment of his chances to capitalize on situations.

The zones intermingle occasionally, but without interfering with the excellent legibility: he can combine material advantages with ambitious idealism, a rare quality which must lead to success.

His small 'a's and 'o's are carefully closed, even rolled-in, indicating that he has acquired a bit of diplomacy and is fairly tight-lipped about his plans. He has learned the hard way — the last stroke of his signature wants to keep people at a safe distance.

The last two letters of the signature gradually decrease in size showing that he has been taken for a ride more than once. He tries to prevent this from happening now, and he generally succeeds as the large lasso-loop under his name shows. The lasso reaches far to the left, as does the loop in the 'P', and some other lines have a leftward trend, such as the 't' in 'this', the 'h' in 'handwriting', and the 'e' in 'expert'. This indicates that his childhood memories are still dear to him.

Now look at the way the letters 'x' and 'p' in the word 'expert' go elegantly into all three zones. This shows an ability to organize and plan and a use of economy in fulfilling complex assignments.

The wide lefthand margin indicates that he leaves a safety-margin between himself and his objective; he is a man who thinks carefully and plans exactly before he acts. The relatively narrow righthand margin indicates that he is keen to establish contact with the outside world and anxious to please.

The general flow of this script and its large and generous size say that this man is a charming extrovert who will not let anyone influence him beyond the moral and ethical limits he has set for himself. He is almost old-fashioned in his romanticism, but shrewd enough to look after himself very satisfactorily. He is not completely without pride, as the little extra loops in the lower zone show.

He is a successful man who enjoys his achievements and admits it honestly and freely.

Biographical background

John Wayne . . . 6 foot 4 inch blue-eyed brown-haired Gemini . . . born Marion Michael Morrison, Winterset, Iowa . . . nicknamed 'Duke' as a youngster . . . moved to California in his teens . . . graduated from Glendale High School . . . scholarship grant to University of Southern California . . . worked summers at Fox Films as a 'props' man and met director John Ford . . . cast in a small role in Ford's 'Hangman's House' and went immediately back to the props dept. . . . . director Raoul Walsh call him 'John Wayne' (more appropriate for a cowboy) and gave him lead in 'The Big Trail' . . . during the Depression, he became 'Singing Sam' the screen's first musical cowboy, but couldn't sing a note . . . handed over to an unknown called Gene Autry and launched into a series of Westerns called 'Three Mesquiteers' . . . in 1939 friend John Ford cast him as the Ringo Kid in 'Stagecoach', the role which catapulted him to stardom, where he remains . . . by 1949 listed as one of ten most popular stars in the United States, where he has remained, usually in the top spot . . . in 1959 formed his own production company, Batjac, of which his son Michael is executive producer . . . produced more than a dozen films, including 'The Alamo', which he directed and starred in . . . has made more than 200 films and shows no signs of stopping . . . show business newspaper Variety calls him 'Boxoffice Champion of the World' since he has starred in 17 of the highest-earning films in movie history . . . authenticated grosses of his films have topped the 700 million dollar mark . . . in 1969 awarded the Academy Award for his role in 'True Grit', a critical and box-office success . . . seven children, four by his first marriage, and three, aged 7 to 15, by his Peruvian wife Pilar . . . now lives in Newport Bay, California, where his yacht, a converted mine sweeper christened 'The Wild Goose' can be moored a few yards away at his private pier . . . says he has no patience for golf, but he will spend hour upon hour poring over a chess board . . . plays bridge, deep-sea fishes . . . he's a devoted movie fan, who screens several films a week in his private projection room . . .

Key to John Wayne's handwriting

[2a]   Active, positive; knows his own ambitions.
[7c]   Power to concentrate, conscientiousness; critical.
[8a]   Another sign of conscientious nature.
[9b]   Idealism; ambition; intuition.

[10a]   Keenness, optimism, will to succeed.
[13c]   Desire to put a safety margin between himself and his objectives.
[17b]   This is normal; shows balanced easy-going personality.
[18b]   This is normal and shows ability to sort out ideas.
[21a]   Impressionable, receptive nature.
[22a]   Spontaneity, expansiveness.
[24c]   Drive and spontaneity.
[25b]   Energy, elasticity. This is average.
[27a]   Spontaneity, drive, action.
[28c]   Polite, conventional.
[29d]   Dogmatic attitudes.

[30b]   Speed and quick thinking.
[31c]   Self-respect.
[33c]   Talkative, strong personality, a sense of style.
[35d]   Conscientiousness.
[35e]   Pride, self-respect.
[37c]   Balance between private and public life.
[38d]   Close, discreet.
[40a]   Warm-hearted.
[42c]   Sexuality.
[44b]   Thinking ahead.
[44f]   Spiritual, intuitive.
[45n]   Self-protecting.
[45o]   Protective towards others. A capacity to help others, take them under his wing.

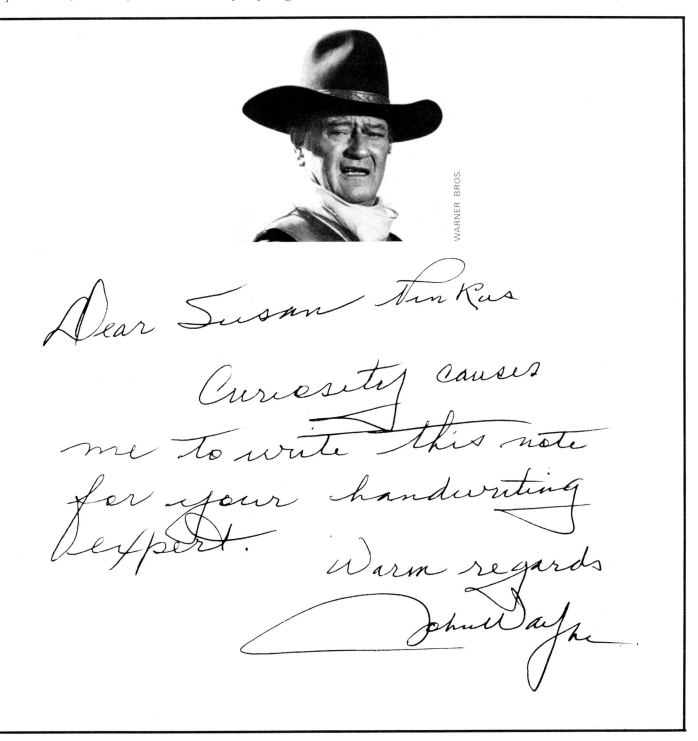

WARNER BROS.

Writing letters

By now you will have a basic knowledge of the graphological skills and you will be able to practice them on your own or your friends' writing. Probably your first sample will be in a letter or on a postcard, though letter writing as an art seems to be going out of favour. Quite apart from the analytical possibilities, it is worth remembering that the extra effort involved is always appreciated more than the usual impersonal telephone call.

This is the age of the telephone. We use it to arrange meetings, to keep in touch with those we love, to announce our good and bad news. We call one another up to gossip, to settle arguments, to quarrel, to make up, to offer comfort, to express love. However, the telephone has not always dominated our lives in this way. As little as 20 or 30 years ago, people would write letters whenever they felt the need for contact with their friends and relatives.

Parted lovers undoubtedly used the telephone occasionally, but they softened the pain of absence with letters which expressed their deepest feelings for each other. Husbands and wives who were parted wrote to each other. Grown-up children sent news home regularly. Families remained in touch and closely-knit through the letters they exchanged and friendships were kept alive for decades.

There are many rewards to letter-writing. Letters link those who are parted and keep friendships alive and meaningful. They also allow us to enter into really close relationships with our special friends. It is often much easier to express innermost thoughts and feelings in a letter than in person. Letters, because they give the reader time and privacy to react, can also be used to ease a difficult situation; to break news gently; to explain awkward events tactfully; to mend quarrels gracefully.

Perhaps the greatest value of letters is that they give lasting pleasure. The amusing telephone call from a girl-friend is over as soon as the receiver is replaced.

Letters should give great pleasure to both the writer and the recipient. Try to think of letter-writing as an art and not as a chore.

Half an hour later it will be hard to remember three phrases from the conversation. A quick telephone call will give lovers instant togetherness, but this sense of nearness vanishes as swiftly as it came. Letters provide a lasting record of the significant moments in life. Like entries in a diary, they have the power to conjure up vividly the situation which existed at the time they were written.

Letters can be broadly grouped into four categories: formal letters; social letters; letters to close friends; and love letters.

Even the most reluctant letter-writer will not always be able to avoid writing formal letters from time to time. These are the letters which have to be written to total strangers: when applying for a job, returning a completed income-tax form or making a hotel reservation.

The essential thing about these letters is that they should be clear, brief and strictly to the point. The letter to the hotel, for example, must specify the date for which the reservation is being made, the number of rooms required, and any other details such as whether the room is to have twin beds or a double. Unnecessary information should be omitted as the reservations clerk will have countless letters to process.

Letters applying for jobs fall into a slightly more sensitive area, for here a hint of personality can be allowed to creep in, to distinguish one application from another. But this is dangerous territory and, strictly speaking, letters have to do two things only: express the candidate's interest in and enthusiasm for the job in question, and outline the qualifications and experience that make him or her suitable for the post.

Letters of application must be organized to convey the necessary information in the clearest possible way. Employers tend to be busy people and may impatiently dismiss a rambling letter. The director of a marketing company will not be at all interested in the fact that his prospective secretary is a brilliant needle-woman. But the fact that she speaks French, although the advertisement for the job may have made no mention of languages, will attract his attention. A talent for needlework would, however, be

worth mentioning if the vacancy were in the office of a school of embroidery design, as it would give the candidate a clear advantage over the others.

A useful way of applying for a job when there is a lot of information to convey is to send in a typed curriculum vitae [resumé] which gives details of age, sex, education, qualifications, employment, spare-time occupations, and anything else that could interest a prospective employer. This should be accompanied by a short, handwritten, letter which expresses interest in the vacancy and perhaps draws attention to the most relevant achievements. Jobs for which one has to fill in a printed application form should be returned with a similar letter.

When a hint of individuality can be introduced into a letter for a job without sounding coy, flippant, or slick, so much the better. But this should always be done with the very greatest of care, for it is of secondary importance to clarity and conciseness and can often misfire. If in doubt it is far better to limit the letter to straight facts expressed in as natural a way as possible.

Even the most impersonal letters to strangers can be formal in tone without sounding stilted. There are, however, fairly strict conventions governing the style of address and endings of formal letters which, although not really complicated, can be difficult to negotiate without a little practice.

Very formal letters open with the words 'Dear Sir' or 'Dear Madam' and end 'Yours faithfully' or 'Yours truly'. Some very staid institutions continue to address their correspondents in this way long after they know their names, but this is becoming increasingly unusual. Normally, as the correspondence progresses, 'Dear Sir' very soon becomes 'Dear Mr Smith', and then perhaps 'Dear Charles'. 'Yours faithfully' leaves the scene a fraction earlier than 'Yours truly', giving way to 'Yours sincerely' 'Yours ever', or just 'Yours'. So the least formal letter will begin with 'Dear Charles' and end 'Yours ever' or 'Yours'.

In formal letters each ritual step from one stage to the next is an unspoken acknowledgement on both sides that the relationship is moving away from formality towards near-friendship. If you are unsure about changing to a less formal style, take your cue from your correspondent. If he bypasses the

Simple, everyday language will always convey your message best, whatever the content. Try to write naturally and briefly even in a formal letter.

'Dear Sir', 'Yours faithfully' stage altogether and plunges in with 'Dear Mr Jones', 'Yours sincerely' from the beginning, do the same; when he starts addressing you by your christian name, address him by his. If you do not you may unintentionally offend him. Addressing someone as 'Dear Mr Smith' when he has written 'Dear John' to you can be interpreted as a signal that you think he is being over-familiar and wish to restore the correspondence to its earlier formality. The only exception to this is when there is a great disparity in age or status, as, for example, in the employer-employee relationship, when the employee may feel that it is more respectful to continue to use the more formal 'Dear Mr Brown', although she herself may be being addressed as 'Dear Jane'.

Party invitations come into the category of formal correspondence. They are usually specially printed and follow the format 'John Smith requests the pleasure of the company of Jane Brown at his 21st birthday party'. Until recently the convention was that you should reply to such an invitation with corresponding formality, no matter how well you knew the sender. So Jane Brown would reply 'Jane Brown thanks Mr John Smith for his kind invitation which she is very pleased to accept'. This still remains the correct way to answer such an invitation, but in the relaxed social climate of today, many people find this artificially rather embarrassing. Except for very formal functions and replies to hostesses who might be offended by a casual approach, it is now accepted that the response to these invitations may be in a more informal vein.

Two further points are worth remembering about formal letters. First, always quote the date and reference number of any earlier correspondence – large firms have very complex filing systems. Secondly, avoid business jargon such as 'Referring to yours of 7th inst' or 'the 12th ult'. It is unnecessary, ugly and old-fashioned. Simple, everyday language is more attractive.

Social letters range from short thank-you notes for presents or hospitality to long epistles sending news to your grandmother. The easy, relaxed letters which fall into this category are letters to enjoy. They have none of the difficult style points encountered in formal letters. Friends can be addressed in any way and any conventional, quirky or affectionate ending can be used.

Style in social letters, in so far as it exists at all, is a simple question of suiting the tone of the letter to the degree of friendship involved, so that what is

written is appropriate to both the person and the occasion. They can be as lively and interesting as can be managed without sounding contrived.

Common politeness makes some social letters more or less obligatory. Letters of thanks, congratulations and condolence fall into this category. In many cases the correspondents may not know each other very well, but it should be possible to convey some feeling without being hypocritical. Write naturally, briefly and sincerely rather than at length. (The recipient can often tell when the writer has struggled to think of something with which to fill the page.) A good social letter should make the recipient feel that their gift or hospitality has really been appreciated, or their loss or success, genuinely acknowledged. A friendly, lively, communication should really brighten the recipient's day. In time the writing of such letters can become an art in itself, giving enormous pleasure not only to those who receive them, but to their writers too.

Letters to close friends are everything letters to more casual friends are, but they convey deeper feelings. There are no rules for composing them except to write with the same warmth, naturalness, and lack of inhibition which would be shown in a face-to-face situation. Letters like these simply provide a means of sharing the highs and lows of everyday life with friends who are absent. They can be written on many different levels but, with real trust on both sides, communication by letter can be a very enriching experience.

Love-letters will be the most treasured letters of all. They have to make up for separation. Because they will be read as if the writer were present, they should be written warmly and tenderly. Above all, a lover should respond to the other's warmth and love. Nothing is more hurtful than a correspondence between lovers in which one is tender and forthcoming and the other reserved and cool. Indifference in love-letters can damage a relationship more surely than any word of anger spoken during a personal exchange for the writer will not be there to put things right with a look or a touch. Sensitively written, however, love-letters can be the next best thing to being together. They can lead lovers to an even better understanding of each other and bring them closer on all sorts of levels, from shared jokes to deep thoughts and feelings.

Whatever its purpose, a letter is a personal and lasting way of communicating. And while people continue to enjoy writing to each other, the art of letter-writing will not disappear.

Doodles

The previous pages have shown you how to analyze handwriting: but there is another form of writing well worth considering which in very many instances appears more like drawing: the doodle.

It may prove surprising but doodles — freely-drawn Freudian slips of the pen that they are — often come straight from your subconscious: that part of the mind which in all of us consists of a wealth of unadmitted desires, inhibitions and fears and which lies hidden far behind the public mask we all wear. As such, they are not as trivial as most people mistakenly believe, but often all-important clues to personality.

Most of us doodle. Research has proved this: so that those who are quick to deny that they ever do have probably always ignored their doodles in the past or completely destroyed the evidence. Patterns vary enormously, but most of us tend to have one particular design which we repeatedly put on paper, whatever variations on the basic theme we may sometimes employ. Women, for instance, most commonly doodle flowers and leaves: hardly surprising when one considers the obvious feminine symbolism of 'coming into bloom'. On the other hand, boxes — and three-dimensional figures generally — are more masculine doodles, though this is not to say that they are never drawn by women. Series of straight lines and boxes which have obviously been built in an upward formation are usually pointers to methodical, logical thinkers. Houses, adolescent film-star-type facial doodles and hearts either cruelly pierced with an arrow or lavishly bound with satin ribbon are obviously idealistic, wish-fulfilment doodles — doodles that show a marked subconscious desire for glamour, love and security. Many more abstract patterns are taken up simply because they are satisfying shapes to draw, since repetitive even strokes are required. They are often 'S' shapes, with the treble clef and snail shapes by far the most popular.

Some people find it equally pleasing to fill in open letters in newspaper headlines or in advertisement copy. They are probably not particularly original or creative, but excel when working within a given structure or framework, operate well in a team and follow orders and instructions admirably.

The size of doodles and the intensity of ink or pencil lead while doodling are, as with handwriting, often indicative of the emotional state at the time of doodling. Spot a repeatedly scored-through doodle, dark and uneven, and it is likely to have been penned in anger. Softer, more 'open' doodles suggest a happier frame of mind and perhaps a more easy-going temperament. But investigators have found that large, dynamic doodles are not always the doodles of out-and-out extroverts, Large doodles taking up a vast amount of space on a clean sheet of paper are often habitually drawn by the introverted, shy and retiring personality who really desires to be more outward-going in company, regrets his of her inability to be sociable and who resorts to displacing a repressed largeness of personality on to paper. Those doodles which you find yourself scribbling while on the telephone or listening to the radio can in fact tell you an enormous amount about yourself. And the information you glean should in turn, if used wisely, help you to fathom much of the iceberg — the real, underlying you. Study the doodles of family, friends and colleagues, too, as you find them lurking in notepads or on blotting paper. A doodle will, of course, never provide total personality analysis; but it could be a step towards greater understanding and thus an enrichment of relationships.

Search your notepad and you're sure to find one of these common types of doodle! Clockwise: flowers, spirals, s-shapes, animals, patterns, boxes.

Part 3
How to read your Dreams

Frances Kennett

Introduction

Dreams have always fascinated man – ever since 5000 BC and before we have been delving into the world of sleep and trying to find answers or give meanings to the extraordinary visions which appear there. And now we know that exploring dreams can be positively helpful and rewarding. Most psychologists believe that your dreams can reveal the things which preoccupy your mind deep down, even if you don't recognize them immediately. Once you know what to look for, you will be amazed how much you can learn about yourself, your friends and family and, perhaps, how you can overcome the problems which are at the root of most dreams.

No matter how humdrum you feel life to be, if you look into your dreams you will find a whole new imaginative landscape that would be hard to think up during your waking hours.

Here is the background you will need to understand the importance of sleep and dreams, and how to extract the information from a puzzling jumble of dream pictures. Past ideas and future possibilities are all included, and there is a dossier of genuine dreams from all kinds of people for you to compare and contrast with your own personal dreamscape.

Contents

Dream
for
yourself

Most people think that dreams are some kind of night-time joke. How often has a friend come over at work or in the shops and said, 'I had the oddest, funniest dream last night'? This is usually the start of a good story, usually a jumble of strange ideas perhaps involving a mutual friend, set in the most unlikely circumstances or filled with such terror and fear that no one can understand the reason for it. The normal reaction is to marvel at the oddity of it all—and then forget about it. But you can get much more out of dreams than jokes or strange stories. It is interesting to note for instance that people always want to tell their dream

to someone, as if there is a natural desire to go back over the experience, to try and think it out. With a little knowledge and experience you'll be able to learn some valuable things about yourself and your friends— about character, aims, ambitions and the problems which are bothering your unconscious. You might even find a solution to a dilemma which has been worrying you for days.

The most important step is to realize that dreams are not disorganized nonsense. Your brain isn't resting by

Night-time experiences can seem as vivid as waking reality.

CHRIS YATES

DREAMS 5

Dreams have their own logic – a car can be the driving force in your life; (right) falling can suggest a sense of losing a grip on life.

scrambling up thoughts and turning everything upside-down for a few hours while your body relaxes. Neither are dreams some frightening glimpse into the 'dark world' of the mind. There is nothing dangerous or harmful about dwelling on your dreams, though you don't need to be obsessive about it.

Psychology and dreams

Many people think that all the talk about 'the mind' and 'psychoanalysis' involved in dream interpretation is nonsense. But you should not make the mistake of thinking it is a pseudo-science, fit only for ridicule. The work of famous psychoanalysts like Freud and Jung has helped thousands of normal, healthy people, to say nothing of many cases of extreme mental disturbance. Their findings can be applied in a simple way to everyone's own experience of life. You don't have to be neurotic, obsessive or anything else so serious. Just as doctors can treat grave physical diseases but also show the world in general the basic rules of personal or home hygiene, so psychologists have shown well-balanced human beings how they can be more self-aware and lead, fuller happier lives.

What are dreams?

What are dreams exactly? There are many theories about the meaning of dreams but everyone basically agrees that they are a product of the unconscious mind. This is best explained by looking at what happens when people daydream. The mind is wide-awake and aware—that is, conscious. You might be going out shopping, knitting or filing cards in a perfectly ordinary way, but your thoughts wander on their own. Perhaps you go over what happened last night, or more often, what you hope will happen in the future. Sometimes these daydreams become quite divorced from reality; people imagine themselves on Caribbean beaches or married to millionaires. While it lasts, a daydream seems vivid and true, but when you 'snap out of it' it is easy to forget. Something of the same process occurs in dreams which take place during sleep. The conscious, controlling part of the mind becomes relaxed (although it does not switch off all its powers) and a submerged layer of thoughts, ideas and feelings wells up. Because this part of the mind obeys its own logic, it describes things in its own direct way, using word-pictures and seemingly irrational chains of connections. This is why in dreams people do impossible things or shift quickly from scene to scene. The unconscious mind is going direct to the point without needing to progress in a logical sequence as the conscious mind does.

The other characteristic of dreams, which everyone who recalls them will recognize, is that they are often unusually vivid—either visually or in mood. Sometimes the feelings they generate can be so strong that they affect the dreamer's mood for the next day—sometimes called 'getting out of bed on the wrong side'. For instance, a successful businessman related a series of dreams he had during the early part of his career, all of which were set in a war situation. (War is one of the classic images of pressure or tension.) At first, while he was working on his own, his dreams involved his own attempts to avoid some nameless terror which came in a variety of guises. After he took control of a large department in a big company the war dreams continued, except his main preoccupation became trying to get the other people in the dream to cope with the attack, or whatever it happened to be. Significantly he could not recall the visual detail of the dreams—apart from the wartime setting—but the feelings of fear, panic and frustration associated with them re-mained particularly vivid.

On the good side, it is quite common to have a very happy or successful dream and to wake up feeling particularly pleased with yourself. Small children for example often dream of receiving gifts: they wake up feeling curiously elated and can be very down-hearted when they realize it was only a dream! Typical is the story of a small boy who was telling his mother in great excitement about his dream of the night before. He was being chased by a wolf and had tried to run into the house for protection through the kitchen door, but it would not open. He struggled and struggled as the fierce wolf drew nearer, then finally at the last minute, the door handle gave and he got inside to safety. The boy's mother replied in the usual way, 'Oh well, never mind, it was only a dream', to which the child retorted, 'Well, next time I have a dream, you leave the door open!' Children have to learn to distinguish between the 'inner space' of the unconscious and the 'outer space' of consciousness. Some primitive tribes still make no differentiation between the two.

This 'alternative reality' of dreams is very important. Allied to it is the fact that dreams happen entirely of their own accord, and we cannot make them happen or control their contents.

What dreams do

What are dreams for? Basically, they are the method by which the unconscious mind sifts and sorts experiences. If you can visualize the brain as an enormous receiving station, with all kinds of information going into it every day, then you will see that it has a large task to perform. During sleep, while the conscious part of the mind is inactive, the unconscious, (or subconscious) processes a vast jumble of material—new facts, situations, past experiences, unsolved worries, fears, desires and much more. It draws up emotions from the deepest recesses of the mind and memory and takes into account all the new information which the conscious mind has received. Then, in its own unique style, it presents a visual and emotional image to you—a dream. Perhaps you have a problem which you are consciously putting off because you do not wish to think about it. But it is still there and may well present itself to you in a dream. The sorting station is sending a message, 'Don't forget, don't overlook this'. Sometimes a dream will even offer a possible solution to such a problem.

As well as the unconscious, there is that deeper part already mentioned where the instincts, intuitions and emotions originate. These too are drawn up into dreams through the sorting house function, producing a very powerful effect on the mind. Just as people push problems to one side consciously, so also they ignore real feelings. It is interesting to note that people often say, 'What do you think about So-and-so, really, deep down?' or 'In my heart of hearts I believe such-and-such', as if in common speech they acknowledge the existence of this innermost part of the mind where strong, genuine feelings are to be found.

By recognizing where the material that goes into dreams comes from, you can begin to understand more of your true nature—your real views and attitudes, your feelings and needs, and by relating the dream-pictures to your everyday existence, get a better grip on your life-situation. Not all dreams are exactly problem-posers or -solvers, but they are a representation of some part of your life, often that part with which you cope least successfully.

> 'I dreamed I was dying in a lonely room. This funny doctor was there but no-one else. The doctor said there was nothing he could do but I was going to die. I wasn't in any pain — it wasn't a nightmare. I didn't really remember it until going to the office next morning. I kept thinking about it all day.'
> Businesswoman, 29

People who don't dream

What about people who say they never dream? If thinking about dreams is so helpful, why do some people never recall them—are they missing out in some way? Most of them are perfectly happy, average human beings, with no apparent disadvantage in comparison with those who seem to dream regularly. Laboratory experiments using the electro-encephalograph (EEG) machine to record brain 'waves' have revealed that people who do not recall their dreams have exactly the same trace patterns as those who remember their dreams vividly. In fact everyone dreams for regular periods during the night and people who think they never dream either forget them or have 'thoughts' in the night which they do not consider to be dreams—more like daydreams. If you are one of these 'non-recallers' try discussing dreams with people who do remember them. You will probably find that you begin to recall them more often.

What dreams can tell you

For those who can remember dreams, the next step is to uncover the real meaning behind them. The key to the subject is that dreams are what a famous American psychologist Calvin Hall once termed 'a letter to oneself'. Once you have learned to read this private letter, some fascinating home truths will emerge. Do not believe that dreams will necessarily show you the answers to all your problems—no dream ever repaired a damaged bank balance or turned an ugly duckling into a swan! But it might help you to see that money is not all-important and that a good face or figure is not the be-all and end-all of life.

The best way to start examining your dreams is simply to recall them during the following day. Just mulling them over, even if they seem quite non-sensical, will be of help. Sometimes a thought will suddenly spring into your mind as a result of these ponderings. It might appear at first to have no connection whatsoever with the dream, but a little more thought will reveal the link. For example, it often happens that a friend introduces you to someone about whom you have heard a great deal of praise and glory. You feel a small prick of doubt, but immediately dismiss it and try to socialize. In the end, you come to the conclusion that this new individual is 'not so bad' after all. It is possible that you will have a dream after such an encounter in which this charming and apparently successful person is turned into a ridiculous figure, a hideous monster or a creepy-crawly insect—depending on the nature of your real view. That first 'suppressed' reaction will come back in dream form, and conversely, dwelling on the dream could bring back the reaction.

Recording your dreams

Another way in which dreams can inform the dreamer is if they are studied over a period of time. Keep a notebook, writing down each dream either at night if you wake up from a particularly disturbing one (which will also help you to return to calm sleep) or first thing in the morning before getting up. Do not simply make a note of the basic situation of the dream—like 'Climbed mountain'—but try to catch in a word or two the essential feeling involved: 'Climbed mountain, made great effort, seemed to take a long time, but felt very pleased when top reached'. It is also very important to follow the sequence of events as they occur in the dream. You often find that you do things for reasons which, in waking life, you might think were totally

Below: Richard Hamilton's 'Interior II' conveys in pop art terms the theory that dream images are all reflections of the dreamer's personality. You can evaluate the significance of each image separately —combined together they will form a coherent expression of your inner state. The objects in this painting are familiar but fragmented; in the same way, dream images are drawn from everyday objects but are presented in stark juxtaposition.

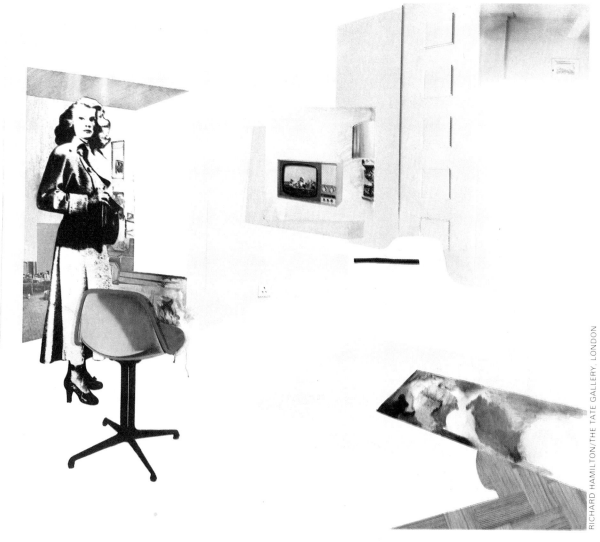

irrelevant or illogical. Next time you tell a dream to a friend note how often you say 'I did such-and-such *because*'. This feeling of compulsion is often very strong during dreams. Take the following example: 'I was running down a narrow dead-end street because a huge tank was bearing down on me.' The chain of events is part of the dream's private language—its message to you. Suppose the tank represents a person's sense of ambition. Perhaps the dream means that if the ambition is followed single-mindedly, without other possibilities being taken into account, it might be a mistake, for it will lead into a dead-end situation. The dream gives a clue to help you work out its contents by the order in which events are presented.

Dreaming in series

Similarly, series of dreams can be especially revealing. Although the dreamer may see himself very differently in each isolated dream, if they are put into a sequence, a pattern will emerge, revealing at least the area of his preoccupation.

Sometimes a series of dreams will show a progression in thinking. If you have some underlying conflict, such as an inability to get along with a relative, a series of dreams may play out numerous alternatives, like being very aggressive or being loving and submissive, or even murderous in hatred. What is difficult to recognize in one dream may be more easily seen when two or three dreams are put together to look for common features.

This serial aspect may seem difficult at first. Take the two dreams described here:

'I was going to a big, strange house in the country which my family had just moved into — but it was empty. I was being driven there in a car in my night clothes, all wrapped up in a blanket in the front passenger seat, but there was no one in the driver's seat. Suddenly I was there — I don't remember arriving — and I went up to a room where there was a man putting up wallpaper. It was incredible wallpaper, in three parts. The first part was a collage of sparkly Christmas cards. The second was a boat — a galleon made out of gold paper — and the third part had a Teddy bear stuck on to it. It was about 2 feet high, and in a running position, stuck on sideways. I was talking to the decorator. I can't remember exactly what I said, but it was something about how much work must have gone into it, and the decorator was going on about how wonderful it was. Then suddenly I was dressed in my day clothes. Sue, a friend of mine, came in dressed in a funny coat and said, "Today's my day for learning". (I knew it was Tuesday, even outside my dream, and she goes to college on Tuesdays). Then I found a piece of paper which said "Please phone Clive before 19.19". Then the phone rang and I woke up and Clive was on the other end.'

'I was in this travelling show and there were many players but I was with the guy who owned the show and I looked like one of those "Barbie" dolls... you know... those "Cindy" dolls ... and not looking at all human. I did all these astounding things which only a doll could do and which a human would hurt herself doing. At the end of the show I had a metal comb which I had to hold in my mouth and make it go round so it made my mouth bleed ... the whole of the inside of my mouth was bleeding. I had to put my finger in my mouth and hold it up to the audience to show the blood to prove I was really human!'

There are certain elements common to both these dreams, even though at first glance they appear very different. For a start, there is a feeling of passivity around the dreamer in both cases: in the first dream she is being driven—as opposed to driving the car herself—and is all wrapped up, motionless, powerless, like a little child or baby. This ties in with the second dream's idea of being like a 'doll', that takes orders from a boss-man. Secondly, both dreams are connected with children. The doll is an object associated with childhood. In the first dream, the girl enters a room that sounds like a fantastic nursery, with pretty Christmas cards and Teddy Bear wallpaper. The dreamer herself could probably add greater meaning to this part of the dream by looking in her memory for incidents connected with boats, Teddy bears and Christmas. In general terms, these pictures suggest she is looking back into her childhood as a time when everything was done for her, with a 'lot of work going into it' as she says in the dream.

Obviously, connections with childhood in the second dream are the doll, but in the main it is concerned with the present. The girl is on her own and somehow associated with a man who makes her do terrible tricks. It does not take a great deal of analytical skill to start wondering whether in real life this dreamer is mixed up with someone who is or has made her hide her real feelings and has hurt her. It might even be a more general situation: the girl might be afraid of having any relationship with a man at all. Only she can tell. Yet, even you as an outsider can progress quite far with this series of dreams. You can see clearly how the same problem-area is covered in both. Here is a girl, who remembers a comfortable happy time at home, now confronted with a new way of living and

'I walk through the stage door of a huge theatre and then discover that to get on to the stage itself, I have to walk down a really enormous, long, but wide, flight of stairs. It is almost like a ladder — there is no rail or handhold — but the steps are flat like a staircase. I am terrified of heights, have always been, but I manage to make it all the way to the bottom without falling. Then, I discover that I'm in a huge complex of caves and one is so small that I'm afraid to go through it for fear I won't be able to get back again.'
Copy editor, 31, female

relating to people, on her own and feeling apprehensive, even hurt, by her new experiences. The first dream moves on further from the happy childhood picture: there is another girl in it saying 'Today's my day for learning.' The message for the dreamer is 'Buck up and don't look back, let's get on with living, however difficult it is'. This links up quite specifically with the end of the other dream. The outside stimulus of the telephone ringing brings to mind the subject area of the problem, that is, dealing with men on an adult level. Comfortingly, the dream is urging her with a 'message' to make contact: 'Go on, give it a try'. The second dream about the doll sticks to the same situation but expresses the girl's fears about the possible outcome —being used and hurt. Incidentally, the dreamer was astonished at the accuracy of the insights in this inter-

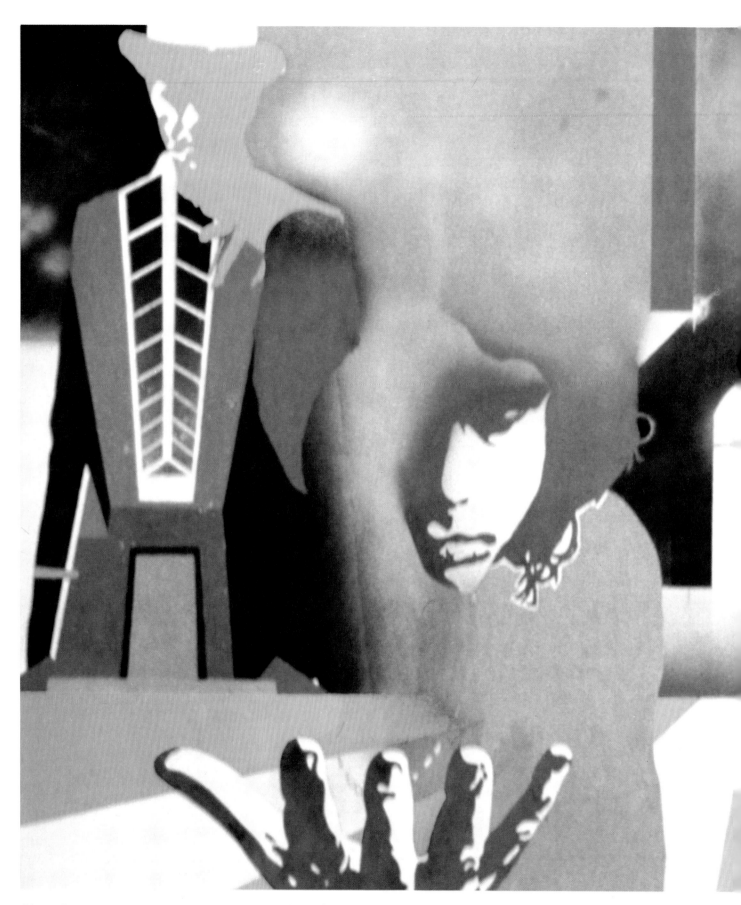

Above: Images can be drawn from any time in your past. They could be zebras from a childhood visit to the zoo combined with last week's holiday flight. These images in turn might be expressed in the style of some science fiction film you saw the evening before.

pretation, which was made without any background information.

No time in dreams

Another aspect of this link-up in dreams of different kinds of pictures is that the dreaming mind takes no notice whatsoever of time, which is part of the conscious mind's experience: it simply doesn't need it. In a dream, something that happened to you ten years ago may be relevant to something that is part of your life today. Look for

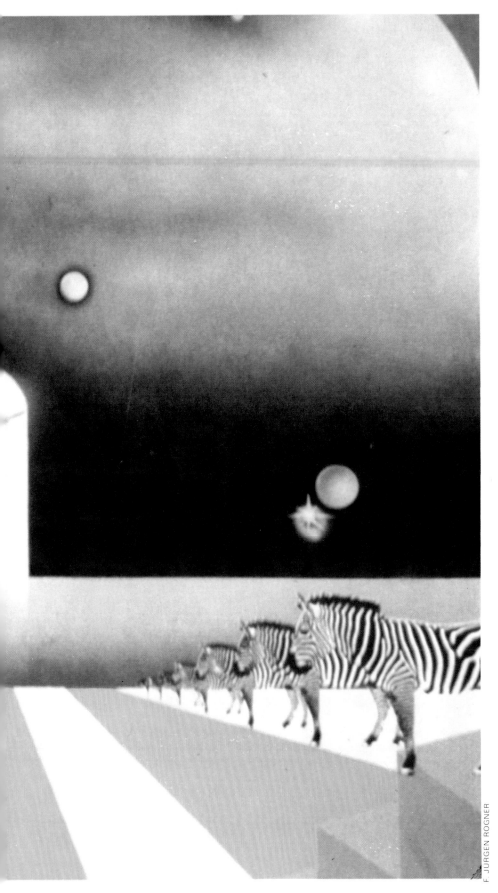

very helpful. To use the examples just discussed: if the girl's recollection of childhood was of a time when she was very unhappy and lonely, then obviously the dream would have a different message. The series might be saying 'You'll be hurt again just as you were before, so be careful'. Either way, the problem is a common one, that of reconciling the past with the present and growing up.

How to recall your dreams

For those people who seldom or never recall a dream and feel a little frustrated at the prospect of missing out in this personal 'fortune-telling', some comfort can be derived from the fact that telling yourself 'I'll have a dream tonight' can sometimes produce interesting results. Ann Faraday, a well-known British dream researcher, has formulated some rules to help people catch their dreams. She recommends setting an alarm clock to go off at two-hourly intervals from the usual falling-asleep time. In this way, you can be fairly sure of catching yourself during a dreaming patch. Even a once-nightly interruption will do, if the idea of more sounds like torture, but in this case, set the clock for much later in the night—between 3 and 5 am.

If you do wake up this way, it is essential to write the dream details down then and there or they will fade very quickly. Better still, use a cassette tape recorder if you have one, and keep it by the bedside. Failing that, tell it to your sleeping partner or say it out loud—this helps to get the details up into the conscious mind which then stores it in the recent memory.

At whatever time you awake with a dream whether in the night or in the morning, it is advisable to move slowly —do not jar yourself into reality if you want to catch the most details possible. Leaping out of bed to rush across the room for a pencil will probably result in your stopping dead in your tracks with a sudden blank in your mind. Move gently, slowly, into a sitting position— some people find it helpful to keep their eyes closed for a few moments while they capture as many details as they can. The small things in a dream can frequently be significant, as for example in making a serial record over a period of time. Perhaps a small detail in one dream may become the central part of another, or a picture with a similar connotation may appear subsequently. Either way, it is important to lose as little as possible so you can have plenty of material to ponder over.

common links in events, and do not concentrate on writing down only those dreams which seem to be the most coherent or the most like waking views of life.

It follows from this that if a picture or incident in a dream reminds you

immediately of something in your past, you must note it down as well. Psychoanalysts have found that one of the most useful interpretations of a dream is that made by the patient himself. So even in studying your dreams in a non-clinical way, such connections will be

Analysis: nine dreams

If you could ask one hundred people what they thought was the mood conveyed in their dreams, about forty would probably answer that it was apprehension. About eighteen would say anger, then perhaps six would mention sadness. Only a lucky eighteen individuals would be able to state that happiness was the main emotional content of their dreams. The remaining eighteen would describe sensations of surprise, excitement or interest.

These figures were established in a very wide-reaching survey conducted in the early 1950s, just fifty years after the first publication of *The Interpretation of Dreams* by Sigmund Freud. In that space of time the issues he first investigated have been confirmed and modified. Nowadays we have a fairly clear picture of the sort of things people dream about. The following samples are typical of normal sleep experiences.

Sex on a desert island

Freud's great contribution to the understanding of dreams was his realization that they reflect unconscious thought processes, especially with regard to sexual drives. Sex can be presented directly, as in dreams which actually involve making love. More often the sexual message is hidden in some way. This is especially true where the dreamer has some sense of guilt or conflict between his desire and his conscience.

'I dreamt I was on a beautiful desert island, green parrots were flying overhead, and suddenly Marlon Brando appeared. I was wearing a very brightly patterned sarong thing, and he said I looked like a flower . . . the next thing we're sitting in a beautiful clearing in a thick shady forest, and there's a mass of fruit and food piled up for our picnic . . . the rest of the dream was all about . . . well, making love.'

The setting
This is a classic example of a sexual dream in more ways than the obvious ending. 'A beautiful desert island' is an exotic, faraway-from-it-all setting. Sex is often suggested in such lush or luxuriously different places. It is essential to notice the background setting of any dreams. Domestic, familiar places occur most frequently. Places of pleasure or sport, such as football grounds or swimming pools, are almost as common, whereas work places are much less frequent, in spite of the amount of time spent there in waking life.

The setting or background can reveal something about the meaning of a dream when evaluated in relation to the events taking place there. Here, clearly, the desert island reinforces the out-of-the-ordinary character of the dream and suggests that it is pure wish-fulfilment.

The hero
A glamorous film star like Marlon Brando may be part of the same desire for romance and sexual excitement. It is quite common to dream of famous people, colleagues from work or social acquaintances (like other people's husbands or wives) in this situation. It does not necessarily mean that you want to make love to that person in reality. You might simply be linking up a wish for sexual satisfaction with an example of the sort of person you like. Consider the character of the film star or friend in the dream, for it may give you some insight into the qualities you admire in a partner in real life. It is perfectly normal for a married person to dream about distant individuals in preference to real lovers or spouses. If your actual relationship is satisfactory then you will probably not reflect upon it often in a dream, which is usually a time for satisfying unmet desires or sorting out problem situations.

The role of the dreamer
In a dream such as this, you should also look at how you place yourself. Is the 'I' figure really like you? Do you find it laughable to think of yourself dressed in bright colours or hearing pretty compliments? Perhaps you think you are not very attractive or that your personality lacks real colour. Your dream may be compensating for these feelings. How do you respond to the idea of all that food? Do you eat it with appetite and pleasure or just toy with it? Remember that food is often a sexual symbol, representing the idea of appetite for sex as well as for sustenance. This is a good example of the way the sexual message of a dream can be hidden under another subject.

The great escape

According to Alfred Adler, another of the great dream psychologists, the commonest drive besides sex is that for power. Dreams frequently reveal the hidden desires of a personality or release some urges that do not find satisfaction in real life.

'I had a really vivid dream of being with a group of men, we were prisoners in a sort of castle — there were soldiers on guard duty everywhere. I organized the men into an escape group. I seemed to be able to speak several languages, so I was the leader, and we dug a tunnel to get out. Then we were climbing over a very high wall . . . it seemed to take ages. Lastly I remember standing on an open train carriage, and rushing through countryside, feeling excited we'd escaped, but worried in case we were being followed.'

You might have guessed already that this is a man's dream—not that women do not also dream of action and power, but proportionately more men than women are concerned with these issues in dreams. This is a reflection of the differences in physical characteristics and the roles usually assigned to the two sexes in society.

The role of the dreamer
Here, the 'I' in the dream is significant again. Is the dreamer rather timid in real life, working at a job that lacks any outgoing action? If this were true, then the dream would be compensatory—making up for the lack he feels in his situation. It might also be an expression

Right: Doorways, staircases, castles, churches—however remote from everyday experience—are common dream images because of their general emotive value.

Jungians believe that everything in a dream is a reflection of some part of yourself, so being alone in a bare room might suggest a need to look inward. A Freudian interpretation might give this image a sexual connotation.

of a man's need to dominate, to organize, to be brave and tough. Alfred Adler, who started out as a disciple of Freud but subsequently developed his own views, placed a lot of emphasis on this aggressive drive in people, believing it was as important as sex.

The influence of recent experience

Such a dream might be prompted by watching a Western or wartime adventure at the movies or on television. However, it is important not to overestimate the 'trigger' of a dream as its cause. The recent experience might produce the particular situation of the dream, but it has nothing more to do with why that particular event—of all others in the recent past—should be retained and re-created in the dream.

Private doubts and fears

A very large proportion of dreams dwell on feelings of doubt, fear or inadequacy. There is a trace of that in this dream, for the escaped man is still worried that he is being followed. In other words, even after he has shown himself to be brave and resourceful, he thinks that it is still not enough and he hurries away on the train to the next challenge. This dreamer probably pushes himself too hard and should learn to accept his limitations. He might not appear like this at all in real life. It is surprising what doubts are expressed in this private way.

Black cats in the basement

'I went into a tall house, down a dark staircase. I don't know why I was there but I seemed to know which way to go. I got into a dark room, it seemed empty, then suddenly I realized it was seething with cats. Black cats. Then I realized that I had a baby in a kind of papoose, strapped to my back. I turned to get out of the room, and a cat jumped on my back and was clinging on to the baby. I tried to get out of the house and was running along trying to get the cat off my back all the time.'

Animals and instincts

Such a dream leads inevitably to an analysis of images and symbols in dreams. What do the pictures suggest to the dreamer? There are two main levels of interpretation here. Take the cats first. By and large animals represent the instincts, the emotional, intuitive parts of a person's nature as opposed to the rational, controlling parts. But it is also significant to find out what the dreamer actually thinks of the animals in her dream, in this case black cats. If for example the person had a favourite pet that died, there might be a strong sense of loving and deep loss associated with cats in her mind. By contrast, the girl who related this dream had always rather disliked them. Their feline movements were too 'creepy-crawly' for her, and she did not like the suddenness with which they bare their claws. This relates back to the general symbolic values associated with them: intuitive, instinctive, especially female emotions. Notice how this is linked in the dream with the picture of the baby tied to the girl's back. A fear of her own feelings is being expressed.

The setting

The setting of the dream as always yields some meaning too. Houses occur frequently in dreams. Living rooms, bedrooms and kitchens turn up most, in that order. Basements and cellars are places where 'base' deeds are committed, where deep feelings are allowed out. The dream seems to suggest not only a fear of discovering deep-hidden feelings, but a hint of the anxiety or hurt that could result from giving way to them.

Different parts of the whole

It is worthwhile analyzing a dream as if everything in it, including people, is a part of the dreamer.

This house stands for the girl herself: the cellar, her own instinctive feelings; the baby may not mean another human being or a desire for children, but a part of the girl herself that she is afraid to express. She is afraid of getting hurt if she does. Obviously, the dreamer herself can tell best to what the images refer. This dream does not answer the questions, but poses them. Somewhere in her unconscious there are deep feelings trying to be expressed.

The turquoise pool

Other dreams work through a problem to a solution. Most of us have had a dream at some point which is repeated, perhaps even over a span of several years. These are known as 'recurring' dreams. Quite often they relate back to some incident in childhood, if you think

The cat is a familiar image of mystery, associated with magic or religion. In general terms, it represents the intuitive, instinctive, feminine qualities.

closely about it. These dreams are often nightmares and it is the old, familiar quality of only half understanding that is especially frightening.

'I dreamt I fell into a lovely turquoise pool — a beautiful blue, with sponges and ferns floating in the water, growing down the sides of the rocks. At first it looked very pretty and I swam about. Then I realized that it was getting darker, deeper, and I was going down . . . I couldn't breathe, I struggled to come up, and I woke up trying to gasp and take in air.'

Re-living the birth trauma

The endurance of an experience from childhood or birth is partly due to the extreme vividness of the incident in a child's mind and partly results from any reinforcement in later life. This dream is typical of 'drowning' dreams which have been explained by Freud as a lingering remembrance of the birth experience or 'trauma', the uterine waters and the journey from the womb, just as he interpreted 'flying' dreams as a manifestation of sexual ecstacy. If later life brings a sense of insecurity and fear to add to the original experience, then a fear-expressing dream on the same theme may result.

Resolving childhood experiences

Sometimes nightmares refer not to birth experiences but to some childhood incident not resolved or coped with at the time. Even a memory of learning to swim or slipping in the bath might be so vivid that a repeating nightmare remains. Dreams can then be helpful: they go over an incident many times but modify the experience until the difficulty is resolved.

In this case, a child had been playing near a pool and had overheard someone remark on its depth. Her dream was a realization of what might have happened if she had slipped—acting as a very vivid warning.

The collective unconscious

Another theory from the great psychologist and theoretician Carl Gustav Jung suggests that monsters in dreams or other terrifying experiences in nightmares are part of our 'collective unconscious'—a sense of shared experience accumulated over thousands of years of evolution in the unconscious minds of all human beings. These experiences manifest themselves in dreams, always in repeated, 'archetypal' ways. Drowning in seas, oceans or lakes is one such motif. (This difficult concept is de-

scribed fully in the section on Jung's theories.)

A legal salad dressing

On the brighter side, a number of delightful dreams seem to satisfy our wildest hopes in improbable ways. Children especially dream in these wish-fulfilling ways because in real life they have little power to do things for themselves. This idea of wish-fulfilment is central to dream interpretation.

'I dreamed I was looking for a job with a firm of lawyers, and I went for an interview to a place. When I got in, one of the partners was mixing up a lovely salad dressing, another was carefully warming glasses for drinks over a roaring fire. The secretary was sorting out beautiful new books — pretty books on all the things I like — crafts, biographies and so on, and putting them on the shelves. I said to myself, "I hope they take me on here, it looks like a good place to work". I felt very happy and decided about it.'

The value of images

Here is a clear case of wishful dreaming, for the girl involved was in real life looking for a job at the time. Why does the dream translate it into such unlikely, incongruous terms? It shows the value of the images of a dream, for all these things—cooking, drinking, reading—are the things that give the dreamer pleasure. Putting them all in one place is like saying 'It's got everything to make me happy'. It could also define a conflict between the job hunting and domestic life. The dreamer, a woman, might secretly be wondering whether she would be better off staying at home. However, the domestic details are highly idealized, with roaring fires and cosy drinks. It suggests that the first analysis is appropriate, merely bringing together images of happiness.

Following the plot

Always follow the sequence of events in a dream: here the conclusion is very significant, for there is a definite decision that getting a good job would be very nice. The dreamer expresses her aim, after a possible conflict.

Parents in the pavilion

Contrasts or comparison between two possible lines of action is the major area of dream experiences. The one above shows a typical problem for a

woman, the choice of taking a job or taking care of her home. Even more fundamental to both sexes is the battle between the desire for freedom and the need for security, especially when growing up and leaving home.

'I'd just got married to someone who in real life is a friend I've known a long time and I'm very close to, but my parents have never met him. The two of us were standing in a huge playing field, like a football ground, and 'way, 'way in the distance inside the pavilion my parents were standing with the rest of my family. We were just about to go off when my parents called, "Haven't you forgotten something?" I thought, "No, I don't think so, I've got enough money etc." They called again, "Haven't you forgotten something?" and again I couldn't think of anything else I needed. They called again, so eventually I relented and we went back all the way over this field to the pavilion where they were standing. When we got there, they said, "We haven't been introduced", so I introduced my "husband" to them and we went off.'

Dreaming about marriage

It is surprising but true that when girls dream about marriage they often put someone they would not expect to marry in the role of bridegroom. This seems to express the general importance and apprehension that women attach to marriage. Men much more normally dream of marriage to girls they do intend to marry in reality. The conflicts inherent in marriage do not seem to strike them to the same degree.

The setting

The choice between family ties and starting a life with a man of her own is expressed here in the image of the football field. The step she had taken means standing out alone in the 'playing field' of life. An element of competition, or striving in the face of the crowd, is suggested. In the pavilion everything is snug and friendly. There is the companionship of the family to be enjoyed. Also, pavilions are places where people relax from the rigours of the game. No one has to bother about the rules of the field.

The spoken words

So in the dream, the conflict is stated and the choice is made, but the dreamer is still not sure. 'Have you forgotten something?' her parents call. The dreamer could be expressing guilt that she has broken her family ties rather sharply and ought to keep in touch more often. It could be that she still feels that she has to be 'sent off' by her parents, just as a little girl gets dispatched to a party: 'Make sure you're good: have you got a clean handkerchief?' It seems to be that sort of question here. Finally, the dreamer relents and goes back—after the mystical 'three calls', a detail which Jung, with his insistence on religious and folkloric elements would have found very important. The girl makes the introduction—that is, makes the link between her new life and her past—and then goes off.

Problems and solutions

This is a very clear demonstration of the way that dreams not only present a problem or a conflict, but frequently come up with some suggestion for a solution. In real life this girl would probably feel much better about her independence if she matched it with a family contact. It could be that she has always fought hard to stand on her own two feet, whereas in reality she now lacks a little of the kindly assurance that good family ties can give. As with all dream analysis, it is the dreamer herself who must sift the likely explanations and accept the correct, meaningful one.

The woman on the cliff

Perhaps less commonly identified are those dreams which not only offer a solution, but positively inspire the dreamer. Most famous people whose lives have called for tremendous courage in adversity or for a particularly strong sense of ambition can recall dreams where their goal was presented to them in some uplifting way. On a more personal level, we can dream about our better natures, pulling through or surviving a difficult time in life. Jung developed a theory that certain male or female figures in dreams are not necessarily sexual partners, but representatives of the 'opposites' in each person. For a woman, this is her Animus, or male counterpart; for a man, his Anima. These figures can appear in inspirational or guiding roles.

'This dream I had about 12 or 13 years ago but I remember it clearly, it was so vivid. I was in a car being driven along — I was in the passenger seat but I never saw the driver full face, only in profile. We were driving along a coast road with the sea on my side and fields on the driver's side running right down the road with no fence or ditch. The grass was incredibly green. After a while the road began to climb steeply up a cliff, and there was a sheer drop now on my side. On and on, up and up we drove until suddenly the road stopped at the bottom of a sheer crag. At the top stood three figures in dark clothes — two men with a woman between them. I didn't recognize her, though she seemed familiar. I got out of the car to take a closer look. The driver remained seated. I couldn't see any way of getting up the cliff, but then the woman, who was quite good-looking and well-spoken, said to me, "It's not as difficult as it looks. I for one would be most disappointed if you didn't make the effort". Then I started to climb the cliff-face up to her and to my surprise found it wasn't too difficult; as I went, I found handholds and footholds. As I got to the top, the woman leaned down and gave me her hand, helping me up. Then I woke up.'

The search for a goal

This man's dream is disturbingly vivid in its sense of striving and searching for a goal. Hopefully, the dreamer derived some comfort from this vision of a way out of his problems, which in his real life were causing him a great deal of unhappiness.

The car

First, the image of the car stands for a 'journey through life' that contains strongly mechanical or dissatisfying elements. Compare this with dreaming of riding a horse, a natural and exciting method of transport. The suggestion is reinforced by the fact that the dreamer is a passenger, carried through life by a person he doesn't really see properly. Remember that all parts of a dream may be analyzed as reflections of the dreamer himself: this driver is the 'front man' of the dreamer's own personality, not really matching up to his own true sense of himself, but somehow going through the motions of living.

The setting

Dreams are remarkably accurate in the location of an event. Here, the dreamer has the sea on his side. The sea is a symbol of the unconscious, creative forces of the universe and of the 'psyche', or mind. This is the potential area of the man's mind, whereas on his driver's side, there is green grass. You might overlook such a very familiar connection in your own dreams—this image suggests the common phrase 'the grass is always greener on the other side'. Is this the way of life that the dreamer really wants? Is it perhaps just a general discontent that things should be better, more interesting or exciting?

The climb

The steep climb is a widely-found way of expressing a problem, a difficulty encountered in life. Unfortunately for this man, the endless struggle just leads to more difficulty, until part of him thinks 'I can't go on like this.' This is symbolized by the end of the road at the bottom of the crag.

The three figures

But there are figures at the top of the cliff—the two sides of himself and a kindly encouraging woman, who represents his Anima. For the first time in the dream, the man does something positive. He gets out of the car, leaving his driver behind. The inspirational force leads him to face the challenge of

William Blake's 'Ascent of the Mountain of Purgatory' combines three major dream symbols. The ocean represents the unconscious, the untapped source of creative potential; the climb of the mountain suggests the upward struggle through life, the vision of the woman, a perfect example of the Anima, stands for the inspiration and encouragement to carry on.

his problems and to surmount them. There are footholds in the cliff, just as there are remedies for life's crises.

The will to survive

This dream is a wonderful expression of a man's unconscious will to survive against the odds, to search out his true identity and make a better life for himself. No one can doubt the sincerity of his inner voice, which in a moment of weakness will not permit him to give up. It is not surprising that this man still remembers his moment of truth over a decade later.

A tractor in the living room

The sense of urgency that imbues many dreams demonstrates the power of the mind to force messages up from the unconscious to the surface. Fears, desires, drives or hopes can be expressed in this dream language. Dreams seem to draw our attention to problems or facts consciously overlooked.

'In my dream the living room in my house was extended into a long hall, like a room in a stately palace. The same carpet I've got in real life was laid all down the length of it. What was silly was that some idiot had driven a huge tractor or tank right down this hall and made two great torn-up track marks all down the carpet. A man was lurking about at the end of the room, and I spent most of the dream calling out indignantly, "Who the hell did this?" and trying to get the man to apologize.'

The immediate problem

This dream deals with a most immediate problem. The woman who related it had been dressmaking the night before while watching television and, rather than stand in a cold kitchen, had ironed a few pattern pieces on the floor over a towel. The next day she recalled the dream, but couldn't think what it meant at all. Then, later that same afternoon, her husband noticed a six-inch long stain on the living room carpet. It proved to be a scorch mark where the hot iron had accidentally gone off the towel on to the floor the night before. The woman had not noticed this at all at the time—in fact, it took some minutes for her to realize

Many people have recurrent dreams of their ideal landscape, possibly recalling a happy incident in the past. Distortion of size is often characteristic of childhood memories.

how the mark had been made. Somehow, the incident had registered in her unconscious mind, and her dream had tried to bring it to her attention.

The missing marquee

Dreams can range from the sublime to the ridiculous in their content and intention, as these last two analyses show. A general principle seems to be that dreams very rarely deal with outside, important events in the world, but only with those that have a strong emotional value to the dreamer. Even wars only come up as expressions of man's aggressive tendencies.

The vast storehouse of the unconscious turns newly received information into a message of personal value. Just as we are serious one minute and silly the next, so our dreams reflect the gamut of human experiences. Take this example of a nationally significant event:

'I was invited to a reception at the home of Mr and Mrs Peter Phillips, parents-in-law of Princess Anne. When I got there, the place seemed very small: a thatched cottage of smaller-than-life size, with a large expanse of green grass in front. I went up to the door where Mr Phillips stood waiting to receive me. "Where's the marquee for the ball?" I asked. He laughed and said, "Oh, we're not having one, the party's out at the back." People seemed to be going through the house, but I turned into a room sort of tacked on to the side of the building. It turned out to be a very pretty, attractive child's bedroom with flowery wallpaper. A boy aged about twelve was asleep in bed. Somehow I knew it was Mark Phillips' younger brother, (although I know he hasn't really got one), but at the same time it was my own son. I was pleased about this, because it meant that I could check if he was all right, tuck him in and give him a cuddle.'

Scaling things down

This dream shows just how much more interesting than fact or fiction your dreams can be. The most obvious explanation is that the dreamer had been watching the wedding of Britain's Princess Anne on television the day before. This is reflected in the detail that some things seemed smaller than reality, like watching a little screen. The transformation into a cottage and the homelike detail 'It's out at the back'

brings the occasion down to a more immediate scale of values—a good example of the unconscious feeling that importance in social, public terms has little to do with genuine experiences of living. Incidentally, it echoes a happening in the dreamer's own life, for extensive building alterations were taking place at the back of her own house.

Motherly love

The final part of the dream is a picturesque and sincere expression of maternal care and affection. In the midst of this personally exciting occasion, the mother thinks of her child. It may seem unlikely, but puns in dreams are very common, and the whole association of royalty, and the 'marquee' bring to mind the picture of a little prince, (in French, *marquis*). It is a nice way of referring to one's offspring!

The bedroom

There may be more than sweetness and light in this apparently loving dream. Is there any significance in the situation of the bedroom just 'tacked on' to the house? It could be an expression of worry or doubt about the dreamer's way of combining her roles as a socially interested person and a dutiful mother. The dream gets round the problem by having a party and putting the child in the next room. Thus, any guilt feelings are overcome.

Looking for the answers

These dream samples demonstrate the enormous variety and depth of meaning that you can find in a superficially nonsensical experience. All the analyses show you how to progress, step by step, through the various stages of the dream. Clearly it is best to start your own efforts by contemplating complete dreams if you can.

Fragmentary recollections are more puzzling at first, but if all you have is 'snatches', then try to keep a record of them over days or weeks and then approach them with the same lines of thought shown here. The individual theories and meanings are described in depth in the sections following. You should always consider the pros and cons in your analysis. Do not write off a dream in one dimension, that is, 'Oh, this is pure wish-fulfilment/expression of fear/sexual fantasy/compensation/ etc . . .' Try to mull over all possible explanations. If you grow accustomed to this habit, then your final choice of an interpretation is more likely to be accurate, helpful and revealing.

Psychology and dreams: the theories

The pictures and stories presented to us in sleep are so strange and varied that it is not surprising to find so many different theories about their meaning. These range from the pure fantastical to the downright mechanical, comparing the mind to a machine.

The main reason for looking at the more important of these theories is that it helps to put your own ideas into perspective. Your interpretation will be more successful because you will have a solid background from which to work. You will be able to consider all the major factors that have been discovered about the world of dreams and to apply them to your own experiences.

Freud—the great innovator

One of the first great contributions to the study of dreams was made by Sigmund Freud. For many people he symbolizes the psychiatrist, the 'head-shrinker', more than any of the other famous names.

One possible explanation for this is the emphasis he laid on sex. All the cartoons showing patients lying on couches and doctors with notepads saying 'Tell me about your childhood' are based upon the Freudian view of psychoanalysis. He believed that everyone is born with basic urges which are suppressed as we grow up and learn to conform to society. So it can be helpful to go back and find out exactly when a certain urge was first curbed in childhood.

Perhaps some of Freud's ideas are laughable today—in stating his views, he had to exaggerate them; otherwise, no one would have paid any attention. If his theory about dreams seems 'sex-mad', consider that in a recent survey, 85% of the men admitted they had sexual dreams and 72% of the women agreed. It is the commonest of all dream subjects—and after all in real life, a good sexual relationship is one of the major reasons for a person's happiness and peace of mind.

What exactly did Freud believe? First, that all dreams are 'wish-fulfilling' of the sexual or aggressive impulses in human nature. These urges are with you from birth, but social training keeps them under control. Obviously,

to live in an ordered society you cannot go around gratifying your basic urges all the time.

Only in dreams, when your conscious mind is not on top of the situation, can these suppressed urges have a chance to come out. Freud believed this and explained why we dream in a different 'language'; not like real life, but doing absurd things with no clear sense of logic as we usually know it.

Because these urges are totally controlled by the conscious part of the mind, it is as if they can only be allowed out at night 'in disguise', using strange combinations of events and a secret sign language to get past the 'guard'—the conscious mind on patrol.

> 'There was a couple that I was watching. They were almost in silhouette. The girl was sitting semi-crossed legged, and the guy was sitting next to her and they were both naked. He just leaned round and touched her on the side of her hip, and she let out this incredibly sort of ecstatic sigh. Every time he touched her, she just went into an incredible convulsion and she started really arching her back. Then her legs came round and she just put her arm round him . . . it was very sensuous. Then she came round on top of him.'
> Motor mechanic, male, 22

The sexual sign language

Even if dreams do not appear to be about sex at all, Freud maintained that under the surface they invariably are. If a dream merely seems to pick out an event from yesterday or a recollection from the past, Freud thought that the incident was chosen out of all other possibilities because it linked up specifically with the urge being expressed in the dream.

Freud's list of sexual sign language seems endless: in the attempt to disguise the true nature of the dream, the unconscious uses a wide variety of

normal everyday objects to stand for sexual things: 'All elongated objects, such as sticks, tree trunks and umbrellas, may stand for the male organ, as well as long sharp weapons, such as knives, daggers and pikes. Boxes, cases, chests, cupboards and ovens represent the uterus and also hollow objects, ships and vessels of all kinds. Rooms in dreams are usually women.' With this means of disguise, the conscious is not alarmed and so allows us to sleep on peacefully. The 'watchful' part of the mind does not see through to the basic urge that is being expressed in a wish-fulfilling dream.

This theory may at first seem ridiculous but if someone has a sexual problem, it is more than likely that Freud's method will help to interpret their dream world. A young girl at college, worried about finding a boy-friend yet unsure of her ability to cope with sex, dreams of a large black gun firing off into a bare white room. There can hardly be the need for a psychoanalyst to help her see the wish-fulfilment suggested by that dream!

The sexual urge is very often expressed through other basic desires, like the appetite for food. Anyone watching the scene in the film *Tom Jones* in which the hero enjoys a frankly flirtatious meal with a loose lady must admit that their smacking of lips over the roast chicken hints at more than stomach hunger. In a dream, enjoying a meal with gusto can stand for an open, eager attitude towards satisfying sexual desires. A common type of man's dream goes like this:

> 'I walk into a beautiful dining chamber with glowing lights and a magnificent feast spread out on the table in the centre. Other people seem to be helping themselves freely to the food and wine, enjoying it all enormously. I want to go and help myself but cannot move forward. Finally a beautiful girl comes over and gives me a plate of food. I accept but, when I eat it, it tastes like liver and makes me feel sick.'

According to Freud, this dream represents a man's fear of sex—his inability

Sigmund Freud (1856-1939), born in Moravia, moved to Vienna at the age of four. His first passion was science, but he made medicine his career and explored the treatment of mental disorders. He dealt with people suffering from hysteria and soon developed the idea that by bringing to the surface the original reason or experience that caused a condition, the patient could be cured. This 'psychocatharsis' (*catharsis*: Greek for purging or cleansing) expanded into the field known as depth psychology or psychoanalysis.

He believed that the unconscious mind exerts a powerful influence over the conscious one and that fundamental instinctive urges are often coped with by pushing them out of sight or making them more socially acceptable by the process of 'sublimation'. More startling was his idea of 'infantile sexuality'; that is, from birth we experience sexual urges, at first directed solely towards the mother, who supports life.

His key work, *The Interpretation of Dreams* (1900), sets out his basic theories. Unlike Jung, Freud always maintained an 'analytical', scientific approach to the human personality, reducing problems to causes, which he saw sexually. This 'reductive' approach reduces the patient's present situation to its component parts through deep analysis of his past experiences.

Towards the end of his life, Freud gained wide recognition, especially in America. Because he was Jewish, Freud fled the Nazis in 1938. He settled in England and died the following year in London.

Alfred Adler (1870-1937) was born in Vienna, Austria, and after studying medicine became a disciple of Sigmund Freud. He defended Freud's views vigorously in the early days of their friendship but after nine years, his own ideas diverged from Freud's emphasis on the sexual urge underlying man's behaviour, and he set up an independent school of thought. Adler developed 'Individual Psychology', the study of people as goal-oriented individuals seeking personal perfection and wholeness.

His most significant theory was that everyone has difficulty in relating his own self-centred satisfaction and happiness to a contentment derived from fitting in to a group or society and his idea of 'will-to-power' led to wide acceptance of the 'superiority' and 'inferiority' complexes. Through dreams, Adler felt a person could better understand his aggressive impulses and desire for fulfilment. He sees what he really thinks of himself. The aim of Adlerian psychology is to help people fit their view of themselves into an acceptable social form. His studies were mainly concerned with the misfits of the world—criminals, drug-takers, drop-outs. He wanted to help people fit in. Freud and Jung were concerned with freeing the 'real' person inside and gave no emphasis to the world that this newly emerged self would find around him.

Adler achieved widespread recognition in his later years. He taught at Columbia University in New York City and at the Long Island College of Medicine, New York. He died on a lecture tour, in Scotland, in 1937.

Carl Gustav Jung (1875-1961) was a Swiss psychologist and psychiatrist. After studying in Basel and Paris, he became a disciple and friend of Sigmund Freud, the foremost psychologist of the time. After a few years, however, Jung developed a separate view and in 1914 formally broke away from Freud and his views. Jung took a much more religious, philosophical and mystical approach to the human personality than Freud's more scientific method, which delved into the root causes of problems.

Among Jung's contributions to the field of psychology was his explanation of the personality, or psyche, in terms of three systems that interact with each other. These are the conscious, the unconscious, and the 'collective unconscious'. The last was of great importance in explaining the meaning of dreams, for Jung was able to show that all people in the world show certain basic, inherited ideas, experiences or concepts expressed in eternal themes. These he called 'archetypes'. Jung was especially interested in mythology, alchemy, and world religions. During the 'thirties and 'forties he made various trips to Africa, Mexico, North America and the Far East to gather information and inspiration for his numerous books and essays.

Jung survived two world wars—he actually forecast the coming of the first in a vivid dream—and died in his homeland at Zurich in 1961.

Dreams can express repressed sexual fantasies and unconscious aggressive desires.

to find a happy sexual relationship. The fact that he sees everyone else around him enjoying it only makes him more inadequate and unable to cope. Interestingly the girl takes the first step, by giving him the plate of food (that is, making an advance). In real life, this man probably worries about girls a great deal, thinking they are a bit

> 'I am standing on a bank on the edge of water, but it isn't really water. I'm standing with my mother, my sister and my cousin. Then I dive in and as I dive in I look down my body and I've changed. I am now a girl with a female body in a black bikini. Then I hit the water and I come up and now I'm back to me again as a guy. I look up to the bank and everyone has blank faces and there are all sorts of breakers, breakers across the water. There are breakers all across the beach . . . like a beach I used to go to when I was a kid. I start walking down . . . but it carries on and gets a bit vaguer . . . it's no longer water, but in a building and I walk down into a room and then it becomes an old concert we had when we were at art college and I am in the cloakroom with Andy Fraser and people from the pop group Free. It's really weird. I recognize the room, but it's not the same and we are all standing there going, "Oh it's no good, it's not like it used to be".'
> Student, 20, male

'forward'. To tie in with Freud's view that personal recollection may support the sexual nature of a dream, it might turn out that the young man was often given liver as a child: his mother would say 'It's good for you, eat it up'. This would suggest a confused attitude about women, that he has not grown up sufficiently to be on his own feet and out of his mother's influence. (Freud believed that sexual feelings start with a child's desire for the mother in boys and the father in girls.) Perhaps the dream is also expressing the man's fear that if he does give way to his sexual urges, punishment will result as it did when he was a child.

Nowadays, people have a much broader view of sex and the Freudian view seems a bit one-sided at first. But in his lifetime during the late 19th century, young people (especially women) were brought up to regard sexual feelings or any other impulsive, natural outburst of emotion as socially forbidden. The upper middle classes of Vienna, where he lived and worked, were particularly straight-laced and admiring of controlled intellectual pursuits. No one spoke about feelings or passions and they were only given way to in deep secret, in the boudoirs and brothels inhabited by 'fallen' women. No wonder that most of Freud's patients were more confused and anxious about sexual feelings than anything else. His thoughts were naturally concentrated on this area and this is reflected in his findings.

A main difficulty with Freud's theory is that not all dreams are concerned with wish fulfilment. Later in his life, Freud too began to change his mind about this part of his work. Take the example given above: Freud's earlier interpretation would be more appropriate if the man in the dream took the plate of food from the girl, gobbled it all up, and asked her for more! The bad endings are explained by saying that the conscious mind on patrol is sufficiently alerted to these feelings coming out that it steps in and puts everything in order once again. It adds on the 'right' ending to crush the urge once more. In this way, Freud managed to keep up his theory that all dreams do express the wish-fulfilment of a basic sexual or aggressive desire.

The influence of Freud

Much of what Freud uncovered in his study of dreams has passed into our everyday life. A large proportion of film or television advertising is based on the wish-fulfilment principle. Just like a dream, the cigarette or alcohol promoter says, 'Here is an ideal world—fulfil your urge to be a sex king or goddess of love by using our product'. If you want some practice at recognizing objects with a Freudian sexual link, try studying the advertisements. Long sleek cars, full of power, that 'respond' to every command; 'satisfying' cigarettes, smoked by two in a field of corn; 'long cool drinks' in exotic places, followed by high dives into deep blue seas —the underlying sexual tone soon becomes very evident. What about those after-shave lotions that have women falling at the feet of judo champions? In these pictures, sex and aggression are, very directly combined.

Letting off steam in dreams

Aggression is not necessarily the desire to go out and fight with guns or boxing gloves. In a much wider sense it means the basic drive for power or domination. Alfred Adler, one of Freud's best-known followers, expanded this view. He put forward the idea that everyone has an equally strong drive within them —the need to dominate. Furthermore, this usually springs from some basic inadequacy or lack which is subconsciously recognized at an early age. The rest of life is spent trying to compensate for it. Adler's theory has been popularized in such ideas as small men like Napoleon lusting for power or that bald men are very sexual to make up for their supposed lack of looks.

It may seem that both Freud and Adler take a fairly dim view of human nature. Their ideas are based on a sort of unending warfare between basic drives and the need to keep them under control. Letting these drives out in wish-fulfilling or power satisfying dreams is like letting the steam out of a kettle: if they are permanently bottled up, a severe nervous breakdown could result. So dreams provide a convenient escape valve.

This does not explain why many people actually wake up from their dreams. If the Freudian view was entirely right, then everyone would always sleep peacefully after a dream, having worked off some infantile wish or urge. But quite often the reverse occurs and we are very disturbed by the things that take place during dreams. It seems sometimes that a dream is acting as a voice of conscience, especially in terrifying dreams or nightmares.

Jung versus Freud

Carl Gustav Jung disagreed quite forcibly with Freud and his followers over this idea of dreams, as well as the view that repressed sexual or domination drives are the key to understanding the sign language of dreams. Jung saw clearly that Freud's great achievement was in drawing people's attention to the idea of the unconscious mind and how he related it to dreams. But he disagreed with Freud on a number of fundamental points. For one thing, Freud always used dreams as a way of getting back to the basic cause of a problem. Usually he found it in some important event in childhood—even in the moment of birth—which had affected the patient's view of himself throughout his life. Freud believed that unearthing the problem through psy-

choanalysis, including a discussion of a person's dreams, could often lead to a cure. Once the basic urge is recognized and coped with in real life, the obsession or fear produced by keeping it forcibly locked up inside would disappear.

For example, Freud describes a young man he once helped who had a morbid fear of going out in the street because he thought he would kill everyone in sight. It gradually emerged from his dreams and remembrances of childhood that he had at one stage heartily disliked his father, so much so that at the age of seven he had made a feeble but deeply-felt attempt to kill him. When his father eventually died the young man felt

very guilty, or rather felt that he should. He transferred his feeling to everyone outside and punished himself by locking himself up in his room all day. Once he recognized the urge dating back to early childhood, he was able to come to terms with his fear and greatly improved.

Jung however, took an entirely different view of dreams. He admitted that a great deal of what Freud had discovered was true, but he believed that the language of dreams was not just some secret code for basic drives, for wishes to be fulfilled. 'Going back' in Freud's way, seemed to reduce people's dreams to a set of rather unattractive, self-centred needs. He wondered why

Above: In dreams of a sexual nature it is interesting to see if natural or artificial images are used to express the dreamer's attitude.

dreams so often seemed to inspire people, to encourage them in their waking lives to do bigger and better things.

He was fascinated by the strange array of mysterious objects and creatures that occur in dreams. Freud's theory seemed to relate all parts of a dream to something inside the dreamer's own make-up. But to Jung this did not account for the pictures which appeared to come from a fantasy world outside the dreamer's everyday view of life.

Jung and the Collective Unconscious

Jung's solution to this mystery was that all human beings have two parts to their unconscious. Freud had looked at the part which hides personal, instinctive urges away. Jung now identified a part that is filled with strange primitive imaginings, which are common to everyone everywhere.

For example, why do all children love stories of witches, ogres and fairies when they have no real-life experience of these creatures at all? Why do people invent monsters in their dreams when there are no such things in the world? Jung suggested that we all share a Collective Unconscious, for we all respond to these basic fancies.

Many civilizations in all parts of the world have created exactly the same pictures in dreams, fairy stories and myths and they are readily understood by people from another country or from another age.

'I was sitting on top of Popocatepetl, playing a card game with three friends. Out of the volcano came beautiful soap bubbles which rose into the air, then floated down the conical sides of the volcano to join the sea of bubbles stretching away on every side as far as the eye could see. The sun came up and the bubbles glistened iridescently, first mauvy-blue, then peachy, then watery green, then all sorts of mother-of-pearl colours shimmering together.'
Student, female, 20

Throughout time, various nations have created remarkably similar stories about their heroes. Moses was found in the bulrushes; Jesus was born in an equally humble stable. The Greek goddess Aphrodite was born out of the sea just as the first ancient Inca ruler came out of a lake. There is no apparent reason for this similarity in legend, folklore and religion. Jung suggests that everyone has a natural tendency to think in these globally familiar ways.

Jung first drew attention to people's fascination with monsters. These fearful images seem to come from a universally shared mythology, equally recognizable to people from all civilizations.

Archetypes

These universal ideas were termed Archetypes, which means the original of a type. They are basic ancient beliefs which, according to Jung, we inherit rather than learn. So old and general are they that we do not need to ask what they mean when they appear in the mind's eye; we simply recognize them deep down without having to question them. These Archetypes are the language—the 'secret code'—of dreams.

Putting the theory into practice, look at the familiar figure of the hero. There are many instances in classical myths, such as the adventures of Hercules, Odysseus or Prometheus; in Britain there was the ideal of King Arthur and Sir Lancelot or St. George slaying the Dragon; in Australia Ned Kelly became a hero of mythic proportions, and there are countless examples from the Old West of the United States. Even in modern dress, the hero persists in comic strip characters such as Superman. Jung is simply saying that no one has to tell you what a hero is. You know what the person stands for as soon as you see the type.

Most of the Archetypes to which Jung drew attention were of a religious nature. Jung was for a long time Freud's disciple, and when he broke away from him because he disagreed with his views, he also developed a great interest in eastern religions. In turn people have disagreed violently with Jung, saying that this Collective Unconscious is a lot of mumbo-jumbo and cannot be proved scientifically. At least Freud had some factual basis for his beliefs. But in one sense the Jungian view is easy to accept, because he also believed that the Archetypes, as they appear in dreams, are reflections of ourselves. Many religions have a similar philosophy when they say God is really inside the individual.

But what if a dream contains a friend that you can recognize or even no people at all? Jung maintained that the friend is there because he or she reflects part of yourself. A room may stand for your own mind—the inside of yourself. In this way, all the Jungian Archetypes are simply representations of the human condition. Where they come from no one can say, but they are made concrete in the world of dreams, appearing like well-known actors on a private stage. Monsters are a 'projection', a representation of our own innermost fears. Heroes are a real-life realization of our own tendency to do good, brave deeds. A witchwoman—another familiar

Archetype—represents the destructive feminine impulse in human beings. Because these Archetypes are showing us to ourselves, they are easily recognizable, even by children. No one needs to explain to a child that the giant in Jack and the Beanstalk is all bad or that the Fairy Godmother in Cinderella is completely trustworthy. In the actual stories neither of these characteristics is proved: it is just known and accepted by the children hearing the tale. The same is true of the Archetypes of dreams. We do not read them up in books for they come naturally to mind. There is a mystery about the source of the Archetypes: if you are religious you will find it easy to believe that they spring from a force beyond human understanding. Others might accept that there is a basic energy in human nature which has over the

> 'My girlfriend and I are in a cottage in the country — not our real one, which stands by itself — but in one that is part of a group, but fairly isolated. There is a huge bomb explosion; the cottage of some people we know has been blown up and is burning ferociously. We know that they are dead, so we go indoors. But then we realize that the flames are spreading into our neighbors' houses, closer and closer to ours. I throw water on — and then buckets of pins and needles — to douse the flames. It is very powerful and scary.'
> Financial journalist, male, 32

centuries responded to certain unconscious forces. These are revealed in the Archetypes.

Archetypal symbols

One thing is sure—Archetypes occur time and time again in the same form. These are termed symbols. Just as a child instantly 'knows' the giant or the fairy godmother, so we all 'know' the meaning of the symbols. Take the story of the Garden of Eden. Eve is persuaded to eat an apple by an evil serpent. Everyone knows what the apple stands for, without having it spelled out for them. 'Forbidden fruit' is a symbol we can all understand. Another example is the standing stone. It is used to suggest permanence in many forms: in Stonehenge, in gravestones or in monu-

ments like the Cenotaph in London or the Washington Monument. In the Bible, Jesus calls his disciple Peter the 'Stone' or 'Rock', for that is the translation of his name from the Greek. Everyone recognizes the meaning behind the idea—even in today's conversation we refer to a reliable man with the phrase, 'He's as solid as a rock'.

Unknown Archetypes

More surprisingly, Jung discovered that people can dream using certain symbols without being at all clear of the Archetypal meaning at the time. People seem to inherit certain motifs in their thinking patterns without being aware of it. In one case, a girl dreamed of crossing a bleak moor with a good friend. On the way they met a large number of ape-like creatures with funny, friendly faces. They all proceeded together—arm in arm, cuddling up to the apes—towards their destination: a beautiful fairy-tale city glistening in the sunlight.

Only on thinking over the dream, which seemed to have no connection with any events in real life (no visits to the zoo!), did the girl discover that the ape-monkey is a very common symbol in eastern religions for the Self—the intuitive, emotional part of a person as opposed to the intellectual, logical part. A picture in a book of the Hindu monkey god Hanuman was so uncannily like the ape-monkey of her dream that the girl was very surprised. The friend was probably included in the dream because the dreamer admired her for her creative abilities and her warm personality. In Jungian terms, it all added up to a message that she should let the intuitive part of her nature guide her towards her goal—symbolized by the city—not just her thinking, logical self. Jung has written about many such incidents that occurred when he was treating his patients. If you cannot think of any private recollection connected with a symbol, it can be very helpful in your own attempts to understand dreams to try to find out something about the universal cultural symbolism described in the case above.

Anima or Animus: your dream reflection

Jung continued to explore the idea that dreams reflect the Self: one of the most fascinating ideas he put forward was that we have an opposite side to our personalities. In men, this appears as an idealized female figure called the Anima, in women, as a male, the Animus. In contrast, Freud would have believed that the appearance of a male

figure in a woman's dream represented sexual desires for someone, but Jung suggested that it could be the male aspect of her own character. We associate this with aggressive, extrovert, decisive qualities—some bad, some good. In a way, dreaming about male movie stars may even show a woman some aspect of her own male character. In men, the Anima is embodied in all the poets' ideas of an inspiring muse, who gives them the power to write beautiful things. In religion, she is the perfect figure of Mary, the mother of Jesus; in Chinese myth, she is the fertility goddess, Kuan-Yin; in classical times she was Aestarti, Venus or Ceres; nowadays she could be Marilyn Monroe, Maria Callas or even Queen Elizabeth II.

> 'I have a vast number of sales reports to make—but I haven't got round to it and I've forgotten what they're even supposed to be about. There's a great compulsion to get them done—but then suddenly I'm off on another business trip, involving a great deal of packing and preparation, none of which has been done and I have a ship to catch in a matter of hours. I always end up wondering whether I can conceivably get a car to get to the port on time.'
> Retired salesman, 60

The Persona and the Shadow

Two other parts of your self can appear in dreams in a symbolic form.

The first is the Persona, which Jung explains as the character or image you project outwardly. This acting figure who faces the world and says what it should do is often not your real self. In dreams, your Persona rather than your real self often takes part. You must recognize that this is not your innermost honest being. Jung tells the story of a woman who in real life was impossibly stubborn and full of fixed opinions. No one could ever win against her in an argument or even get her to admit she was wrong. One night she dreamed that she was going to a very important social occasion. On the doorstep, her hostess greeted her and said delightedly that all her friends were ready waiting inside. Then she led her through a doorway—into a cowshed! The dreamer's unconscious was giving her a picture of what her Persona

or image was really like and which she would not consciously admit to herself. Finally, a very helpful aid to understanding dreams from the Jungian point of view is contained in the Archetype of the Shadow. This is just what it suggests. It is the other side of your personality which does not see the light of day very often. It does not necessarily mean the evil or bad part of you, it might just be the secret part you feel least able to bring out into real life. It might be tender, imaginative and romantic and so you keep it lurking behind an agressive facade. It might also be truly destructive, as characterized vividly by Robert Louis Stevenson in *Dr. Jekyll and Mr. Hyde*—a story which came to the author during a dream.

The Shadow can be good or bad and can make your dreams very confused because you have to decide if the dream is about your outward personality or the Shadow behind. But life is pretty complicated too, and dreams reflect the conflicts experienced in it. It is interesting that small children seem to have an instinctive knowledge about the fundamental Archetypes of the Persona and the Shadow, for at some stage most play with an imaginary friend—who somehow seems to be the one who causes all the trouble in the household!

Although at first sight the theories of Freud and Jung seem to be poles apart and quite irreconcilable, they are not basically very contradictory. What matters most is that if a dream points out a problem area, exactly which way you take it will depend on your personal circumstances. Other symbols in the dream, especially those of a personal remembrance or of an Archetypal, general meaning, will help to make the central issue clear. Some people are more prone to follow Freud than Jung or the other way round. People who regularly visit a Freudian psychoanalyst tend to dream with lots of sexual pictures, while people who become interested in Jung start to fill their nights with magical visions of weird beasts and religious figures. The mind is very suggestive and responds to outside influences in surprisingly quick ways.

Dreams as problem solvers

Most modern dream researchers have established themselves on the basic principles of either Freud or Jung, and most have tried to find a less extreme position. J. A. Hadfield is a British psychologist who believes that dreams are basically problem-solving. He pays

particular attention to the fact that over a period of time, dreams will concentrate on a specific problem area trying out one possible solution after another until one dream comes to a realization of the issue. A simple example is the habit of dreaming about an accident. Drivers tend to have the same dream over and over again. At first the dream will make the accident take place as if realizing the dreamer's worst fears. Then gradually the content changes and the dreamer finally sees himself actually avoiding the accident by fast reaction and good steering. The dreams have worked off the driver's sense of anxiety and possible guilt about his behaviour on the road. So your dream may warn you where you are going wrong and why. It may reveal parts of yourself, consciously overlooked, which you should take into account in the future.

> 'I am on a paddle steamer—it's hot and sunny.
> Snow White and the Seven Dwarfs are sitting in deck chairs, surrounded by wicker travelling trunks. I go inside into a dim bathroom with no windows. The walls are covered with green tiles and the bulb is broken, leaving a glowing filament. Everything is dusty and dirty, and when I turn the taps on, rusty nuts and bolts come out.' Girl, 8.

Act out your dreams

An American psychoanalyst, Fritz Perls, developed the problem-solving aspect of dreams in an unusual way. One of his teaching methods was to have people act out the events of their dreams as if they really happened. It can be surprisingly revealing, and sometimes very amusing to do this.

Perls once had a teenage girl patient who had dreamed several times about her mother but had no idea what the drift of her thoughts intended. She thought she had a good relationship with her mother, all things considered. Perls asked her to talk as if she were the mother-figure in the dream and then to reply as the daughter. It rapidly emerged in this invented conversation that the voice she gave the mother was louder, more decisive and altogether more on top of the situation. As 'herself', the girl seemed unable to reply and changed physically as she acted, hanging her head and mumbling her words. Clearly, the girl did not really feel that she had found her feet. Nor was she free of her mother's domination, although she had said aloud that she got along with her mother pretty well. She automatically assumed the hangdog, feeble Persona of her dream.

You can try this simple experiment yourself—even if the dream is about objects, not people. For instance if the dream has a tree in it, why not imagine what kind of tree *you* are: 'I'm a tall thin sapling. I may not look very strong, but actually I can withstand winds and rain well, because I can bend and not break'. Over a period of time, you can build up a very revealing commentary, especially if you keep a journal of these thoughts.

The off-line brain

If however you dislike the idea of so much imagination being involved in understanding your dreams, you may prefer to consider the very interesting theory put forward by another British specialist, Dr. Christopher Evans. Remember that the unconscious has been described as a 'sorting house', taking in all kinds of information, sifting and absorbing it and then telling you in a dream how things stand in your real self. Dr. Evans has developed the idea of the sorting-house into a comparison with a computer. A computer is just a very elaborate calculating machine whose operation is controlled by large numbers of 'programs'. Programs are nothing more than special instructions which tell the computer what to do. With modern computers these programs have to be continually revised and brought up-to-date, a process which is best done when the system is (to use a technical term) 'off-line'. When a computer is off-line it is not switched off but rather uncoupled from its environment. Plenty of activity can go on inside but it doesn't interact with the external world. You might say that it's a little like a library which is put out of bounds to the public at regular periods so that the staff can do some cataloguing and rearranging. If computers don't have their programs revised in these off-line periods then they get muddled, out-of-date, inefficient and ultimately breakdown. Dr. Evans argues that the brain itself is a computer—a biological rather than an electromechanical one—and it too must be controlled by programs. Furthermore these programs must also be revised and updated and this must be done when the system is 'off-line'. So when we are asleep our brain is off-line and dreams represent the brain sifting through its

old programs, rewriting them, discarding dud ones and putting in new ones. We do this, Dr. Evans believes, for a large part of the sleeping period and it is this program revision that is the basis of true dreaming. The kind of 'dreams' we remember over breakfast in the morning are the fragments of the major programs which were being rewritten during the night and which were interrupted for one reason or another as the conscious mind briefly came awake.

If you look at each individual incident or object in a dream, it will relate to some new information, some newly-absorbed experience in your recent past. It might be from words read in a newspaper, from pictures seen on

Women in dreams may not only be the subject of sexual fantasy, but alternatively a symbol of the feminine aspects of a man's nature.

television, overheard remarks or friendly conversations. All these bits and pieces will be sifted and processed by the computer-brain in sleep.

All these theories, old and new, are evidence of the vast amount of research that is going on at present to understand the significance of dreams. No matter which view appeals to you most, at least consider that dreams are not completely random and absurd. They are proof that the brain is a complex, delicate organ with a potential that has barely been recognized.

The language of dreams

Dreams give their message in a direct, non-verbal way: they present a series of ideas inside your sleeping brain. Some of the ideas come in a very clear visual sequence which you can recall in the morning and relate to someone else almost as if the whole experience had really happened or had been read as part of a book. At other times the pictures are so fragmentary and jumbled that you can only remember one particular action.

Psychologists attach a great deal of importance to the way things are presented in dreams. To understand the message, it is vital to know what to look for. For instance, if someone you are talking to yawns while saying 'how interesting' and looks over your left shoulder, he is trying to tell you that the whole subject is really a bore. Dreams often use the same mannerisms we use in conversation and these tricks of speech give a clue to what is really being conveyed.

The meaning of symbols

First, learn to distinguish between symbols and images in your dreams. They are both dream pictures, but the possible meanings are very different. Symbols say something to everyone. They have a general significance which can be grasped by all people everywhere. **The 'magic man'** is a traditional symbol, of which many examples can be found. Merlin the Magician, the Wizard of Oz, the witch-doctors of Africa or the medicine men of American Indian tribes have the same powers.

The Garden of Paradise is another well-known symbol. This is a vision of a perfect place where everything is good and nothing goes wrong. People of all eras have found ways to express this symbolically. There is the Garden of Eden in the Bible, the Elysian Fields of Greek myth, and Mahomet's beautiful Paradise of the Islamic faith, where lovely girls or 'houris' wait with musk perfume, wine and the promise of love for the faithful. Nowadays, the same ideal is used by travel brochures to lure holidaymakers to that perfect resort where the sun always shines, the sea is clear and blue, the beach isn't crowded

and there's a never-ending supply of exotic food, drink and beautiful people. **A ship sailing over an empty ocean** symbolizes man's progress through life. It is a good example of combining more than one symbol to form a widely-understood situation. The ship represents his society—his way of organizing with other people, some system against possible chaos in the world. The sea stands for the age-old unknown forces of the universe or the creative mass which lies unformed below the surface of the mind. This way of imagining life

> 'I set out on a journey with a large open egg tray balanced on the palm of my hand and a carafe of wine clutched in the other. The terrain was rocky and the narrow footpath lined with bushes. The pace was brisk and I had to concentrate very hard not to break the eggs as I tripped up and down the uneven path. When I got to my destination the eggs just broke of their own accord. I thought: "Well I still have the wine". Then I noticed I no longer had it. Concentrating so hard on the eggs, I had left the wine somewhere along the way. So I turned back to find it.'
> Fashion journalist, 36, female

comes to us in the stories of Odysseus travelling the seas in search of home or in Jason's hunt for the Golden Fleece. In the Middle Ages, the 'Ship of Fools' was a favourite theme, characterizing all the types of people you could meet on your journey through life. Perhaps the familiarity of this symbol accounts for its favour with politicians, who are constantly talking about the 'ship of state' and the need for a 'firm hand at the helm'.

If you find something in your dreams that is not clear to you from your own experience of life or from immediate past events you can recall, then try to think more broadly of its possible symbolic meaning. The paradise sym-

bol just mentioned is quite common. Any dream of a beautiful calm place, not necessarily a Garden of Eden in the religious sense, may have overtones of this general symbolic meaning. Sailing on a ship may have nothing to do with sea voyage you have actually experienced: it may simply be a way of representing your progress through life. The phrase 'all at sea' will perhaps help you to understand the function of this symbol.

Images in dreams

An image works rather differently from a symbol. This is simply a more accurate way of referring to a picture. Dreams work in images: they take an idea, a thought or feeling and turn it into an exact picture or image to present to you in sleep. They are generally more commonplace than symbols—like offices, shops and all the paraphenalia of day-to-day life. This word is properly used in the phrase, 'He's the spitting image of his father'—that is, he looks exactly like him.

Suppose someone is 'up in the clouds' in your opinion. In your dream, you may well have an image of him actually sitting on a cloud. Studying hard for exams might show up in a dream as someone being force-fed or sitting in front of a huge plate of food. When you 'can't take any more in', your dream says so with an image of the feeling. If you feel you cannot see the wood for the trees in your life, perhaps you will dream of being lost in a giant forest.

Not all dreams are just images of well-known phrases like this: sometimes your dream invents a new image or picture as a way of saying something. Men who have trouble relating to women often dream of she-monsters. This is a vivid image of their feelings, showing how they respond emotionally to the female. Their shyness may really be a fear that women are too clever or too passionate and will take them over completely.

Images can be very amusing because they are so apt and direct in their message. A young girl who was beginning to visit a psychoanalyst to work out a particular difficulty in her life

Above: Background in dreams is very important. Exotic, faraway places suggest freedom and a lack of inhibition. A desirable and inviting girl is of course a standard male fantasy!

dreamed that she arrived at her analyst's house and found lots of underwear all over the waiting room. It was being aired on the radiators and on chairs round the heater. This could be interpreted as an image of the girl's own misgivings about 'washing her dirty linen' in public, expressing a wish that her analyst would spill a few secrets in return just to even the balance! Of course, this is just one possible interpretation: remember that the image of

ladies' underwear has strong sexual overtones as well.

The tricks of dream language

Once you can begin to look at the apparent 'story' of your dream as a series of images, then you will find it much easier to study. Try to evaluate each picture in its own right, as well as the overall effect of the dream. When you recognize images and see the possible symbolic value of some of them, then you can try to supply the following advice about the tricks or mannerisms of dream language. These points to watch were first recognized by Sigmund Freud, whose book, *The Interpretation*

of Dreams is still considered to be one of the finest and most valuable studies in the field.

Condensation

More than likely, you have already discovered that any one image in a dream can mean a number of things. Do not worry or be put off if several different ideas spring to mind at once it only shows how rich in suggestion and how powerful in meaning the dream language can be. Freud had one fascinating example of this characteristic, which he called condensation. A woman dreamed about some beetles trapped in a small box. At first she thought the

image had been suggested by something she had seen the day before—a moth had fallen into a glass of water. This might indeed have provoked the choice of image but does not go deep enough into why, of all the petty details from the day, that should have come up in her dream. The woman was then reminded of her daughter's hobby of collecting butterflies and this drew her back to memories of her own youth. Finally, Freud helped her to work through to the hidden or latent meaning of her dream. She was concerned about her husband's waning interest in sex and she knew that a well-known aphrodisiac called *cantharides* is made from crushed beetles.

Another image in the dream helped the woman to put two and two together, for she had also dreamed about open and shut windows. This immediately reminded her of a running battle she had with her husband about fresh air in the bedroom, rather than all the windows being shut. That led to a consideration of her relationship with her husband, and the underlying meaning of the beetle image came clear.

What if you do not know all the possible meanings of an image? After all, not everyone knows about aphrodisiacs made from beetle juice! The woman worked round to her own meaning simply by seeing connections—or condensations—in the beetle image of her dream. Thinking about her daughter's hobby reminded her of her own youth and attractiveness and called back memories of old romances. This in itself would have led to the heart of the problem, even if she had stopped there with the beetle image. Remember also that dreams are more often than not about things that worry us. It is not usually necessary to dig very deeply before the problem springs to mind. It is only in serious cases of mental anxiety or disturbance, when the cause is buried in the unconscious, that a lot of pain and effort is required to find it—and that calls for professional help.

Displacement

Almost as important as the condensing process is displacement, when the real concern of the dream is pushed into a small image. The images are skirting round the issue in order to avoid presenting a direct, head-on picture of the problem. If the dream becomes too clear it often turns into a nightmare

Left: The mood generated in a dream is very significant. The landscape could be gentle but is there an air of menace?

which wakes the dreamer up. Freud also thought that dreams are thus disguised to avoid upsetting the 'Conscience' part of the mind—the part that guards the basic thoughts and tries to stop them coming out—but nowadays, like most of Freud's ideas, this view is disputed.

Suppose you are worried about a relative, such as your sister. You might dream of a woman being involved in a car crash. This stranger may look totally different from your real-life sister, except that she is wearing the same glasses or a dress in a style your real sister prefers. This should be enough to tell you the true subject of your dream.

Freud was right in saying that this displacing device occurs when a part of you thinks you are doing something wrong. Suppose you are attracted to someone but you think should not be. You may have a very sexy dream involving a complete stranger, but his name may be similar, his clothing—or even a word he says—may recall the true object of your feelings. But if this were always true, then you would never have very explicit, clear dreams whose questionable parts are not disguised, and you would wake up far less often than you do from disturbing dreams.

A stranger or a shadow in a dream, incidentally, may have some symbolic meaning as discussed in the previous chapter. These figures can stand for sides of your own nature or personality that you do not know or refuse to acknowledge. Obviously, the other images in a dream will help you to decide which is the correct way of assessing them.

Reversal

An amusing trick to try, if a dream obstinately refuses to yield any meaning to you whatsoever, is to turn it round completely. Reversal is a common feature of the dream language. If you dream you are walking over a carpet in muddy boots, then why not consider: 'Am I the carpet, being walked over by other people?' The dream image may be saying, 'Don't be a doormat', in an upside-down way. The feeling of the dream may help. You would probably feel upset or indignant during a dream of this sort, which would certainly reflect the true meaning.

Killing or harming a child in a dream is a common worry for parents. But this too might be reversal; they hope very much that no harm of any sort will come to the family. But according to Freud, it might also be a wish-fulfilling

dream, recalling some moment of intense exasperation when a parent does feel like 'killing' a child. It is better to let off steam in this way in a dream than to harbour the feeling so that it affects your real experience of life.

Killing your own father or mother however does not follow the reversal principle. This merely shows in strong terms your attempts to break away from parental authority. You want to stand on your own feet and be independent. A parent can be concealed in an image of another kind of authority—a king, a ruler of a state or your boss at work.

A more Jungian approach might also consider whether you wish to rebel against some dominant part of yourself, reflected in an authoritative person.

Compensation

Jung also elaborated on the idea of reversal, believing that one of the main functions of a dream is to provide compensation for your real self. If you are a harrassed housewife, you may dream of being a glamorous, cool career woman. A ruthless businessman will tend to put himself in the place of a butterfly collector or a romantic intellectual in an ivory tower. A shy girl will dream of holding court in a circle of admiring boys. All these dreams are making up for the failings or unfulfilled needs of an everyday self.

Animism

Bear in mind also that if a person in your dream seems particularly wonderful, magical or idealized, it may come under one of those symbolic meanings already discussed.

A very beautiful, tender woman in a man's dream might represent his own finer, female instincts—what Jungian's call the Anima. Similarly, a sympathetic, courageous male figure might stand for a woman's own braver nature —her Animus.

Dreams have a habit of showing abstract things or feelings in the more visual form of people or animals. Bravery, just mentioned, will become a brave man; tenderness, a loving woman; Freud called this trick 'animism'. The same term is often used to describe the way objects are given human or animal properties by primitive peoples, for in their waking, day-to-day life they too turn abstract things into people or animals. The wind becomes 'the big man who blows'. Try to think broadly about this kind of image in dreams, for they work in the same way.

A policeman is often the most familiar character to appear in our dreams as the voice of conscience.

A devil figure may represent feelings or urges which you think are wrong but somehow cannot control.

An angel will act as the voice of good, as if from the nobler side of your nature or from your heartfelt faith in something.

A tramp will be an image for some unacceptable part of you or for something of which you are ashamed.

A gipsy will stand for some wild, impulsive, out-of-the-ordinary desire that you have lurking about inside you.

A baby will not just stand for birth or for your own desire to have children. It can just as well signify abstract things such as ideas or creative imaginings. A good example of this was a young man's dream about giving birth to perfectly-formed but very small babies. It was not some peculiar urge to be a woman! His profession was graphic designing and the babies stood for his wish to produce 'perfectly conceived' finished artwork or design ideas.

The cat image normally stands for supposedly feminine qualities such as intuition.

Dogs not unnaturally act as images for more traditionally masculine attributes such as adventurousness, aggression or faithfulness. This is an image that can contain many different abstract references, so you have to consider your own particular view of dogs (especially pets you know well) and add those ideas to the suggestions given here. For example, a scruffy, mongrel-type dog could indicate a low opinion of someone—possibly yourself—coming out in your dreams.

Other animals that commonly occur as dream images are wolves (fear, sexual aggression, hunger), rats (despicable, underhand people or feelings), rabbits (fertility or soft, easily-hurt characters) lambs (sacrifice, innocence, purity) and sheep (easily swayed, timid people). Sometimes the very nature of an animalistic image will help you to see the true meaning.

Horses for example are frequently chosen by female dreamers to symbolize the act of sex. A wild, strong stallion with a flowing mane is a beautiful way of imagining the power and force of sexual feeling. Notice how different this is from that other favourite sexual symbol—the automobile.

The car is sleek, powerful and shiny, but it is also automatic and mechanical underneath. If you dream of being driven by someone or sitting in the passenger seat, this indicates a more passive role in the situation. You should look into the dream to see if taking a more positive, outgoing attitude is being suggested to you.

Jokes and puns

Not all dreams take a serious approach to your experiences. For some reason, people find it difficult to accept jokes or puns in dreams at first, as if they believe that dreams must always be intense, mysterious and earnest underneath. But some unusual experiments have proved that we use word-play even in sleep.

> 'I was wearing a backless bathing suit and I had to have a school photograph taken in those strange rows they make you sit in. For some reason I had a bra on underneath — and as the costume was backless you could see the bra at the back. So I wanted to find a place to take it off, just a public lavatory or something. But either I couldn't find one or if I got to one, there was always someone waiting outside and I was feeling a bit coy about the whole thing, so I was having a terrible time. I think I eventually did get the bra off and I felt much happier, then I went and sat down in my place with an enormous sweater over the bathing suit so that the whole thing was pointless anyway, with sort of little pink knees showing and wondering whether anyone would mind about the fact that I didn't have a school dress on.'
> **Package designer, female, 24**

Ian Oswald, the British dream researcher, describes how the whispering of certain names to sleeping people, for instance the name of an ex-girlfriend or a former work colleague, will draw a response from the dreamer. A girl who heard the word Robert inserted a rabbit into her dream! The brain seems to mishear the word and includes an image whose word sound is close to the word actually said. Don't dismiss word-play or punning when looking for the meaning of a dream image. Someone who places the events of a dream in a football field for instance may in fact mean 'field' in its metaphorical sense, as in the 'field' of medicine or academics.

Psychologists find that people sometimes see a joke that is not apparent to anyone else. The dreamer recognizes that a figure represents someone known personally, because of a silly word or a ludicrous situation. If a dream contained the image of a king seated on a throne in the act of re-folding the Sunday newspaper and grumbling about it, then a family member might know instantly that the royal figure was Dad, who always complained about everyone else getting the paper first and losing his sports page!

Absurd dreams

An extension of dreams with jokes or puns are those which are at the time absurd. You wake up thinking, 'What a silly situation!' Sometimes the absurdity is simply the result of a lack of time-span or proper connections. This is a characteristic of dreams in general. They are like films that are badly made, jumping suddenly from one scene to the next, from one image to another without proper observance of the conventional logic of real life. This explains why dreams often contain absurd mixtures of people. Suppose your grandfather is mixed up in a dream with some of your close friends and neighbours, when in reality he died ten years ago. Freud suggests that this is as if you were saying to yourself, 'What would my grandfather say about this if he were alive?' Your dream, with no respect for time or individuals, simply makes that suggestion real. Even if you can't imagine why you should think such a thing—even unconsciously—stop and wonder if there are any characteristics about your grandfather (or whoever it is) that have some relation to the subject matter of your dream. It can be quite revealing.

Although it is sometimes upsetting or distressing to dream about a relative or dear friend who is dead, this explanation will help to put it into perspective. You may be bringing that person back because they held views or values that

Nudity is an expression of a desire to be frank and open without hiding behind a social facade. It can turn up in the oddest situations—but are they really so absurd? A tiger for instance is a clear image of the power of sexuality; a policeman and obviously a priest stand for the force of conscience. In this context, death, in the form of a funeral cortège, could stand for the dreamer's suppression of real feelings.

are significant in your present life. However, Freud also points out that ridicule can be a form of criticism. If you place someone near to you in an absurd position then you may be letting out some critical opinion you formerly kept to yourself, possibly for the best of reasons, like love or a sense of respect. Do not confuse absurd dreams with others which are simply odd or peculiar. Absurd dreams have a strong feeling of mockery attached to them *at the time*. You often feel that things are absurd during the dream itself. Most dreams only seem silly when you wake up and think about them in the cold light of day.

Nakedness. A common dream of this type that causes embarrassed laughs is that of nakedness. 'I walked right down the main street in broad daylight with nothing on, but I didn't seem to care.'

The interesting point to notice is the lack of any sense of absurdity or shame at the time. Freud believed these dreams were purely wish-fulfilling, satisfying a basic exhibitionist streak in everyone. However, Jung and many other psychologists have come to accept this kind of image as an expression of a desire to be frank, open and true to ourselves. If there is any feeling of fear attached to it, then clearly the message is that you are afraid of what people might think if you express your real views, behave naturally or lower your defences.

It is interesting to see how social convention makes us think that being stripped or caught without clothes is a sign of humiliation, shame or degradation. This dream image is really using the idea in a much more basic, true way. How about the traditional story of

'Lion devouring a horse' by the celebrated 18th century British painter, George Stubbs, is a powerful impression of the destructive capacity of aggressive or sexual drives. Both animals are world-wide symbols of these instincts.

the Emperor's new clothes—is it a joke against the court who fell for appearances, or against the Emperor for being so silly that he walked about in the nude?

Swimming is frequently connected with nakedness dreams. By now you will probably be thinking ahead to its possible meanings. People talk about being 'in the swim', or in old-fashioned schoolgirl slang, things went 'swimmingly'. Add to this the ideas already explained about the sea or ocean symbol and it is easy to see that swimming represents being at ease with life or being at one with your feelings and desires, pushing ahead with energy and excitement. Adler would say that swimming with effort stands for the urge for power or achievement; thus swimming upstream or against the tide can be taken exactly as the words suggest. You are going against popular opinion or trying to cope with troublesome issues. If the dream includes reaching land after the struggle, it may be a way of encouraging you in your aims.

Naked swimming can also suggest sexual fulfilment, as you will no doubt know if you have ever watched those old films with native girls splashing around, wide-eyed and flower-decked, while gun-laden soldiers or pith-helmeted hunters peer through the bushes! (Freud also said a great deal about the sexual imagery of guns and other weapons.)

Repetition

At the opposite end of the scale from absurdity or apparent nonsense is the intense feeling that is generated by repetition. This way of making a point in a dream is the most easy to identify. It is explained simply as a way of saying 'very much so' in images.

Climbing up a hill which seems endlessly steep and arduous is a way of saying 'Getting along in this life is very, very hard going'. It could be that the dream is an expression of fear or doubt about a particular goal you have in sight. You might pause and consider if pursuing the aim is really as important as all the effort it will cost.

A very long journey by train or bus embodies the same idea. 'Life is tedious', the dream is saying. It is implicit in the train image that catching or missing it relates to your views about life. Are you missing out on good opportunities; do you worry about success? An endlessly repeated attempt to catch a train would suggest a state of anxiety or tension about getting on in the world. Perhaps the dream is warning you to relax a little and not take things so seriously. Remember that mechanical means of transport also suggest an automatic, driving power in your life. We say someone has 'gone off the rails' if things go wrong for him. An endless train journey, especially if you are a passive individual sitting quietly in a carriage watching everything flit by, suggests a humdrum existence in which you let yourself be carried along. But your dream is telling you that somewhere deep down you know this is not really what you want.

Lucid dreams

Sometimes you will have a dream in which you are passive in a different way. You stand back from the events taking place, saying to yourself, 'I *know* this is a dream, but I'll let it go on'. Other people decide exactly the same thing but enter the dream, changing what happens in it. It is as if they say, 'I don't like this part of the dream; let's change it to something else'. These are called lucid dreams and offer two possible explanations. If you realize it is a dream but stand back and do nothing, then this is a way of keeping the situation at arm's length. You do not enter into the experience of the

> 'I remember sitting in a cafe with a friend. The cafe is a very strange place with lots of different levels and stairs. The table we are at is beside a window which looks out over a large walled garden. The garden seems quite a long way down and is ablaze with flowers and plants of every description. Suddenly I am no longer in the cafe but in the garden, there are lots of loaves of bread about. Then I see a large, green crocodile. I start to climb the wall, which is easy (but I seem to be getting nowhere fast). I eventually reach the top and find myself in a wasteland. I wander off and walk miles until I come to a river. There is a bridge over the river and I see a policeman and another man.'
> Illustrator, 25, female

problem even in sleep. This might be a way of showing that in reality you behave in just the same way—by not facing up to issues or meeting them head-on.

If on the other hand you seem to direct the course of the dream, changing the 'plot' and making things happen, then it is possible that the dream is being helpful or therapeutic. You are exploring various endings or trying out different ways of resolving your real-life difficulties. Dreaming of making things come to life exemplifies the kind of image found in a lucid dream. It is a beautiful way of suggesting that there are latent, unused powers inside you that are beginning to blossom and come out. You should be encouraged by such

a promising dream and act on it as positively as you can!

Secondary revision

The final point to consider when you are looking at dream images is a little more complicated but worth the effort if you find that most dreams respond to your analysis, but just a few evade you. It often happens that a dream seems so clear and recognizable that the meaning is straightforward and comes out at once. This is especially likely if the dream has similarities with a wish or favourite ambition. Knowledge of these ideal hopes and fantasies keeps a public relations man's salary healthy, when he plays up to them in his advertisements! Suppose you dream of moving into a beautiful house, furnished in exquisite taste with everything you have ever wanted. Whatever else happens in this dream, you will be likely to wake up and say, 'Oh well, that's clear, it was just one of my wish-fulfilling dreams', and then forget all about it. Of course you want a house like that—many people do. But dreams are rarely quite so simple. You will probably overlook other parts of the dream in order to fit the whole experience into your favourite fantasy. Freud described this process as 'secondary revision' and maintained that it leads people into making quick, superficial judgements about the contents of their dreams. Look more closely at that house again. Were there any details, such as going down into the basement or climbing upstairs to look at the view? Were there any objects you noticed as you passed—any clothes in cupboards or rubbish left neatly in a corner?

It may not always work, because dreams fade so quickly, especially if you made a quick snap judgement and put the thought aside. But if you can go back over the dream and look at the finer details, you will probably surprise yourself as new interpretations spring to mind.

Looking into your dreams

Do not worry if you feel you will not remember all these different points when you try looking at your own dreams. Even if you only remember one or two the first time, the rest will follow. It is much better to take a relaxed view and simply mull over a few thoughts. You will certainly fail if you sit down with a long list and a red pencil, taking an academic approach to the task. Dreams are natural things and they should not be forced into an intellectual guessing game.

What is sleep and how do we dream?

When you go to sleep you do not merely lose awareness of the world around you. Pronounced physiological changes also take place. The body's temperature is lowered, the heart's pulse rate is slower, and various bodily functions such as digestion are measurably reduced.

It seems that there could be certain areas of the brain which need constant stimulation to keep us awake that is, conscious. Sleep is the state which occurs when these areas cease to be stimulated.

No one can survive without regular periods of sleep, even though it may seem a waste of time—especially to children—to spend about a third of a lifetime in what appears to be a state of 'nothingness'. Furthermore, sleep is required *at regular intervals*: it is not as useful to the body to have 4 hours of sleep one night and 30 hours the next. The body has learned to work by a 24-hour clock and finds it difficult to forget. This clock, based on the movement of the earth round the sun and the consequent periods of light and dark, is known as the 'circadian rhythm'.

There is some truth in the general belief that working on night shift produces less satisfactory work than the normal daytime periods. The body takes many days, even weeks, to get out of the circadian rhythm, and during that time physical co-ordination, alertness and other manifestations of mental ability function less effectively. Anyone who has travelled between continents by jet will know how difficult it is to adjust to a new time scale. Even the relatively simple 'hop' between New York and London means a 5-hour difference in time and many people feel disoriented for several days, even if they appear to have caught up with lost sleep.

In general, the brain needs regular doses of sleep to continue making judgements or decisions and carry on other thinking processes. Experiments have shown that sleeplessness does not impair physical activity—but it does hinder concentration. People become increasingly vague the longer they go without sleep, eventually suffering from hallucinations—literally dreaming with their eyes open.

The activity of sleep

When asleep, the body and brain are not completely dead to the world or unconscious. The body is kept going by the activity of the autonomic nervous system, which controls the essential 'life support systems' of the heart, digestion, cell repair and replacement and so on, which continue during sleep. The senses also continue to be active to a certain degree: when an alarm clock rings, a part of your head registers the sounds of the bell and responds to the stimulus, sometimes dragging you unwillingly from sleep. A mother can be woken by her small baby crying to be fed at 2 am, while other people in the house—even the baby's own father—will not be disturbed.

Another part of the brain allows us to ignore regular noises, like cars outside or mild rainstorms. In this way even while asleep the brain apparently selects the intake of stimuli and lets us respond to some, but not to all. You can actually exploit or train your mind to some degree: many people say to themselves, 'I must get up early tomorrow' and actually wake up even before the alarm clock rings. Routine can play its part, for you can accustom yourself to waking regularly at 7 or 8 am if this is part of a long standing pattern of living. In the same way, many people always feel hungry at noon or at six.

Orthodox sleep

The activity of the brain during sleep is of course very important when studying dreams. Scientists have found that it is possible to measure brain activity by measuring the electrical impulses constantly given off. These can be registered on a machine called an electro-encephalograph (*cephalos* being the Greek work for 'head'), known as an EEG machine. By attaching electrodes to people's heads in various special spots, an interesting record of brain activity can be obtained. It seems that adults have several levels of sleep. At first, while someone is fully awake but preparing for sleep, a steady wave pattern is detected by the EEG machine. These waves are called 'alpha rhythm'. This is not exactly the same as being wide-awake and fully alert, for if the telephone rings or some other circumstance forces a person to get out of bed, these alpha waves disappear, and a completely different pattern is recorded.

After this first 'alpha rhythm' stage, the brain falls into a second stage of drowsiness, and a pattern of much slower, more irregular waves occurs. Then, finally, the person falls into deep sleep, characterized on the EEG machine by big, deep 'delta' waves, punctuated by small patches of shorter, faster waves, which are termed 'sleep spindles'. This state is known as 'orthodox sleep'.

During sleep, people fluctuate from one level to another, rising up and down through the three main stages in 90-minute cycles. So on average (although this is very rough and does not allow for the immense variety in sleeping habits that has been found), most people have three or four periods of deep, big-wave sleep each night.

Although people tend to think that deeper sleep comes late in the night, there is some evidence to show that the brain derives the most refreshment and benefit from the big-wave levels of sleep that occur in the earlier cycles of the sleep period. It also seems that the first hour or two of sleep goes immediately into the 'delta' wave level. So

Right, above: 'Stop-frame' photography has shown that the body changes position constantly during sleep. Below: The EEG machine records the electric impulses generated by the brain during sleep. Electrodes are also attached to pick up the muscular movement of eyes, throat and heart.

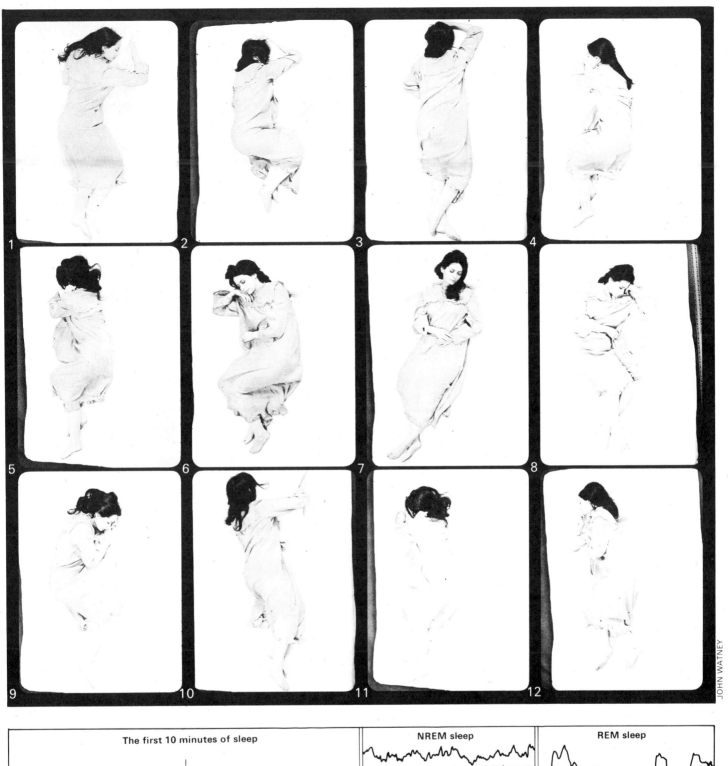

JOHN WATNEY

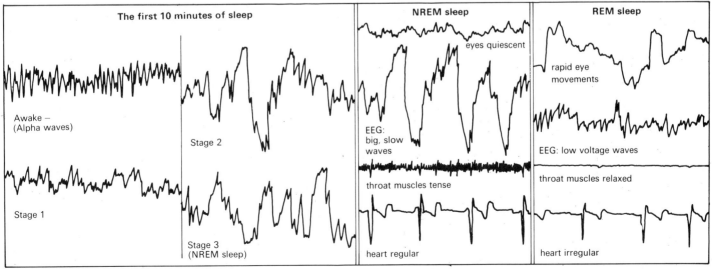

The first 10 minutes of sleep		NREM sleep	REM sleep

Awake – (Alpha waves)

Stage 2

eyes quiescent

rapid eye movements

Stage 1

Stage 3 (NREM sleep)

EEG: big, slow waves

throat muscles tense

heart regular

EEG: low voltage waves

throat muscles relaxed

heart irregular

perhaps there is some truth in the saying that sleep before midnight is better than sleep in the early hours—if a person's usual time for going to bed is about 10 pm. But obviously if someone is accustomed to sleeping from midnight until 10 am, he will draw the greatest benefit from his sleep between midnight and 2 am. In the same way, you do not necessarily need double sleep to recuperate from a very late night. In this case, the body simply makes up the lost resting time by going into longer periods of big-wave sleep on the following night. Most people find that a normal period of sleep, that is about 7 to 8 hours, is enough to repair the damage of a late-night party—although it does not take into account other bad effects which might also be present—like alcoholic poisoning from too much drink!

Paradoxical sleep

There is another level of sleep, however, which, because of its 'contradictory' nature, is known as paradoxical sleep. Although the terms 'orthodox' and 'paradoxical' may seem to be an unnecessary complication in the matter of sleeping, it is important to use this distinction. It is easy to make the mistake of thinking that one or the other of the two main stages of sleep is deeper or of better quality. In fact, you should have a fair share of both kinds of sleep for the mind and body to function efficiently.

In the late 1950's, EEG experiments undertaken by Dr. Nathaniel Kleitman achieved a breakthrough in the study of sleep and dreams. It was discovered that people have periods when the wave pattern changes again, this time to a shallow-wave pattern. Their eyes move rapidly about at the same time, up and down and from side to side, although the lids remain closed. You can often notice this kind of reaction in sleeping dogs or cats: their noses or mouths twitch, their tails swish and their eyes seem to be moving, as if looking at something.

This period, called REM (Rapid Eye Movement) sleep, appears to be the time when humans dream most vividly. It would not be true to say it is the only time, for during experiments, people have sometimes been awakened when their eyes were still and their EEG readings showed big-wave sleep, but they were still interrupted in the middle of a dream. However, it does appear that if a person is awakened during REM sleep he remembers his dream most clearly. Georg Mann, a colleague of Dr. Kleitman's, once described the process as being like a visit to the theatre: the sleeper/dreamer sits in his seat, at first fidgeting expectantly. Then he slowly settles down ('alpha wave' sleep) until he seems spellbound by the action on stage (REM sleep)

'I was at Hawkwell (a house which we had owned in 1949) and my ex-husband was talking about something which was "up the road". In the dream the road was a different road from the one that really ran past the house and I knew we had never been up it. So I asked him suspiciously what he knew about this road. He admitted sheepishly that he had been looking at a new house which was being built up there, which he rather liked. Without actually moving I could see the unfinished house. I asked him what we would get for our house if we sold it. He replied instantly, "£38,000". I thought, "How the hell did he know that?" I knew somehow that the new house was selling for £27,000. So I said, "Why don't we sell this house and move into the new one?" I don't remember any more.' (NB. The house prices are very specifically in terms of 1970's values, rather than 1949, which seemed to be the period in which the dream took place.)
Librarian, female, 56

---

watching everything with his eyes until the curtain falls. Finally, he shifts again as the play ends ('delta' waves).

Studying people asleep in this way has dispelled one very common misconception: that dreams only take a second or two to occur, even though they seem very long to the dreamer. We now know that dreams take exactly as long as the events would take in real life. People who have dreams or nightmares which force them to wake up at night find that they feel terribly low the next day. They have in fact experienced a loss of satisfying sleeping time.

You may think that the time when you dream is the time when you are most 'relaxed', when the mind has all its defences down so that these strange pictures from your private underworld can well up into your brain—but this is not the case. During this kind of sleep, the brain is actually sending messages down to the body muscles to stop any action. The muscles of the body are completely relaxed. Remember the description of the man in the theatre, who sits 'spellbound' by the action. The brain prevents us from acting out the events in the dream world. This discovery has helped to explain the horrible sensation when you want to scream but can't or you try to run but remain rooted to the spot, which characterizes vivid dreams and especially nightmares.

Why you need to sleep and dream

How do we know that sleep is vital? This question is easy to answer: it was common experience during World War II when prisoners were tortured by being kept awake, that after a comparatively short period of time, they would suffer serious personality disorders as well as physical discomfort, and some actually died from the effects of sleep deprivation. The fact that the prisoners were forced to stay awake, rather than being allowed even short periods of sleep, was the worst aspect of the torture. Walking about, prolonged shouting sessions, hot and cold showers —any number of activities had to be maintained to keep them going.

The brain must have its regeneration period of sleep and fights very hard to get it. It is perfectly possible to 'drop off' even for a second or two if you are short of sleep. How often has the rocking of a train or the droning voice of a boring public speaker resulted in your nodding off involuntarily?

A regular rhythm or pulse is a great sleep inducer: the cradle and the rocking chair are domestic proof of that. But strangely enough people fall asleep just as readily through something which ought to be stimulating. They sleep in front of the television or at concerts and plays—and then complain bitterly that they cannot sleep in bed! There is also a danger of accidents or damage in jobs which involve driving long distances or operating machines in a factory. Work does not become easier to do because it is repetitive—it is harder to maintain concentration, and people who work in such conditions cannot help but make mistakes or put themselves at risk. It is part of their human make-up.

Learning in bed

The ability of regular rhythm to induce sleep also counters the science-fiction idea of 'learning in one's sleep'. Many people believe that you can learn a foreign language or the lines of a play by playing a repetitive recording through earphones while you are asleep. It seems unlikely that this could ever happen, since the process of sleep stops the stimulation of the 'wakeful' part of the brain which is normally the area capable of learning and memorizing new information. In fact you are much more likely to be woken up by a recording, just as you would by the telephone or alarm clock.

However, the best time to learn in bed is for a short period when 'alpha rhythms' are present. This is when the body is relaxed ready for sleep but still awake mentally. Perhaps this accounts for the pleasantness of reading in bed—quite complicated material can be well absorbed at this time of night. But don't overdo it—if you're trying to cram for exams or finish vital work for the next day, you'll do more damage by not having enough sleep than forcing yourself to stay awake and learn!

Sleep is vital, in both its orthodox and paradoxical forms, and it follows that dreaming is all important as well. But don't worry if you think you never dream. You do—but you may never *remember* them on waking.

Scientific experiments have shown that if a person is deprived of sleep altogether, then his first night's sleep afterwards will be spent in a greater proportion of orthodox, deep-wave sleep than usual. But after that, on the second or third night, he will make up the paradoxical sleep of vivid dreaming that he has missed. This suggests that both kinds of sleep are equally necessary and work in different ways for our benefit. It might simply be habit to have these two kinds of sleep, but it is also possible that orthodox sleep feeds our body, while paradoxical sleep feeds our mind or brain.

Bad sleepers

It is quite possible that someone who complains of being a 'bad sleeper' might be expecting too much and might be getting quite enough sleep for his own needs. Older people definitely need less sleep—the cells of their bodies and brain are not being renewed at the same rate as a growing child. Remember also that short snatches of sleep—even seconds long—can fall on people, so that in an apparently sleepless night, you can never really be certain that you didn't 'drop off' for a moment. People who sleep badly probably come straight up into full consciousness from deep-

THE VICTORIA AND ALBERT MUSEUM, LONDON

wave sleep more often than 'good' sleepers, who usually have a period of doziness before awakening fully. In other words, bad sleepers remember periods of wakefulness more vividly than other people and consequently believe that they hardly sleep at all.

Sleeping pills

People often believe that sleeping pills will help them to sleep 'well', especially if they are plagued by distressing insomnia. However, there is a great danger in their use, especially the barbiturates. Many psychologists have produced evidence that if you take sleeping pills, you do not get the normal amount of paradoxical sleep—the sleep of vivid dreams and mental regeneration. People frequently find that even though they take sleeping pills, they do not wake up feeling refreshed—a complaint that can now be explained partly by the need for two kinds of sleep.

It may be a temporary relief from the day's worries to force the mind into

Gustav Doré's 'The Exercise Yard' conveys the despair of sleeplessness. Luckily the body has an invincible capacity for snatching sleep.

oblivion with barbiturates. But in the long run, this is only evading the issue. You are actively preventing your mind from facing up to your life-situation and possibly from helping you to understand yourself, so that whatever you are doing can be sorted out. Worse still, as the body really dislikes these drugs, it will make strenuous efforts to overcome their effect. This is what happens when the effect of the drug begins to 'wear off'. It is not uncommon for people to experience far worse sleeplessness and much more intense 'imaginings in the night' than if they had not embarked on pill-taking in the first place.

Sleeping pills can be just as habit forming as alcohol and can have just as serious results. If people would think of them as dangerous, perhaps they would not damage themselves by relying on them habitually.

An interesting sidelight to the problem of drugs can be seen in the immense reaction that many individuals experience after an operation under full anaesthetic. An anaesthetic immobilizes the body, cutting out physical pain and conscious awareness. However, it could be that part of the brain does register what is going on, which is why anaesthetics can give a nastier shock to the system than the surgery performed under it. Even a minor event like having tonsils removed can bring about very vivid dreams for days or weeks afterwards. If one isolated, safely supervised event can have such marked repercussions on the brain, no wonder that prolonged pill-taking is so destructive, even if at first it seems a dull, wonderful relief.

No-one would suggest, however, that prolonged periods of sleeplessness should be ignored, and no doctor would discuss them as mere complaining. Severe insomnia can be successfully treated—but not merely by popping in a pill every night year after year.

Sleepwalking

Sleepwalking is a severe form of night disturbance, often incorrectly associated with insomnia. It is, on the contrary, linked with the deep orthodox sleep where no eye movements occur. Sleepwalkers are not acting out the events of their dreams, but the activity seems to indicate that there is some form of mental activity going on in orthodox sleep. People have reported dreams when awakened during this stage, but they are generally less vivid and more difficult to remember for any length of time. The exact nature of the mind's activity during sleepwalking is still a mystery, but it may indicate emotional disturbance. In a child it appears most commonly to be a sign of anxiety or upset, so a doctor should be consulted if it persists. The one excep-

Children are especially prone to visions of 'bogey men' during the dozey phase before sleep.

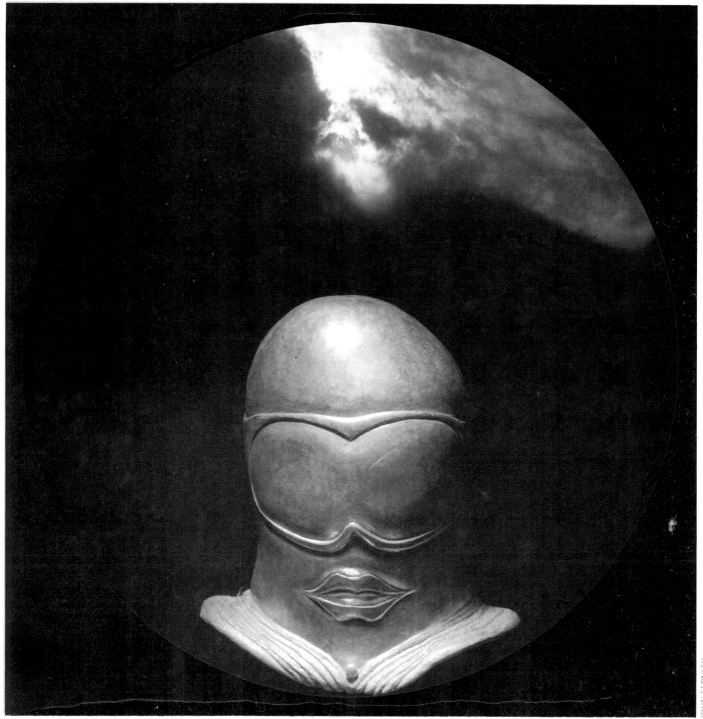

tion to this advice would be if the family had a long history of sleepwalking—for some reason the phenomenon is quite often hereditary.

Things that go bump in the night!

One of the most familiar and easily explicable forms of night disturbance is found during the 'dozey' phase, which takes place just before deep sleep and also just before normal awakening (as opposed to a sharp jolt into alertness). The commonest effect is to imagine that you are falling or that the whole bed is floating. It is also well-known to have a quick imagining of a car crash and literally to jump or start violently at the moment of impact. For children this is the time when 'bogeymen' stand at the foot of the bed, or eerie faces float before the closed eyes. One man remembers vividly that a head made of black and yellow houndstooth check tweed would hover at the end of his bed almost every night at one period of his childhood! Everyone knows the dread of seeing a menacing stranger in the room—it turns out to be the same old dressing gown on the back of the door. The scientific name for an experience of this sort is a 'hypnagogic' dream, a word which only signifies the time when these visions appear, which is in the period leading towards sleep.

All this activity of the brain is reflected in the wave patterns taken from sleepers wired to an EEG machine. Falling asleep is not a steady flow downwards into deep relaxation, but the 'alpha waves' of drowsiness—although regular —rise and fall on a general downward path. It is like watching the flames of a dying fire: they fade steadily, but there can occasionally be a little burst of life.

Dreams and your body

The idea of linking bodily states with the content of dreams is one that has excited great interest for many years. At one time it was thought that dreams were merely the result of eating a heavy meal too late at night. Certain foodstuffs, such as cheese, were supposed to have a particularly strong effect on people, causing vivid dreams. Any form of physical imbalance, such as the discomfort caused to the stomach from over-eating or indigestion, can cause dreaming, but nevertheless does not account for the extraordinary pictures created in our dreams. If food was the reason for a dream, as opposed to one possible cause, people eating cheese would all have exactly the same cheesey dream—but they don't.

However, certain patterns can be noted in the way the body adjusts to outside stimuli. If someone falls asleep resting uncomfortably on an arm, he is quite likely to have a dream involving something unpleasant happening to that limb, such as paralysis or being wounded. But as dreams tend to draw attention to something we should recognize about ourselves, it would be quite feasible that the mind could choose this bizarre way of letting the sleeper know about the discomfort—forcing him to wake up or at least turn over.

In one series of experiments, Calvin Hall, the American researcher, has proved this kind of influence on dreams by placing a waxed candle in a dreamer's hands on two occasions. The first time, the man dreamed he was playing golf, and the second time, he imagined he was lifting weights in a gymnasium! Hearing a tap dripping is a familiar example which often transforms itself in dreams into something like rain, tears, or pouring wine. Sleeping on one's back can cause pressure on the spinal cord and some dreams recreate the pain in a nightmare.

Nightmares

Nightmares are dreams which create a picture or feeling which is so terrifying or disturbing that it wakes you up. Some scientists believe that certain body functions are behind them. Small children find the emotions of rage or hatred so strange and overpowering that at night they re-create them as a particularly forceful dream-picture. This idea is reinforced by the fact that nightmares start in children just about the age when they develop an understanding of good and bad behaviour. So, saying to a 4 or 5 year old, 'You'll really get it if you pinch Suzy again' impresses on the child a sense that many of its natural feelings are bad and dangerous. Consequently he has nightmares in which he realizes the awful consequences of letting 'naughtiness' get out of hand. In older people nightmares can often be a repeat of these childhood fears and may indicate that there is a problem still unsolved in the person's character.

This idea is taken further by other psychologists who believe that people often have nightmares as a result of half-understood physical sensations. Girls in their teens, waking up to the idea of sex, often have very intense dreams which are representations of their emerging sexual drive. What you do not understand often frightens you —and so the dream becomes a nightmare, with a 'big black thing' chasing you and your legs refusing to move. Dreams of falling from high places can be quite terrifying as well—but they can also occur with no feeling of fear at all! Some of the most disturbing nightmares that adults experience are caused by anxiety. As often as not the events of the dream may seem inocuous enough, but the atmosphere of fear, disgust, anger, sorrow or bewilderment will be the dominant feeling, enough to wake you and leave you feeling disturbed and agitated for some time afterwards.

Dreams and illness

There is an extension to the physiological aspect of dream-making that occurs rarely, but cannot be overlooked. It has been known for someone to dream of being seriously ill, in a very specific way, such as dreaming of suffocation, when in reality the dreamer is a victim of asthma. There are also notable instances of precognitive dreams about illness, in which people have dreamed of having a heart attack or a brain tumour several months before the conditions have actually been diagnosed.

Many people dream about things of which they are afraid or worried, so in most cases a dream about illness will have this simple cause behind it. It expresses the worst fears of the dreamer, so that the problem of anxiety is brought into the open. In rare cases, it could be that the heart trouble or other disorder is present in some slight form, and this registers on the unconscious mind before the conscious one, producing a dream-picture of the trouble. No one should believe that 'bad' news in a dream will necessarily come true: a dream about cancer probably indicates that you have a real anxiety about this illness and the best way to cure that is to have regular checks, as advised by most doctors.

Whatever the factors which cause a dream—outside noises, inside stomach grumblings, or imagined fears—the pictures which are presented to a dreamer are unique, private and endlessly varied. The poet Keats once described sleep as a 'soft embalmer of the still midnight', and asked,

'Save me from curious Conscience, that still lords
Its strength for darkness, burrowing like a mole'.

But research has shown that sleep, while essential and refreshing, still allows the burrowing to continue for our own good.

Dreams without Freud

Dream interpretation is not new; it is one of the oldest and most widespread arts. Ever since man has been capable of coherent communication he has been fascinated by the meaning of the strange frightening and inconsequential meanderings of the unconscious.

The Mesopotamian theory

Of the early civilizations known to man, Mesopotamia developed the most comprehensive and sophisticated explanation for dreams and their language. The emphasis laid on sex by Freud's theories is not as revolutionary as you might think. In ancient texts written by the Babylonians and Assyrians, some dating back as far as 5000 BC, a large amount of space is devoted to explanations of sexual images in dreams.

If a man dreamed that his urine streamed out directly against a wall and spread in the street, then he would have many children. Dreams of flying, which Freud interpreted as symbolic of sexual pleasure, were a subject of great interest to the Mesopotamians. They wrote long books on the various meanings, but most agreed that flight signified danger or death.

These early books about dreams contain many images and symbols of everyday actions, especially eating and drinking, and deal with animals such as donkeys, horses, goats and cats. The Mesopotamians believed that dreams came from evil spirits or demons and that they were like spells, bound to come true unless the dreamer did something to avert them.

The Babylonians had a goddess of dreams, Mamu, to whom they prayed and whose priests performed rituals to stop dreams from being fulfilled.

Nebuchadnezzar's dream

In the Bible, the Babylonian king Nebuchadnezzar dreamed of a strong flourishing tree, cursed by a 'holy one', which turned into a withered stump. The Hebrew prophet Daniel, who was renowned as a dream interpreter, told the King that the image forecast madness. The Bible relates that one year later, Nebuchadnezzar did indeed become insane, 'till his hairs were grown like eagles' feathers, and his nails like birds' claws'. This can be seen either as an example of an evil spirit's dream come true, as the Babylonians would have believed, or as showing that Nebuchadnezzar felt within himself a premonition of his own illness and downfall. Certainly the dream is a good example of the Jungian view that all images are reflections of the self: the tree was the king's mind.

Dreams of the Egyptian dynasties

Egyptian relics of dream books show that their beliefs were quite similar to those of the Babylonians and Assyrians, although they do not date back as far in time—to about 3000 BC. They too were concerned with sexual dreams, and incest and bestiality crop up very often. No one is certain whether this means that people really did make love to their close relatives or to animals, or simply had fantasies about it. The Egyptians subscribed to the theory that dreams come from evil spirits who had to be appeased in some way. However, there were dreams from good spirits, too.

Pharoah's dream

The Old Testament is full of stories about dreams, the best-known being those told by the Pharoah to Joseph. Seven well-fed cattle came out of a river to feed in a meadow, followed by seven lean ones, who then ate the fat cattle. On the following night, Pharoah dreamed of seven good ears of corn that were eaten by seven thin, blasted ears. Joseph interpreted these dreams correctly as a forecast of seven years of plenty to be followed by seven of famine. Notice how the dreams go over the same ground on two consecutive nights, using different images to convey the same message. This trick is still recognized in modern theories as a part of the dream language.

Dream temples—Epyptian style

The Egyptian word for dreaming means the same as 'to keep awake' and shows that they connected dreams with some great state of knowing or seeing things in the dark. So deep was their faith in dream messages that they built temples to which they would go to pray for helpful dreams. Skilled dream-interpreters were on hand to explain the contents next day. If a revealing dream would not come, then there were a host of spells and incantations to make one appear. One remedy was to 'take a cat, black all over, which has been killed; prepare a writing tablet and write with a solution of myrrh the spell and its destination and put it into the mouth of the cat'.

Dreams in ancient Asia

The ancient Chinese and Indian people went much further with their studies of dreams. They did not simply work out lists of what certain images in dreams meant, like the Mesopotamians and Egyptians had done, and they modified the idea that dreams come from outside forces, from good or bad spirits.

The ancient Chinese made a distinction between the different levels of consciousness long before western psychologists began to discuss its existence. They accepted that dreams are produced by the unconscious mind and wrote many books studying the different symbols used in dreams, including the I Ching which is arousing great interest nowadays among people interested in the workings of the mind. Its approach seems to many to have a deeper insight into the subject than many books of western philosophy.

The Chinese rationalization

Chinese writers tried to work out some overall reason for dreams, drawing on astrology and taking note of the time, season and bodily condition of the dreamer. Dreams were classified into several types: ordinary, terrifying, thoughtful, waking, joyful and fearful. (These were mentioned in a book written around 500 BC: the Lio-tzu). Like many ancient peoples, the Chinese believed that in sleep, a part of the body is able to wander, to experience dreams, and that great care must be taken not to rouse the sleeper too suddenly, before he has time to return to himself. Nowadays this idea is still given credence by spiritualists and others who believe in 'astral projection', the idea that everyone has an 'astral body' capable of leaving the physical one and wandering at will, usually during sleep.

This quaint medieval view of Nebuchadnezzar's dream shows the effects of his later madness. His dream was a classic example of the subconscious revealing death or a future illness.

Indian understanding

The idea of different states in the body intrigued the Indians, who also developed a subtle understanding of different levels of consciousness. They thought there were four states: waking, dreaming, dreamless sleep, and a fourth, which is a mystical union with the god Brahmin. It is extraordinary to think that several centuries before Christ, the notion of distinction between different types of sleep was already being considered, although it

has taken years for modern scientific research to confirm this with EEG machine experiments.

One of the earliest Indian dream books is contained in the Atharva Veda, an old collection of writings dating from around 1500-1000 BC. Among its many fascinating ideas is the suggestion that if a man has a series of dreams, only the last should be considered important. This ties in neatly with the modern concept that several dreams work through a problem in different ways until they find a solution. The

Indian theory suggests that they realized that dreams could have a purpose.

They also accepted two kinds of imagery in dreams: those relating to common experience and those having a more general wide symbolism. This is a feature of modern understanding that finds echoes in the early writings. Images which Freud took to be sexual—swords, axes, flags—were taken to mean happiness. Symbols such as the sun or moon falling from the sky or dreams involving the sea or mountains suggested messages of a different kind,

usually dangerous or fearful. This is rather like Jung's explanation of archetypal images, which people everywhere can recognize, whatever their own personal experience. Basic emotions are expressed through them.

Perhaps even more remarkable insight is found in these early Hindu writings in the practice of looking at the temperament or character of the dreamer. This was only hinted: the main drift of ancient Indian belief was to think of some mysterious 'other force' at work, but nevertheless, even a suggestion that someone's personality is related to his dreams is a very modern idea.

The Classical idea

Fundamentally, the eastern religions of Hinduism and Buddhism are much more contemplative than those of the western world, so perhaps the emphasis on states of mind is understandable. In comparison, the classical worlds of Greece and Rome used dreams more as signs about how to act or what was going to happen. Famous writers and poets such as Homer give many instances of people prompted to action because of some message from a god revealed in a dream.

Dream temples, Greek style
The hero Achilles in the story of the fall of Troy, the Iliad, believes that the god Zeus will aid the Greeks with advice revealed in a dream. So widespread was this view that the Greeks took up the Egyptian idea of building temples where people could go to sleep, to dream and to have a 'divine' message descend on them.

The temples were dedicated to Aesculapius, the Greek god of healing, for it was also believed that medical cures could be achieved through dreams. A dream could specify the right kind of treatment, besides revealing to someone a proper course of action. Hippocrates, (a medical man from whom we still have the 'Hippocratic oath' which doctors are supposed to swear) wrote a book about dreams, one of the few that have survived from the classical era.

The Hippocratic theory
Hippocrates explains in great detail a belief shared by the Greek people with other parts of the early world. Everything that happens to a human being, in sickness or in dreams for instance, is a reflection of some larger state of affairs in the universe. A man is controlled by the powers that cause the sun and moon to shine or the earth to bear crops, and so an event like an eclipse or a flood has

a terrifying effect. It also explains why the idea of some outside power or god speaking in dreams would have been credible.

The Platonic theory
Not all Greek thinkers shared this view. Plato developed an explanation of dreams that bears some resemblance to Freud's line of thought. At night, he said, we have a 'wild beast' roaming around inside us, while reason sleeps. The passions in us which drive us to commit murder, sacrilege or incest can come out in dreams. Freud also narrowed down the kind of drives that make us dream to those of sex and power. There is a noticeable link in his theory of the conscious and the unconscious with Plato's idea of reason being asleep while the wild beast roams.

Dreams and Romans

The Romans held to most of the views of the Greeks and were prompted by their dream images to do things with just as much sincerity. Hannibal crossed the Alps after being encouraged in a dream, and Julius Caesar came to power in the same way. When returning to Rome at the head of his army, he dreamed one night of sleeping with his mother. This he took as a sign of 'entering the mother land' and promptly crossed the Rubicon into Roman territory with his troops. This entry was forbidden unless a general disbanded his forces first and was symbolic of seizing the power of the empire.

Artemidorus: linking past and present
The most famous of all books about dreams to come out of the classical world was written by Artemidorus of Daldis in the second century AD. Throughout his life, he gathered together a vast store of ancient documents relating to dreams in order to write a major study of the subject. He actually used material from the great library of the Babylonian king, Asurnasi at Nineveh. In this way, a clear tradition of dream interpretation survived from the earliest days of civilization to the first centuries of the Christian era. Perhaps these strange connections account for the disrepute which fell on Artemidorus: he was taken up by magicians and quacks seeking to prove some mystical line of authority back to ancient prophets and seers. But if all this is left aside, the real value of Artemidorus' work is immense. He was the first person to see clearly that dreams are made up of a number of

images, strung together in a sequence. He believed it was very important to study the whole dream and to see the images in their setting. This has long since been accepted as an essential method for worthwhile understanding of dreams. Second, Artemidorus said that it was always necessary to have a good knowledge of a dreamer's personality and his life situation—and that is exactly what modern psychoanalysts try to discover and what you should apply to the interpretation of your own dreams.

'I was riding down the road on a bicycle and somebody started following me, also on a bicycle. He started terrorizing me — I was terribly frightened and I kept trying to get help, but I could not speak or shout. All the time my hands kept getting caught in the spokes of the bicycle wheel.
I got to a phone booth and two traffic wardens walked by laughing and talking and they saw me struggling and screaming trying to get into this telephone booth but I could not actually get anything out of my throat at all, and they obviously were thinking "How cute, this young couple you know, having a lark", and that frightened me even more. Eventually I got in the phone booth and I tried to telephone Mike, my husband, to save me, and then I realized that he was the one who was terrorizing me at the same time. Eventually I actually managed to get the words out and I actually shot up in bed screaming for help.'
Picture researcher, 25, female

There is more than a grain of truth in another suggestion from Artemidorus: many dream images have a strong sexual element, he said. The plough in the furrow, the horse and carriage and the granary store were all studied in what we now call 'Freudian' terms. He also commented, 'a mirror means a woman to a man and a man to a woman', which neatly expresses the same idea as Jung's description of the Animus and Anima. These two are our sexual opposites, acting as an expression of our aggressive, masculine nature or passive, more feminine side.

Muslim dream theory

Dream interpretation began to go out of favour in Europe once the magical associations surrounding Artemidorus' theories became known. Only the non-Christians, the Muslim Arabs, continued to be fascinated by it.

They studied all the writers from classical times and from the far eastern part of their empire, where information filtered through from China and the Indian sub-continent. Subtle and mysterious explanations were put forward, and hundreds of books, from dictionaries and encyclopedias to religious treatises and magical poems, were written by Arab scholars.

Mahomet's explanation of faith

Mahomet, the founder of Islam, used dreams as a way of explaining the faith. He relates in the Koran a dream in which the angel Gabriel takes him on a journey through the night, riding a silvery grey mare, all the way to Jerusalem and then up to heaven. He meets Adam, the four Apostles, Jesus and finally sees the Garden of Delights. He meets God, who gives him instructions for his people about how many times a day his people should say their prayers. Then the beautiful grey mare flies through the dark sky, back to the spot on earth where he had fallen asleep.

Although there were many knowledgeable dream interpreters, the Muslims tended to explain dreams in a way that fitted in well with their religious beliefs. And there are some amazing insights in Arabic works:

'He whose soul is pure is never deceived by his dreams, whereas he whose soul is blemished is continually deluded'.

There also was an attempt to understand symbols, especially those which we now consider to be Jungian archetypes. But in the end, the skill was limited by the main purpose, that of explaining people's thoughts in terms of the rules of the Islamic faith.

Dreams and Christianity

In the Christian world, dreams fared even worse. The Church frowned on 'interpreting', believing it was involved with sorcery and black magic. It only allowed the possibility that dreams could be divinely inspired. It is very interesting to see that all the dreams reported by religious figures in the New Testament and in early Christianity do not require any interpreting at all. They are nearly always straightforward mes-

Mahomet used his dream of a journey to heaven on a silvery grey mare to inspire faith, but it could be seen as an expression of his own ambitions as a spiritual leader.

sages of encouragement from God. There was no thought of foretelling a man's future, for that was in God's hands.

Francis of Assisi

St. Francis of Assisi recorded many dreams which he had at important moments in his life, all of which gave him the strength to carry on in his life of poverty and to continue the establishment of his order of Franciscan monks. One striking image came to him just before a very difficult interview with Pope Innocent III. He saw a tall tree with wide, thick branches before him. As he looked at it in admiration, he felt himself growing and growing until he was the same height as the tree. He touched it with his hand and it gently gave way, bending down at his touch. St. Francis saw this as a sign from God that the Catholic Pope would give way and accept his ideas. (Notice how both St. Francis and King Nebuchadnezzar took the world-wide symbol of a tree to express their wishes and fears.)

Famous precognitive dreams

This limitation on dream interpretation continued for many centuries, and only in the last hundred years have people begun to look at dreams from the point of view of the personality. The other aspect of their contents that fascinated thinkers was the occurrence of dreams that seemed to foretell the future.

Nearly all biographies of famous people contain such startling incidents.

Francis Bacon, Elizabethan writer and scientist was staying in Paris while his father was lying seriously ill in London, England. One night when his father was near death, Bacon dreamed of his family home in the country, and that it was plastered with 'black mortar'. This led him to believe that there could be some form of telepathic communication between blood relatives.

Oliver Cromwell when a young man had a dream in which a huge female figure drew back the curtains round his bed and told him that one day he would be the greatest man in England. Cromwell especially noted later that no mention had been made of the word, king. (The female figure could be interpreted as the Jungian concept of the anima: while Cromwell's remark could be a good example of 'secondary revision' as Freud would say – adding in a conscious detail to an unconscious experience.)

Queen Marie Antoinette, overthrown and imprisoned by the French revolutionaries, had a dream of a glowing red sun rising above a column, like a temple pillar. Suddenly the column cracked in half and fell to the ground. Her image has been understood to represent the fall of a powerful figure.

Shelley had a dream no less than a fortnight before he drowned in the Mediterranean, sailing from Leghorn, in which friends came into his bedroom, seriously wounded and bloodstained, with staring faces, warning him that the house was being flooded by the sea. He also dreamed in the same moment of strangling his friend, Williams, who did indeed drown with him.

Charles Dickens had a dream in which he saw a lady in a red shawl with her back towards him. She turned round and introduced herself with the words 'I am Miss Napier'. Dickens had no idea who this person was, but the very next night, after giving one of his famous readings, some friends came backstage, bringing with them the selfsame woman, and introducing her as 'Miss Napier' in real life.

Bismarck, the iron ruler of nineteenth century Germany, dreamed of the rise to power of Prussia over the other German states. This actually came true and was one cause of the First World War.

Abraham Lincoln dreamed of his own violent death, with his body lying in state on a catafalque.

Adolf Hitler had a most extraordinary dream as a young man during the First World War. He was a member of the German Infantry and found himself in the trenches on the French front. One night, he dreamed of being buried beneath an avalanche of earth and molten iron and of being severely wounded. He woke up and felt compelled to leave the trench in spite of warnings from his comrades. No sooner had he started to scramble away from the dug-out than a fearful explosion thudded behind him. Hitler turned back to see the trench completely collapsed and all the soldiers dying under a mass of earth and hot metal. It has been said that the event encouraged Hitler to believe that he could not fail in his plan to dominate Europe.

Nowadays, a large part of dream research is directed into this area of dreams which foresee. Sometimes of course it can be argued that they are merely another version of wish-fulfilling or problem-solving dreams. Both Marie Antoinette and Bismarck might be expected to have such dreams, given the circumstances of their lives. But not all, certainly not Hitler's dream, could be brushed off in this way.

Lord Tennyson dreamed of Prince Albert coming to see him and kissing him on the cheek. 'Very kind but very German' he said to himself in the dream. The very next day, he got a letter from Windsor Castle informing him that he was to be Poet Laureate.

The Duke of Portland, who was involved in arranging the Coronation of Edward VII, had a dream that the king's coach got stuck in the Arch at Horse Guards on its way to Westminster Abbey. Although the State Coach had been used before, he insisted on the arch and the coach being measured, and found that the top of the coach was too high to pass under the arch. Since its last appearance, the road surface had been raised due to repair work, and everyone had overlooked the fact.

Dreams in primitive cultures

These are the traditional views and mysteries of dream history. Now that you have seen how many ideas date back to the earliest civilizations, you will not be surprised to learn that psychologists have gathered some very useful information in recent years from looking at present-day primitive tribes, some nearly extinct. The data collected can yield valuable comparisons and sidelights on the way that all minds work, primitive or sophisticated, and shows how widespread and fundamental certain ideas are.

The Siriono of the Amazon
Looking at tribes all over the world has proved that people dream to a large extent about the everyday facts of their lives, wherever they are. We might have dreams situated in houses and motor cars, whereas the Siriono natives of the Amazon in South America dream about

hunting in the jungle. Just as we use the image of the car to suggest other things besides transport, (mechanical emotions, sexual drive and so on) so the Siriono people dream about hunting, even when they are not hungry. They turn hunting into an image to suggest other things. This leads to the conclusion that all human beings use typical parts of their living pattern to make images in their dream world.

The Sioux Indians
Many discoveries about so-called primitive people suggest that perhaps they have better ways of living than we do ourselves! The North American Sioux Indians, for example, dealt very kindly with the misfits of their society. They somehow fitted them in, instead of shutting them away in a kind of institution. They did not regard the criminal, the insane or inadequate as shameful or

stupid. They put all the blame on evil spirits who had infected the dream world of these poor people and treated them as best they could. In a way, this recognizes that people have an unconscious part to their minds that produces drives without respect to the conscious part. Other tribes seem to have understood this too, although it took western civilization many centuries to come to the same conclusion through psychology.

The Iroquois Indians
The Iroquois Indians worked out a theory that dreams may say one thing

In primitive societies, the barrier between the world of dreams and ordinary daily experience is not so sharply defined. The Sioux bear dance was a symbolic enactment of the roles of hunter and hunted.

but mean another, and they devised special techniques to help people discover the true meaning. The Iroquois used a method rather like that suggested earlier of writing down or recording all the thoughts that spring to mind in association with a dream image to build up some impression of what it represents.

Once the Iroquois dreamer had a clear idea of what wish was being expressed or what problem was being confronted, then the Indians would 'make it come true' by acting it out, either in reality by staging an argument or in a ritualistic way. More developed societies also have ways of releasing some urges as a ritual — all the howling and shouting at a football game could be viewed as a fairly healthy way to express aggression!

The Hurons

The Huron Indians had a theory which has quite noticeable resemblances with modern ideas about dreams. Like many primitive cultures, these Indians believed that the 'voice' of the dream world was a guardian spirit, which gave revelatory messages, but in disguised form. These could be warnings about enemies, disclosures of special cures for diseases or good advice about the best places to go hunting. Especially interesting is the belief that this 'spirit-voice' could reveal the hidden wishes of the scul – rather like the Freudian idea that dreams are expressions of unconscious urges or wishes. The Hurons came even closer to modern thought when they suggested that perhaps the 'spirit' or 'soul' inside is made happy or satisfied by expressing its desire in dream form. This led them to wonder whether in fact physical illness or emotional upset is caused by the 'spirit' rebelling because its desires are not recognized – not far off present-day thinking about psychosomatic illness.

The Diegueno Indians

These Indians of Southern California have been studied with great interest because they devised a technique of psychotherapy through dreams – a development not found very often among primitive people. The 'treatment' was confined to people who were suffering from a particular type of obsession or fantasy. This was sexual and consisted of excessive dreaming on the subject, in mild form, or hallucinations, when it was considered serious. These visions would be of a 'spirit-lover' plaguing the sufferer. The treat-

ment would be to have a lengthy conversation with a shaman or magic man, who encouraged the patient to confess his fantasies and discuss why they are so absorbing. The shaman declares that he might as well tell all, because he knows all about it anyway, through his magic powers. He might also recommend the sufferer to go on a special healthful diet – or get married! But the significant aspect of this Diegueno custom is that the remedy takes the form of a consultation – a talking-out with an expert – much the same as a modern analyst works. In most primitive groups, remedies are usually more physical: people 'act out' the dream or dance away the affliction.

> Two recurring dreams:
> 'I'm in some play or other, but I've been idle about learning my lines. I've lost my script so I search high and low, but I can't find it and no one else will lend me one. Then it's time to go on stage, and I still don't know my lines.'
> Librarian, female, 56
>
> 'I kept dreaming that I was going down a spiral staircase — like in a castle or church tower, As I went down it got narrower and narrower until I was stuck with my shoulders above and my legs round the corner below!'
> Housewife, 30

The Ashanti People

The foregoing examples concern American people, but of course, African studies have come up with equally varied and surprising facts. These too help to build up some basic conclusions about the nature of dreaming, worldwide. The Ashanti of West Africa, for example, had also caught hold of the idea that dreams can mean exactly the opposite of their apparent content, just as Freud has pointed out in his Interpretation of Dreams.

To give an example: someone may dream that a hunter kills an elephant. The Ashanti method would be to look beyond the immediate images and find the real answer by association of ideas. The elephant is the most powerful animal of the jungle, so he must represent a king or chief. The Ashanti would

say therefore that the dream is a warning that a chief will die in the near future. A similar explanation is given for a dream of a house without a roof. This is a symbol foretelling death because for the Ashanti, spirit people live in a world of roofless dwellings.

The Ashanti also share the common idea that the 'voice' of a man's dream is a spirit, and they believe that it can be someone's ancestor speaking. It is a widespread notion, and takes many forms. With the Ashanti, the ancestor often appears in dreams in animal shape. Some anthropologists have been led by this idea into linking dreams of ancestors with totem worship. This is simply another way of saying that primitive people maintain a strong sense of their tradition and identity by worshipping their ancestors and by personifying them as animal or half-imaginary beings. This sometimes involves making actual totem images of them, which are respected and revered by the whole tribe.

Totems and dreams

There are many different theories about what totems are, but the basic idea explained above is common to several of them. A totem acts as a symbol of the group or tribal identity and is often imbued with magical or beneficial powers. This story from a Canadian tribe reveals how totems work for primitive people: A man went out hunting and met a black bear who took him home and taught him many things. After a long stay with the bear the man returned home. At first he looked and acted so like a bear that everyone was afraid of him, but someone rubbed him with magical herbs and he became a man again. After that, whenever he went hunting, the bear helped him catch his quarry. The man built a home and painted a bear on it and his sister made a blanket with a bear design too. Then all the descendants of his sister used the bear crest and were always known as the bear clan.

Such legends occur all over the world and very often the origin of the totem comes from a dream picture. Totems can be personal too: among some Australian aborigines, witch doctors adopt a special totem after dreaming of a particular thing, such as a lizard or a kangaroo. A rather attractive custom from the Dyaks of Borneo illustrates

The most striking characteristic in dreaming among African cultures such as the Ashanti is their belief that dreams are as real as waking experience.

how far and wide this dream influence extends: if a man dreams that something of value is given to him, then when he wakes, he picks up the first curious object he sees – perhaps a shiny stone on the ground. He takes it home and hangs it over his bed, and when he next goes to sleep, he addresses it and says he wants a dream with good pictures about some matter or business which is important to him at the time. If he has such a dream he keeps the object and it becomes valuable to him, but if the dream is unhelpful he throws it away and waits for another such opportunity.

Dreams directing reality

It is quite common among primitive people for special talents or careers to be marked out by a dream experience. Among the Blackfoot Indians of North America for instance a man became a medicine man after he had had a series of dreams in which a dead relative came to him and gave him detailed instructions on how to work cures or cast spells. In many tribes, a young man who intends to become a priest can only do so if he has a dream of making contact with a god first. This is a reminder of the Old Testament story of Samuel, who as a child heard a voice in the night and thought it was his priest, Eli. But the priest, who had been sound asleep, realized that the boy had heard the voice of God.

General conclusions

It seems that primitive people have two kinds of dreams: those that relate to their own personal situation and which come to them quite spontaneously, or those that are more important, containing messages or visions about the whole life of the tribe, its identity and importance. This second kind is sometimes called a 'culture' dream and is obviously considered valuable. In many tribes, special customs exist to induce this kind of dream. They help to keep the group sense of security and well-being, or they can result from the dreamer's wish to be blessed by his ancestors or receive good omens from the 'spirit' of the tribe. In our own culture, we have examples of this kind of dreaming, like Joseph's dreams, and their importance in Bible history. Dreams are used by primitive people for a number of other social functions, like choosing a person's career or guiding his work. In fact, primitive people use dreams in ways not far removed from those which present-day interpreters suggest they are considered for problem-solving and help towards better self-understanding.

'True' dreaming

The most general belief that characterizes primitive people's dreaming life is that at times they can be just as real and 'truthful' as everyday life. There are endless variations on this theme. If an Ashanti dreams of adultery then this

> "I'm in London and for some time without explanation, the streets have been getting sinister splits in them and steam and smoke start oozing out. Men with wheelbarrows of tar keep trying to fill the cracks. Nobody talks about it but every time you go past a street that's been newly tarred, you know that's another one where the steam has got through.
> I go to visit a friend on the other side of London, in a room with a few large plants, a hickory floor, Bauhaus furniture. We decide we had better get out of London. We run as fast as we can go to Victoria Station. There's a bus like an airport bus, with no seats in it, only some ill-fitting, garishly patterned carpet. A thick, bull-necked man with an SS armband comes up and says "You haven't been members of the Party. You can't leave London."
> We start running, running back to my home, and everywhere the streets are cracking open, melting, boiling, and the smoke is so thick it's dark as night. We rush into a black marbled doorway where there are electric lights and luscious green plants with red and orange veins.
> Then the lights go out and flames start creeping out of the crevasses."
> Magazine editor, 36.

results in his paying a fine just as if he had committed the act. The Didinga people of the south-east Sudan had the custom that if a man dreamed of another as a victim of witchcraft, then the dreamer had to go and see him the very next morning and avert the evil by a series of elaborate ritual acts. If a member of the Dyaks of Borneo dreams of falling into water, he believes that this has actually happened to his spirit and so has to summon a shaman or priest-figure. The shaman 'fishes' for the lost spirit in a basin of water with a little hand net until he catches it and returns it safely to its owner. A tribe in Brazil called the Bororo once deserted a whole village in a panic because one of them dreamed that he saw enemies approaching on the attack. But perhaps the most famous anecdote on this subject comes from the distinguished pioneer scholar in anthropology, Levy-Bruhl, who wrote how a chief in equatorial Africa had a dream that he travelled to Portugal and England. When he got up the next day he put on European clothing and announced his journey to his friends, who all gathered round and congratulated him on his wonderful luck!

The power of dreams

Primitive people may use dreams to predict the future or direct the actions of the tribe or clan. Or they can use dreams to sort out some personality problem, or even a physical illness. The interest for us lies in seeing how primitive people believe so absolutely in the power of dreams. It is easy to see that if a young man dreams that he is in contact with a god, for instance, and accepts this as a message that he should become a priest, then probably it is his own desire or motive that brings about the dream. The curious thing is to note that if a tribal custom requires a dream of this sort, then it will occur.

Old and new

Some anthropologists are specializing in studying primitive people whose lives are being radically altered by contact with the outside world. In some cases, people seem to adjust quite well and incorporate Western ideas into their dream patterns, alongside the old beliefs and customs. This could provide an interesting application of dream study. It might help to show if a group was acclimatizing to the new way of life at a fundamental level or whether their adaptation was only successful to the casual outside observer. The strain of coping with a new culture, a new way of living and thinking, could be detected through changes in their dream pictures.

Many primitive peoples chose their totem or clan symbol from dream images, which in turn were usually drawn from the natural world around them – animals, birds, trees, the sun, moon and stars are often featured in this way.

Only a dream?

You may have come to the conclusion by this stage that you can read just about anything you like into a dream and interpret it in at least a dozen different ways! Of course you have to weigh up the possibilities in an image. Is it a symbol? Is it an image for something of a sexual or other nature? What did you feel about these images at the time of dreaming, and what do you feel now, thinking about it?

The chances are that there will be some overlapping between your answers, especially if you are getting close to the purpose of the dream. If you construct a 'theory' about a dream, you will immediately know inside yourself whether it is rubbish or not. But you will find that you cannot impose an idea like 'reversal' or 'displacement' on any old dream and come up with an answer. When you feel a little click in your head, or a lurch in your stomach and a voice saying 'That's it!', you will have no doubts about it. Dream interpretation only has real value if you recognize and accept the truth for yourself.

Inspiration while they slept

Through the centuries, man has used dreams in most remarkable ways to enrich his life. A wide range of achievements have been made possible through these bizarre sleep experiences. You can learn something of yourself and, if you are lucky, about the world outside.

In sleep when the mind is sifting information and the input of data is reduced, there is a greater chance of putting two and two together.

Archimedes leaping out of the bath shouting 'Eureka!' is a story everyone knows—he had suddenly worked out the secret of measuring the volume of solids by their displacement of water. In a lovely state of slumbering relaxation, with no effort from his conscious mind, he hit upon the answer to a problem which had occupied him for weeks and months.

Niehls Bohr, the famous Danish physicist, offers a more up-to-date example. When he was a student, he had an extraordinarily clear dream of a sun composed of burning gas, round which planets were spinning, attached by thin filaments. He awoke to realize that this dream image showed the structure of the atom which gave him the inspiration for further research into atomic physics. However, these flights of inspiration do not always involve such abstract scientific concepts.

Elias Howe was an American who wanted to design a really practical sewing machine. He dreamed that he was captured by savages and ordered by their king to produce a perfect sewing machine—or else! He tried and tried, but without success. His fate approached: the savages advanced raising their spears to kill him.

Suddenly Elias noticed that all the spears had eye-shaped holes in their tips. He awoke with a start and realized that the dream had uncovered the secret for which he had been searching: the thread on a machine should go through a needle hole near the tip in order to run smoothly. A small detail, but it revolutionized the design of sewing machines.

Friedrich Kekule's was probably the most well-known dream discovery. He hit upon the exact shape of the so-called 'benzene ring'—the atomic structure of the benzene molecule—with a dream image of a snake swallowing its tail. The instantaneous and accurate nature of this discovery led him to say to a group of scientists in a speech: 'Let us learn to dream, gentlemen, and then we may perhaps learn the truth'.

Thomas Edison, the inventor of the telephone, was so sure of the value of dreams that he developed the habit of snatching forty winks between hours of work and believed that a great number of his best thoughts and inventions came to him in these drowsing moments. (He was also a great believer in ESP.)

Of course, these kinds of experiences also happen to people in waking life: a flash of intuition, a sudden moment of truth is as much the way of scientific discovery as slow plodding progress. But what fascinates experts is that during a dream, which is supposed to be a jumble of images from the unconscious mind, a real insight into the workings of the world can so often be revealed.

Dreams and art

Not only in the realm of science, but in art too, dreams have their part to play.

Freud once said that it was not himself, but the poets who 'discovered the unconscious'. Throughout history, art and literature have been greatly enriched by the fantasies that have stirred in creative minds.

Shakespeare often described dreams through his characters, as a reflection of their state of mind. Lady Macbeth is a dramatic portrayal of a mind haunted by guilt: a clear image of hand-washing represents her desire to wash away her sin. In *Richard III*, the king has a tormenting dream before the battle of Bosworth—as if his unconscious is forcing him to see the tragic, drastic consequences of his lust for power. Shakespeare rightly suggests that King Richard's fear lies within himself—in the conflict between his urge for power and the pain that such destruction brings him.

Wordsworth wrote many poems as a result of dream visions—he once said that he felt he had 'lived in a dream'.

Coleridge's poem *Kubla Khan* was dream induced, although the poet also took drugs, which may have affected his imaginings.

Novelists have often found their plots and characters through dreams.

Jules Verne's *Twenty Thousand Leagues Under the Sea* certainly explores that dark underlife populated by Jungian archetypal creatures, monsters of all shapes and sizes.

Charlotte Bronte used dreams to great effect in her classic novel of childhood, *Jane Eyre.* Through the little girl's dream images, the author conveys better than any other words could express the loneliness, fear, and frustration of her life:

'A feeling as if I had a frightful nightmare, and seeing before me a terrible red glare, crossed with thick black bars. I heard voices too, speaking with a hollow sound, and as if muffled by a rush of wind or water: agitation, uncertainty, and an all-predominating sense of terror confused my faculties.' This is an authentic and vivid description of a typical childhood terror which perhaps Charlotte Brontë experienced herself, to be able to use it so well in her book.

Edvard Munch's Anxiety *captures the blank dread which must have clouded much of his own dreamworld.*

The Surrealists

After Freud's theories were first published, many artists began to dwell on the idea of the unconscious mind and thought that they too should invesigate this new way of looking at the personality. The paintings of the Surrealist movement perhaps capture the peculiar style of dreams better than any other school or generation of artists. Surrealism really began in France in the 1920s. It was defined by one of its founders, the writer André Breton, as an attempt to create art from the mind's eye, to express the real functioning of the mind 'in the absence of all control exercised by reason'. Breton wondered, as many dream theoreticians have, 'Couldn't the dream be applied to solving the fundamental questions of life ?'

In capturing dream visions in paint, the Surrealists have helped people to recognize the amazing depth and richness of the unconscious mind. Their work has made people realize that there are many different kinds of 'reality' besides the one we see in during waking hours. Surrealism attempts to reach a new awareness, to lead to a better harmony between the conscious rational mind and unconscious forces. The word itself means 'over-real', a new level of consciousness, with the two levels of the mind better integrated.

Celluloid dreams

The Surrealists did not only use paintings to explore this possibility. Many of them realized the great flexibility of the motion picture to express it—notably the French writer Jean Cocteau and film directors René Clair from France and Luis Buñuel from Spain. Buñuel is still making brilliant surrealist films, superbly adapted to modern ideas. Many other film directors have played with the distinctive characteristics of dreams to convey the working of the mind very successfully. Early examples of 'dreamy' films were mostly confined to movie-fantasies, just as many dreams are pure wish-fulfilment. Women sighed over Rudolph Valentino or Clark Gable, men over Loretta Young or Jean Harlow, and the expression 'dreamboat' for handsome men is still around. But later directors began to look more deeply into the style of dreams.

The dislocation of events in dreams can be perfectly captured on film. Among the best are Alain Resnais' *Last Year in Marienbad*, Fellini's *8½* and *Juliet of the Spirits*, Antonioni's *Blow Up* and Ingmar Bergman's *Wild Strawberries*. Not just 'intellectual continentals' can do it—consider *2001: A Space Odyssey*, *Yellow Submarine*, *Barbarella* or *A Clockwork Orange*. They all have sequences that perfectly convey that mad, floating 'alternative reality' of dream experiences. Audiences have become so adjusted to this film technique now that if a person suddenly moves from one place to another—say from smiling at a child to seeing her run over, as in *Sunday, Bloody Sunday*—they know it means that the first is what is happening, while the second is what is being thought at the same split second. The essential feature of dream

Salvador Dali's 'Impressions of Africa' is a striking example of the Surrealist attempt to capture the 'other reality' of dreams.

technique in films is that so far it has only tried to imitate the way minds work during sleep. A whole new movement in the arts is trying to break down the barriers between consciously imitating and actually releasing this unconscious working of the mind through hallucinogenic drugs. The dangers behind this kind of experiment are obvious. But some people find the results so overwhelming, so startling and original however that they are prepared to take the risk. The feeling of 'breaking down the walls of the mind' was strikingly captured in the final sequence of *2001*—other examples can be seen in *Performance* or *Easy Rider*.

It's easy to see the continuing preoccupation with the 'freewheeling' processes of the mind in the 'pop' culture of today, whether the images are stimulated artificially or not. Look at the LP covers in any local record shop and you'll soon see that many have designs or photographs which draw heavily on strange juxtapositions, weird landscapes and representations of the archetypal symbols and images of all schools of dream interpretation.

Present-day research

Many psychologists believe that the brain acts as a filter, hindering our perception of 'supernatural reality', shown to some extent in dreams and the effects of hallucinogenic drugs. Present-day research is moving more and more into this realm of 'another reality'. But no one really knows the full extent of the mind's powers. Are those midnight inspirations nothing more than freak occurrences, or could dreams be used to release more knowledge? This whole area is usually termed 'psychic research' and means investigation into 'paranormal phenomena' which are not totally explicable by the present laws of science. Until fairly recently, this field of the paranormal was regarded in a dubious light, only attractive to eccentric old ladies and deluded gentlemen who liked to dabble in the occult. But now it is gaining ground as an area for serious work, and no wonder, with an overwhelming mass of well-authenticated evidence waiting to be studied.

Foreseeing the future

One of the main areas of study is precognition in dreams—those hundreds of cases where people have foreseen events during sleep. A typical incident comes from the novelist J. B. Priestley. He had a vivid dream in the 1920s of sitting in the front row of a balcony,

FOX-RANK

M.G.M.

looking out across some dimly-seen, majestic and colourful spectacle. More than ten years later, he found himself visiting the Grand Canyon in the United States. The canyon was covered in a thick early morning mist and as it cleared, the vast, impressive Colorado landscape spread out before him. At once, Priestly recognized it as the identical place of his dream.

There are countless cases of people reading newspaper headlines in a dream announcing an earthquake or similar disaster before it occurs or at the same time, and during the First and Second World Wars mothers frequently dreamed of their sons being

Top: Buñuel's film 'The Discreet Charm of the Bourgeoisie' incorporates a common dream situation: the fear of sudden exposure. Below: the park sequence in 'Blow Up' by Antonioni brilliantly conveys the 'other sinister reality' of narrative dreams.

killed, as the event was happening.
It is possible to pass off a sizable proportion of these 'precognitive' dreams with a simple explanation. If a person wakes up for instance 'knowing' that something has gone wrong, it may be that his mind has an acutely developed sense of awareness that comes through even in sleep to give a warning in

CHRIS YATES

extreme situations. This would account for those miraculous escapes from falling bombs or avalanches. Many other incidents are simply the result of worry and coincidence.

But the inexplicable dreams, foreseeing incidents that are quite beyond likelihood or visualized in such detail that they are genuinely 'psychic', pose much deeper questions. It could be that the movement of time as we know it is only one way of arranging events. Perhaps incidents in the future can 'be known' before they happen. Even more peculiar, can we know about the extreme past in great detail?

Reliving the past

Dreams about someone else's past life,

Even the most bizarre images that appear in dreams could contain a hidden meaning for the dreamer.

including names and places, have been alleged and have attracted a great deal of interest. One man could recall a previous existence as a naval gunner at the time of Napoleon and came up with such accurate details that Earl Mountbatten used the material as evidence while discussing naval history with experts. A woman called Mrs Smith seemed to recall the entire life situation of a girl who lived in 13th century Toulouse in dreams, visions and a kind of half-automatic writing. As in the case of J. B. Priestley, Mrs Smith recognized parts of her dreams on a holiday visit.

Dream communication

A theory that is being slowly accepted is that everyone has some degree of extra-sensory perception, or 'ESP'. At its simplest level, this means that you might be able to receive information from other people by a kind of invisible radio, without knowing them—and without even intending to. This would explain dreams relating incidents from the past or simultaneous events across a physical barrier, such as the problems of a relative overseas. But the real 'future' dreams are still a mystery.

Some fascinating experiments in this field have been undertaken recently by two American doctors, Montague Ullman and Stanley Krippner. They have been trying to show that in a dreaming state, people have more powers of telepathy or ESP than they do when awake. Usually these powers are associated with psychically sensitive people, but it could be that in sleep the faculty to perceive things in this way becomes much more widespread.

The experiments usually took the form of having an 'agent' who concentrated on a particular picture or idea and tried to get it across to a sleeping person, or 'subject'. The subject's dream would often incorporate the picture or idea being transmitted. The doctors learned to refine this phenomenon. Just as most ordinary dreams are concerned with people and problems, the best transmitted pictures or ideas were those dealing with these themes. So if an agent concentrated upon a picture of eating, drinking or a beautiful woman, then a male subject would be very likely to dream in a clear way of the subject matter.

How accurate are the results? In one example, the agent was looking at a painting by Monet called 'Corn Poppies'—in it a field of flowers forms the background and a woman walks across the foreground with a child. The subject's dream that night included plants, a lady 'dressed up' and a child. Now of all the things that the sleeper could have dreamed, such exact parallels with the agent's 'message' are remarkable. Multiplied by hundreds of similar tests, the results of Ullman and Krippner's experiments lead to some striking conclusions.

Nightmares could be a transmission of someone else's horrifying real-life experience. Incidents in the past might contain such powerful human emotions that they live on and get 'picked up' by another mind, even hundreds of years later. Perhaps we might even learn to develop this faculty usefully.

KIM SAYER

Leave your dreams to chance

The whole question of 'chance' may have to be re-examined in the future, if dream research continues to explore in this direction. How often have you come across some extraordinary coincidence: you dream of a friend you haven't seen in years, and the next day a letter from that same person arrives in the morning post. Normally you would dismiss this as a once-in-a-million occurrence. Now, as psychic research increases available information it seems that chance occurrences may actually be 'willed' by the unconscious.

Everyone must have experienced the terror of being chased in a nightmare: could this be the transmission of someone else's horrifying experience in life?

Interestingly, as well as exploring the unconscious mind in their paintings, the Surrealists also adopted chance methods of achieving their ends. Anything that came together on the canvas, as if by accident, might perhaps hold some unconscious meaning. The artist Paul Klee once said that his aim was to 'make chance essential'. In the light of these ideas, that is not as absurd as it sounds.

What the future holds

The real understanding of dreams is just beginning. We still have to find out how the mind selects its images. No one knows yet how memory works. The workings of so-called 'primitive' brains have to be compared with 'civilized' ones to find out if there are any real differences as well as similarities.

How much difference is there between the way children and adults dream? Is there some evolutionary progression in the hierarchy of living creatures which governs the way they dream? What exactly is the effect of drugs and other stimulants on the working of the brain, the function of dreaming and the power of extra-sensory perception?

With all these immense questions still to be answered, the personal value of dream study has been widely accepted by experts and ordinary people alike. Some analysts even suggest that life would be greatly improved if families were to institute dream-swapping sessions, or if politicians and businessmen turned their attention to their night

Perhaps dreams will provide the key information to unlock the mind and help understand the true nature of personality.

experiences on a regular basis! Erich Fromm, a leading American psychoanalyst, has more than once advocated teaching dream interpretation in schools and colleges. So carry on dreaming, because that's where some of the most important parts of your personality are expressed and some of the richest and most worthwhile ideas have come from.